CONTENTS

ACKNOWLEDGEMENTS

Thank you, Grazie, Merci, Go Raibh Maith Agat, Gracias, Danke, Arigato, Obrigada, Dzien kuje; Khob Khun Ka!

The creative collaboration of **Sarah Hughes** in the publishing of this book was an enjoyable, first-class journey of her professional proofing, refining, editing...and encouraging. Find her at 2liveanddream@gmail.com

In addition to everyone mentioned in this book, the following people, dear souls, and others made my torrid travel tattling with passion possible:

My grandmother, **Helen Shiels**, who was a travel agent and brought back exotic gifts and photos from each of her trips. She booked my first airline ticket and owned a cottage in Colchester, Ontario, Canada, which was, by car, my first international destination during summer weekends.

My parents **Arthur and Gladys Shiels**, who packed up the car and took us on vacations ranging from Niagara Falls to Houghton Lake to Disney World.

Travel Writer and author **Larry Olmsted**, who has also been a generous colleague and collaborator in crime since the day we met by noticing our matching Omega Seamaster watches during a breakfast in Bangkok.

Brian Lewis, the founder of Sleeping Bear Press, who took a chance on a first-time author and commissioned me to write a biography of J.P. McCarthy, which became a regional #1 bestseller and raised $50,000 for charity.

Vartan Kupelian, the golf writer, advised: "Instead of just being an author, you should also write columns." And then helped me secure my first newspaper gig at the

Observer & Eccentric in Birmingham, Michigan.

...My gratitude, as well, to everyone on this admittedly dreadfully incomplete list:

Jerry Rose, Quentin Lutz, Ben Wright, Karen Moraghan, Kristen Hunter, Brad Packer, Andrea Grisdale, Kayla Schubert, Dennis Lennox, Saul Anuzis, Dan Shepherd, Suzanne Sponder, David Whitaker, Virginia Irurita, Bernard McMullin, Ottie Stein, Ruth Moran, Michelle Gonzalez, Barbara Golden, Emily Gail, Jill Daly, Jim Wise, Camille Cussac, Misty Belles, Mona Mesereau, Alice Marshall, Geoffrey Weill, Chris Follenus, Garrett Kenny, Francisco Glaria Baines, Rita Annunziata, Nicole Bellatti, Carole Petrusini, Janna Graber, Susan Angel, Mickey Hirten, Al Wilson, Angie Miller, Xavier Destribats, EvaMaria Panzer, Liz Ware, Tim Hygh, Tony Cuthbert, Jeff and Suzanne Huard, Matthew Upchurch, Andrea Fischer Newman, Dave Herbst, Rick Sylvain, Dana Debel, JP McCarthy, Len Barnes, Dean Breest, Art Tebo, Stephen Kircher, Jim and Chris MacInnes, Erin Ernst, Judy Booth, Jim Wise, Tim McGuire, Barry Godwin, Joan O'Neill, Stacey Mesuda, Kristen Yantis, Keith Salwoski, Cass Colbourne, Dan Wooten, Austin McConnell, Emily McCormick, Linda Villafane Piergrossi, Chris Moyer, Trevor Tkach, J Mike D'Augustino, Ken Raynor, Lana Wescott, Felix Sharpe Caballero, Noel Cronin, Pat Ruddy, Robert Florence, Donald Contursi, Jim Nantz, Ron Hinrichs, Kelly Schulz, MaryBeth Romig, Gicela Diaz Viera, Johnathan Raggett, Zoe Ward, Michael Caprio, Madeline Austin, Jessica Brida, Jean Armas, Brian Johnson, Ed Witte, Dennis Sutton, Jo Ann Bass, Diana Moxon, Brittany Williams, Kirsten Dunn, Melanee Shale, Greg McNeilly, Andy Hetzel, Ken Dallafior, Danielle Tucker and Rick Gray, Dan Loepp, Jase Bolger, Dennis and Debbie Muchmore, And...Tony Cuthbert

WELCOME

This book is full of tales such as the one I am about to share with you...and it ironically occurred while I was writing this acknowledgments section.

I was typing on my laptop computer at a bistro table under the colonnade at the Beverly-Canon Gardens after lunch at Nate-n-Al's on a lovely, Beverly Hills afternoon. The gardens are in the shadow of the Maybourne Hotel across the courtyard.

Just after I had written the name of the late Vartan Kupelian as one of those I am eternally grateful to, I saw a woman about to walking my direction up the aisle wearing a particularly colorful sundress. I recall nothing about her looks, but I remember the dress.

Just before she passed me, I said to her, "That's a very nice dress."

The woman passed by like a statue on roller-skates giving no audible or visible response.

Then I heard a woman's voice from the other direction.

"Did she even say thank you?" the voice asked.

I turned my head to see and answer the women, a brunette seated alone at the next table.

"Not a peep," I answered. "But that is okay. It happens."

I do not remember what she wore, but the woman had her hair pulled up and looked to be nearly finished with a coffee or a smoothie or something in front of her. There was also and an empty salad plate.

She looked like a working mom, and, perhaps with mothering instincts, expressed disappointment that the woman ignored me.

Her kindness out of an awkward moment resulted in a most amiable conversation that picked up steam for the better part of an hour. We talked about friendliness and life and each other's children and our jobs…the kinds of things one talks about with someone you meet for the first time.

I will admit she had eyes that danced, so I listened to her for as long as she wanted to chat.

Another feature I noticed - she was able to communicate with facial expressions when she struggled to find words or to decide exactly how to put something. "You're a writer: help me out here," she'd finally say.

We were both open books, but the occasional contortions were charming when she was trying to decide whether she should reveal something personal to me.

Less you think she did all the talking, she politely asked questions about me as well, and I talked about my son Harrison who had just finished law school and was, at that moment, off traveling with his college pals in Ibiza, Spain.

"He needed to blow off some steam after taking the Bar Exam," I explained. "Imagine this: he was with me in Las Vegas last week and then flew off to Ibiza. If there is any steam left in him after all that, it will be a miracle. And if there is any money left, I will be even more surprised!"

We laughed for a moment.

"You son – he travels like you," she said.

I admitted I was very blessed and then turned the tables.

"Have you been away at all, recently?"

"I went back to Armenia – to Yerevan – in 2021. It's the capital. Have you been?"

"No," I answered, shaking my head. Though I was still at my own bistro table, I leaned in.

"If you ever go, I will tell you one tip: 'churches, churches, churches,'" she said, leaving me wondering whether, technically, that was one thing or three things. "See as many churches as you can. They each have a different story and different meaning. The locals will tell you to go to Lake Sevan. But I tell you: churches."

"You said you went back to Armenia. You have been there before?"

"I was born there," she revealed. "I took my first steps the day before my family came to America. The rest I took here because I had not yet mastered the skill."

I smiled at the wit she displayed in that detail.

"You're Armenian," I stated. "What is your name?"

"Varduhi."

"You are never going to believe this, but just before we started talking, just now, I was writing, on my laptop, an acknowledgement of my late mentor...who was also Armenian. Like you, he was one of the nicest people I have ever met."

"What was his name?" she asked.

"Vartan," I answered. "Vartan Kupelian."

"That is the masculine version of my name. He is Vartan; I am Varduhi. Vartan and Varduhi. Same name."

I felt a chill run up my spine.

"Our names translate to mean 'rose.'"

I sat silent for a moment but then said, "Vartan died three summers ago. His funeral was right about at this week in August. What are the chances that I would be writing his name, in gratitude, in my laptop, and I would, moments later, in a random moment of kindness, meet a person of the same nationality and the same name?"

Varduhi looked at me with her dancing eyes and said, "That is Vartan waving at you through me."

1

FASTEN YOUR SWEET BELT

 Consider, as we travel the landscape, that some of the most memorable romances in literature and filmmaking are books, movies and "true Hollywood stories" in which the protagonists do not end up together. Their "happily ever after" is...apart.

Humphrey Bogart's Rick put Ilsa on the plane in the final frames of "Casablanca."

The torch F. Scott Fitzgerald's "Great Gatsby" carried for Daisy Buchanan was snuffed out in the same pool Jay Gatsby was in at the end of the book.

The stormy, steamy, bullfight marriage of Frank Sinatra and Ava Gardner ended in divorce, but their adoration for each other never did.

Rhett Butler didn't give a damn when he left Scarlett at Tara in "Gone With the Wind."

Mia and Sebastian cared too much about chasing their showbiz dreams than to pursue each other in "La La Land."

And whose heart doesn't swoon at the "misty watercolor memories" lyric in the title song of "The Way We Were" – the movie that left Streisand and Redford alone?

Billy Crystal's "City Slickers" was a comedic adventure but Jack Palance, playing Curly the cowboy, added an element of the sort of momentary road romance I speak of when he was asked if he'd ever been in love?

He explained that once, while on horseback, he'd spotted a young woman in the field working in the dirt. With a faraway look in his eye Curly described her as wearing a little cotton dress when she stood up to stretch her back with the setting sun behind her.

"I turned around and rode away. "I figured it wasn't going to get any better than that," he explained.

When a chagrined Billy Crystal's character Mitch protested and suggested the cowboy should have pursued the woman because she could have been the love of his life, Curly explained to him, "...She is."

Each of these romantic vignettes unfolded in colorful settings: Mysterious Morocco, Antebellum Atlanta, Tinseltown, the Big Apple and the American West. The locations can tend to heighten the "watercolor memories" so I began to let my mind wander across some of the destinations in which I had experienced some situational sweetness. I am not talking torrid – I'm speaking about the sort of situations that played out more like "Curly" than "Casanova."

These brief relationships were not going to get any better than they were during those golden moments.

In this book, I am going to share some "coronary captures" in a series of stories set at destinations designed to steal your heart.

2

MILESTONE MOMENT AT ONE OF LONDON'S RED CARNATION HOTELS

 I was leaving my lodging in the Noël Coward Suite – room 308 with its' leopard-print carpet, yellow-striped bed, white marble bathroom, and lead–glass window view of Kensington Palace - headed for Harrods.

The historic department store was less than a mile away. Harrod's would be manic – while the Milestone Hotel and Residences, one of London's esteemed Red Carnation Hotels, is the opposite. Cozy, charming, and elegant in every way.

In fact, while savoring my English breakfast and tea and considering a glass of champagne, I overheard the unmistakable accent of a Texan at a nearby table.

"How did you ever find this hotel, in a city full of thousands of them, in the first place?" he asked his colleague. "There is no reason to ever go anywhere else."

As much as I hated to leave the hotel, I had Harrod's and other appointments that day, including dinner at La Famiglia, on Langton Street, in Chelsea. The 40-year, Tuscan triumph is where I would have my last meal were I ever sentenced to a firing squad at the Tower of London, where they spelled torture with a capital "T." The adorable Marietta Maccioni maintains the tradition of her legendary late father Alvaro with her twists in the way Claudine Pepin supports – and spars - with her French celebrity Chef father Jacques Pepin.

"I loved my father, but he was resistant to change. We needed new chairs, and it took me two years to convince him," said a smiling Maccioni. "Two years! I do not describe that as 'winning' an argument with him!"

There is no arguing the Pasta e fagiolo, on the "Alvaro's Favourite" section of the menu, is worth crossing the Atlantic – or Arctic – for. So, I would cross town from Knightsbridge and the Milestone Hotel for the experience.

To do so I got into the Milestone Hotel's tiny wood-paneled elevator wearing a royal purple blazer and tie. As the London phone booth-sized lift went down, the doors opened at the second floor and a woman, in a hurry, was about to step in when she suddenly noticed I was inside. The sight of me startled her.

"I am not a ghost. I am real," I said. The woman, with pulled-back blonde hair, laughed as I allowed, "But I guess I am a little bit scary."

She slipped in, and the white shorts, tank top and sneakers she wore were as bright as her smile. She had pulled-back blonde hair.

The doors were closing on the close quarters when she said, in an English accent, "Sorry I just need to push that the button behind you. Button 'B,' for the fitness center in the basement."

I moved out of the way but still pushed the button for her.

"Shouldn't 'B' at this hour of the day stand for "bar?"

She shrugged. "I know. And it is an awfully nice bar too. Have you been in it?"

"The very moment I arrived from Heathrow Airport." Then I shrugged. "It was morning, but my room was not ready yet."

"Oh right."

"Not a bad situation, really," I said. "A breakfast beer."

The door opened to the lobby for me to get out and the bouncy blonde looked up into my eyes as if the person who'd startled her in the elevator was now a curiosity of some value. She asked, "You are from America, aren't you?"

"How did you know? I joked. "California.

"Well, I'm sure you can tell where I am from," she countered.

I looked at her and squinted. "Hmmmm...India, that's it. India."

She burst out with a laugh. Then, with the lift doors closing, she pointed at me with a big smile on her face.

"You...you are funny!"

3

LOVING LONDON'S LA FAMIGLIA RESTAURANT

I had a date with an old flame, so I dressed my best and took a classic, black London taxi from the Milestone Hotel, just across from Kensington Palace to a restaurant named La Famiglia in Chelsea

It was twilight when I walked between the front flowers and fauna and under the indigo blue, streetside awning through the door and up into La Famiglia – its white tiled walls warmed by candles and subtle lighting. That is, the parts of the white walls which were visible, since most of the space is covered with a patchwork puzzle of framed photos – black and white or sepia-toned, of Maccioni family and friends or significant supporters who had, for decades since 1975, done exactly what I was doing – dining in one of the world's most wonderful restaurants. Bridget Bardot, Tony Bennett, Michael Caine, Peter Sellers, Princesses Margaret, Diana and Catherine, to name a few.

My photo is not on the wall, but I was greeted and seated with the warmth of a family member. This was the mantra of La Famiglia's founder, the late Florentine Alvaro Maccioni, the Godfather of Italian cuisine in London, who insisted, "Every single person who walks through the door is an important person."

I was led to the covered, open-air, back area of the restaurant. It was empty and all mine for the moment, but within 30 minutes would be filled and festive. It's a 210-seat restaurant, but it feels like 50.

The walls in that section, unlike the original front of the La Famiglia, were largely visible and mostly uncovered because they were white-painted, exposed brick. Occasional planters were affixed to the wall and the room is centered by a large, skeletal, wrought-iron, traditional Roman numeral clock with black numbers. Tufts of striped fabric concealed the ceiling except for the directional lights aimed at the tall potted trees dotted along the walls. At either end, where there wasn't brick, lattice wall coverings gave the space the feel of a Tuscan garden.

In my seat, I looked across the crystal-clear and etched wine and water glassware; shiny cutlery; ceramic flower vase; and the white doily on a silver bread dish atop my blue-checkered linen-covered table. The menu, with its black and white photo of an old-time, large Italian family, could wait as I breathed in my joy at being back and soaked in my surroundings.

I felt happier than I had in a long, long time...before even taking a bite.

I could sense I was smiling broadly - from ear to ear - at my date.

But the "old flame" I was meeting was La Famiglia restaurant herself, and I was alone with her again, at last. And admittedly in love.

Seated by myself, I never felt alone at La Famiglia, as any number of the bustling team of servers smoothly and subtly checked on me.

The very tall, dark-haired server Paolo seemed to enjoy himself more than anyone in the room. He did not whistle while he worked – he sang stanzas of classic Italian melodies and tarantellas such as "That's Amore;" "O Sole Mio;" and "Santa Lucia."

Paolo's singing was as sweet as the enthusiasm of a tenured, textured server named Maurizio, especially during the "dolce" conclusion of my meal, when he insisted I taste almost every dessert that came out of baker Raquel's oven, one after another.

"Oh, come now, you must try chocolate salami. It is popular in the south of Italy," Maurizio explained.

"Chocolate salami?" I asked warily.

It turned out salame de cioccolato is actually dark chocolate, eggs and sugar shaped with broken bits of biscuit added and dusted with confectioner's sugar before a night in the refrigerator makes it resemble charcuterie. While it looked like salami, it tasted like a light, dry fudge.

"But now you must try the almond souffle cake," Maurizio insisted. "Souffle con mandorle."

I dutifully obliged and was astonished to find the sponge cake in the layered desert was so light it served only as a delivery method for the mascarpone and Italian meringue.

"Our cheesecake all'Italiana, per favore, is next. It is baked. Cotto al forno. Very light. With berry sauce," he then said.

He was right – very light...and yet very cheesy.

It will not surprise you to learn that Maurizio slipped in scoops of gelato beside the dolce deserts.

And I was soon to learn there was still one more course to come...

"You know you cannot leave without tasting the homemade limoncello," came the voice of La Famiglia's proprietor, Marietta Maccioni.

"How did you know I was here?" I asked her as we hugged.

"I know when and where everyone in here is seated," she said, "even when I am off property."

The limoncello is a family affair-aperitif it turned out. Maccioni's 20-year beau Fabio Cozari, who is also La Famiglia's operations manager, and consultant chef Gonzalo Luzarraga collaborate on the syrupy potion.

Truth be told I was delighted to not leave, especially if it meant sitting and visiting with the adorable Maccioni, who maintains the tradition of her legendary late father Alvaro, who passed away in 2015, with her own twists - in the way Claudine Pepin supports, and spars, with her French celebrity Chef father Jacques Pepin.

"I loved my father, but he was resistant to change. We needed new chairs, and it took me two years to convince him," said a smiling Maccioni. "Two years! I do not describe that as 'winning' an argument with him!"

I asked if Alvaro ever admitted Marietta was right?

"Ha!" she laughed in response.

There is no arguing the Pasta e fagioli, on the "Alvaro's Favourite" section of the menu, is a thick bean soup with pasta worth crossing the Atlantic – or Arctic – for. When my bowl was empty, the only noticeable thing left in it was the embossed "La Famiglia" logo on the lip.

"Your olive tapenade is still as good as it was eight years ago," I told Maccione in an aside leaning toward her at the table to be heard over the lively din and Paolo's singing.

"I think it is getting better," she countered. It seems to be getting sweeter."

Then, Maccione, a woman of Italian heritage who speaks in an English accent, asked me what I had for my main.

"It was not easy to decide from your menu, but Paolo suggested to me the Pappardelle was the dish that best represents the restaurant," I told Maccione. (The menu describes Pappardelle al cinghiale as "fresh egg flat pasta cut into a broad ribbon shape traditionally of Tuscany served with our family wild boar sauce.")

Maccione nodded in agreement with Maurizio. "The fennel in that dish cuts the wild boar ragu which can sometimes have a gamey flavor," she explained.

"If you say so," I said to her, "but I can also tell you those pappardelle noodles tasted like candy."

Maurizio poured me a glass of wine when he could see that the stylish Maccione and I were going to sit and spend a little time catching up on this and that.

"Grazie mille," I said.

"You will see most of the waiters who work here are old school Italian. Service like you would see in the 1960's and '70's. I love that kind of waiting. You feel like you are in Italy," she noted.

Maccione told me of her plans for a La Famiglia 50th anniversary party and while we talked, could not help but keep a keen eye, through her spectacles, on the restaurant. And I could not help but share my admiration and appreciation with her.

"Your restaurant is so crisp and clean and elegant."

"People tell me the atmosphere here is different than any restaurant. I would like it if they said it was the food, but they say the atmosphere," Maccione admitted "One of my regulars, who is in his 30's, was brought here by his grandfather. He held his wedding reception here, and now he has a son of his own, so it is four generations coming here. And we also get people who have been twice in their lives, but they feel like regulars."

La Famiglia is her father's last in a series of successful, high-profile London restaurants and clubs (he served Sinatra), and Marietta Maccione is in lockstep with her father's experience and vision.

"He was larger than life: a character. Everyone loved and respected him. He was born in Tuscany, in Vinci, where Leonardo DaVinci was born. My grandfather was a farmer," she explained. "When my father moved to London, he was part of a group of restauranteurs called the 'Italian Pioneers of Food' for the U.K. When he passed away, The Telegraph and Times and national newspapers carried his obituary. I was not expecting that."

Alvaro Maccione was obviously very high-profile, and Mariatta told me when he was at the restaurant he liked being in the front of the house. "But he also loved cooking, even at home. My mom does not even know how to cook. She was his kitchen porter," she laughed lovingly.

Some of Alvaro's other favourites on the menu include chicken liver pate with toasted Tuscan bread; thick spaghetti of Siena with homemade tomato passata sauce; grilled whole mackerel with fresh rosemary served with a salsa verde of parsley, anchovies and garlic. And named for his daughter, Manzo Marietta is thinly sliced filet of beef lightly cooked with garlic, extra virgin olive oil and served with a garnish of misticanza salad.

"Marietta, what was it like when Princess Diana would come into La Famiglia?"

"It was amazing When she walked in, the restaurant went silent. So many famous people come here, but I have never seen that," she answered, speaking with affection and reverence.

Catherine, now Princess of Wales – the future Queen - has subsequently dined at La Famiglia, Maccione recalled.

"I was at the door, and I did not know she was coming because a friend of hers had booked the table. The Princess walked in and was the nicest, loveliest person ever. It was very busy that night and nobody even noticed her. With Diana there was so much more commotion outside. I was so happy for Kate that she could walk in and sit with her friends. She sat right near where you are sitting now, Michael. Her security police protection sat very discreetly nearby."

Only because I asked her, Marietta told me she is still friends with Barbara Broccoli, the producer of the 007 James Bond movies.

"Barbara Broccoli is such a nice lady. If you get to know her and she likes you, you're in her group of people she can trust and rely on. She knows when she comes here to La Famiglia she eats well, and I look after her. She has brought each of the actors who have played 007 here," Maccione recalled. She told me she was going to a private estate auction organized by the family of Roger Moore, who played James Bond in seven 007 films.

While Maccione wants guests at La Famiglia to feel as though they are in Italy, she ventures to Italy twice a year.

"My mother is Sicilian, so I like to go right down to the Province of Ragusa – to a tiny fishing village nobody goes to called Donnalucata."

Everybody comes to La Famiglia – even the acclaimed London cabbies know its Chelsea World's End location at 7 Langton Street SW10 well.

"This restaurant is part of the cab drivers' 'knowledge,'" Maccione explained. "The Knowledge" is the training London cabbies must complete over three years to familiarize themselves with London's most important, frequent destinations in order to taxi people through the streets without looking.

Once you now have the "knowledge" of La Famiglia, you will never go to London again without booking a table at my beloved Chelsea cucina.

4

SOUTH BEACH SUNDAY

 When, what to my wondering eyes should appear?

Wait 'till you hear!

Some people spy UFO's. Some see "pink elephants." Some look at the Loch Ness Monster, or purport to have laid eyes on Bigfoot.

My Miami mirage, on a steamy Sunday South Beach afternoon, was the view of a glorious woman glistening in the sun...yet I could not believe my eyes.

I savor every moment simmering in the international, diverse, colorful culture of Miami Beach – particularly the vibrant, eclectic South Beach area. The Ocean Drive-art deco vibe is lavish, luxurious, and loco!

Eccentrically ethereal is how I would describe the woman who appeared in my path as I wandered up the waterway called Government Cut. It is an inglorious name for the exciting channel of blue water that flows between Fishers Island and Miami Beach. Cruise liners and container ships float through it from Port Miami to the Atlantic

Ocean. The Government Cut sidewalk is popular for watching the big boats and waving to the cruise passengers as they look down at the crowds from the high-above railings of their ships.

As I walked up the promenade, the Thriller Miami bounced by. It is a cigarette-style speedboat that takes tourists around the port for views of celebrity homes and zips them into Biscayne Bay for a bit. The neon pink, open-topped rocket was kicking up a big, watery, white rooster tail plume behind it.

I figured, if I did not dawdle, I could reach and walk out onto the South Pointe Pier where, from the end, I could watch Thriller Miami round the jetty and turn back into Government Cut on its way back to its marina dock at Downtown Miami's Bayside Marketplace. South Pointe Pier, in addition to bordering the channel, also provides, by looking north, a sweeping view of Miami Beach and its high-rise hotels and, at twilight, the glow of its neon-bordered buildings on Ocean Drive.

Only bright, noonday sunshine was between me and the pier about 50 yards ahead until I noticed I was approaching the aforementioned woman. She was perched in my pathway sitting on one of the few concrete benches spaced along the sidewalk. But this woman was not just sitting. She was occupying that stone bench in the way The David occupies its pedestal in Florence's Accademia Galleria or the way Michelangelo's other sculpted masterpiece, La Pieta, anchors St. Peter's Basilica. She was a work of art, as I could see as my footsteps drew me nearer.

The woman, with long, dark, thick, luxurious, wavy hair, had draped a beach towel across the concrete, backless bench. Atop the towel, using the entire length of the bench, she positioned her bronzed body on an angle with one of her legs dangling over the side at the knee. Her arms were extended behind her with her palms planted on the bench to support her, which set her shoulders broadly beside her and arched her back which, conversely, supinated her shiny, oiled upper torso to the sun. Her head was tossed back in a purposeful pose which surrendered to the sky as if the sun were her flashbulb.

The woman, who I estimated to be 45 years-old, was wearing what appeared to be a very expensive gold-colored bikini with a subtle pattern and the beach bag sitting next to her was as motionless as she was.

If her eyes were open, she would be viewing the water, so I decided, as I was about to pass, I would alter my path to the left in order to not disrupt her view. She sensed me as I strolled by, and her head turned just a little. I acknowledged this by saying hello as I passed.

"Helllllloooo," the woman responded.

Her response came in an elongated, lyrical, friendly fashion. If a single word can go up and down the musical scale, her deep, unbothered voice did it, delivering the greeting like a warm bun just out of the oven.

I could not tell if she had spoken in an accent or an affectation.

So naturally, I had to turn back to hear more.

I was past the woman, but I paused my gait mid-step without stopping, if you know what I mean, in a non-interrupting lean away which I considered to be unobtrusive, non-threatening body language meant to convey that I was not stopping.

Before I spoke, I saw she was still, glowing and glistening, in the same stunning pose.

"Are you missing a photographer, by any chance?"

She laughed – again low and long.

"You look like a magazine cover sitting there," I continued.

"Thaaaank yoooouuuu," she cooed in that same, deep, elongated tone followed by a gracious smile.

I grinned, nodded, and kept moving.

After five minutes on the pier watching the fishermen and teenaged tourists taking selfies, I walked back off under the pier's archway and noticed the bench was empty – the woman was gone. No bikini – no beach bag.

I thought about her "posing for no one" and her haunting voice.

I imagined that, as quickly as she was gone, maybe she was never actually there? Maybe the woman in the golden bikini was an apparition during a walk on a hot, humid day. A Miami mirage.

I was left to only wonder what her story was. Why was she posing like that? Where was she from? What did her deep yet lyrical voice sound like when speaking more than two words?

I shrugged and continued walking. My plan was to spend the day on foot, beginning right where I was, near the pier at Government Cut along South Pointe Park on the south tip of South Beach. The park, full of trees, grassy spaces, paved trails, and fountains, is a placid buffer from which you can see Miami's skyline or dive into the South Beach scene with its stylish oceanfront hotels and artsy, coral-color and bright white/aqua-blue-windowed high-rise condo buildings.

My plan was to walk, in no hurry, up Ocean Avenue all the way to the end at Loews's Miami Beach Hotel. Then, probably linger at the adjacent Lincoln Road Shopping District off Collins Avenue at 16th, which is a scene to itself with everything from streetside hookah lounges to boutique shops scored by street musicians in a fashionable retro setting.

I planned to make my traditional stops along the walk to cool off with refreshments: historic Joe's Stone Crab for key lime pie; Mango's for Latin Music and fanciful bar-top dancers; and, if I want a serious buzz, I might sit and sip a frozen concoction called "Call a Cab" on the second-floor balcony above Lummus Park Beach at Wet Willies.

The open-air, art deco-style endless pool party at Clevelander, at the corner of Ocean and 10th street, is also hard to skip.

But before all that, once I cleared South Pointe Park's palm trees, I like to duck into the South Pointe Tavern, which is on South Pointe Drive, across from the public parking lot in front of Nikki Beach, which is a chic day and night club.

South Pointe Tavern is designed to be a local bar, so it is comfortable, cool, and dark with bistro-seating, exposed brick, nautical-style lighting, leather couches, and bookshelves with classic titles about art, music and design. There are vintage travel posters in the men's room – I have not been in the ladies' room.

I sat alone at the bar, except for a senior citizen who wheeled up in a vintage red convertible, drank a Miller Lite, and left.

I chose a cappuccino, and, since it was just us at the bar, I made a little small talk with the bartender from Argentina, who told me all about how she loved Santa Barbara, California.

"You've been working here for some time now," I posed to the bartender.

"Yes. Two years."

"I remember seeing you before."

As she went about cutting limes and washing glasses, I was surprised to catch myself hurrying through the cappuccino. I tried to slow myself down to a chill state – or, for me, what passes as a chill state. But nevertheless, I paid the tab.

"Muchas gracias. Adios," I told the bartender, who waved back as I went out the front door, turned left, and continued my walk.

I was about 40 paces down the street when what to my wondering eyes should appear? Walking my way up the sidewalk, and soon to pass me, was the dark-haired, deep-voiced, mysterious model from the waterfront bench. Over her bikini, this time, she was wearing a white, elegant, knit cover-up which was more holes than fabric. She was also toting the big bursting beach bag, somehow effortlessly.

As we were about to pass in a parallel intersection, her on my right, I greeted her while walking.

"Hello, again."

"Hiiiiiiiiiiiiiiii," she responded, once again elongating the word in her alluring baritone voice while smiling.

Neither of us stopped strolling in opposite directions.

After a short but respectful distance, I stopped and turned around in the shade to view her. It occurred to me the mysterious woman with the beach bag would soon be passing...South Pointe Tavern.

Then I got a sinking feeling.

"Oh no," I whispered aloud as I watched her walk up the sidewalk. She was 30 yards away, but I could see what was about to happen from 100 miles away. "Please do not do what I think you might do. Don't do it. Nooo."

Sure enough, the woman turned right and into the South Pointe Tavern.

"Jesus," I said to myself, before a torrent of tortuous thoughts cascaded through my mind.

"If I had only stayed at South Pointe Tavern two more minutes, the answers to my intrigue would have walked right in the front door. I was the only person at the bar, so even a tiny bit of banter would have been natural if not expected. But no, I had to rush out to the next stop," I berated myself. "The universe was randomly delivering my answer right to me."

Timing was everything.

"What a dope!" I remarked.

I considered going back in, but not too seriously, because it would have been transparently awkward possibly to the woman and certainly to the bartender.

I know, I know, fortune favors the brave, but this time, the mystery woman would remain just that.

"Maybe," I thought, "the universe wanted me to miss talking to her. Maybe the universe had me rush the cappuccino to make sure I left the South Pointe Tavern right when I did?"

Walking back up the street and going back in, while tempting, seemed counterintuitive to life's rich pattern. Was I being a coward? Or was there power in resigning to the ironic vicissitudes of life?

Let's face it: it is likely the two smiling moments with her were probably as good as it was ever going to get. And they were very good.

Or maybe...she was not real.

Your move, universe.

5

SAN DIEGO SENORITA AT SEREA

She had literally stumbled into my path by barreling toward the coffee table just before taking the seminar stage in a Las Vegas breakout room at the annual Virtuoso Week Travel Conference. We were both wearing facemasks that morning, so our smiles weren't visible but the humor of the clumsy collision of two tall professionals prompted a moment of comical commiseration.

As we steadied ourselves, she shrugged and joked, "I simply cannot make a presentation or speak without a coffee first."

Under my mask one corner of my mouth was lifted in a bemused, entertained grin.

"Perfectly understandable," I allowed. "That was some entrance. Break a leg up there."

Her dress was colorful, and, on the dais, so was she. Compared to the other panelists, who were sharp and smooth with a smidgen of smarminess, I found her entirely authentic and genuine. The other professionals were buttoned-up and fine, but there is a difference between taking your work seriously...and taking yourself seriously.

Her unvarnished enthusiasm made her cliched clunker line "Travel is my life, and my life is travel" tolerable, especially in her slight Latin lilt. But her caffeinated contribution to the industry forum wasn't facts and figures – it was honest, firsthand, beating heart storytelling about her recent "itinerary interruptus" in pandemic-pestered Portugal. I admired the way she described rolling with the necessary, creative adjustments. It made me trust her. And I felt certain clients who rely on her legendary travel advisor company appreciate her honest-to-goodness goodness and on-the-ground experience.

I enjoyed the presentation at Virtuoso Travel Week and learned a lot. But I had more to glean so I emailed the erstwhile, coffee-craving panelist and, from our homes six states away, we exchanged messages for a couple months. The exchanges were plucky, and like a game show we would test each other's travel knowledge by sending photos we'd taken around the world while on the road: "Can you name this seafront European location?"

I nearly fell off my chair when she was able to answer one of my challenge photos by identifying the doorman standing in front of the ornate, colonial, Oyster Box Hotel in Durban, South Africa. This worldly woman knew her stuff!

It wasn't easy but I eventually stumped her by sending a curveball photo of the Fairmont Grand Del Mar. It was a trick of sorts because that magnificent resort property is in her hometown of San Diego!

Speaking of San Diego, other than our momentary coffee collision, we'd never even met or even spoken on the phone. My trails had taken me to Mackinac Island, and Utah's Greater Zion Region, so we made plans to have dinner near her home on Coronado Island when I was scheduled to be just 90 miles away in Los Angeles for a few days.

"I know just the place to take you when you come down to San Diego," she wrote with her typical, natural enthusiasm. (Of course, with all of her travel expertise, she had a plan.)

The night before we were to meet, while still in L.A., I texted over my last travel quiz challenge photo. I snapped it from my table at Spire 73, the rooftop bar at the InterContinental Downtown Los Angeles. I held a slender glass of golden champagne in the frame with the panoramic Pacific sunset and skyline view behind the bubbly. She messaged back something sweet and while I was 73 stories up, we were 24 hours from meeting.

A 120-mile drive south down I-5 the next day placed me checking-in to San Diego's Westin Gaslamp Quarter. Here, $17 million in renovations helped create rooms like the Westin Workout room I was given with a Peloton exercise bike in it. Westin's re-investment in the well-located hotel adjacent to the Padres home baseball stadium and the nightlife of Gaslamp Quarter also created a welcoming lobby bar, which is where I was headed after showering, shaving and dressing for a drink before ducking out for dinner.

I was sipping my solitary glass of red wine to cut my nerves when a couple chatted me up.

"You look like you're going to a wedding?" the woman asked.

"Well, not just quite yet" I deadpanned back with my own private joke.

I was dressed my best, however, and headed to Serea, the seafront seafood restaurant on Coronado Island my dinner companion had chosen for us. Serea, with its organic, "ocean-friendly" menu is in the historic Hotel Del Coronado - circa 1888. As I approached the entrance door a group of three younger men passing me going the other way, looked me over and engaged me.

"Man, you're looking good," one of them said, saluting me in a sing-song cadence. "Yeah, brother. Sharp!"

In a town that once hosted the America's Cup races, that statement put more winds of confidence in my sails.

With my Prada loafers lifted by these random votes of encouragement, it seemed I was walking, or rather gliding, on the right path that night. Until, that is, I got inside "the Del" and found it to be a castle-like campus unto itself: an indoor rabbit warren of lobbies, hallways, pathways, and flowered courtyards. I followed my better angels (ignoring a cliched male stereotype of an aversion to asking for directions) and decided to duck into the Del's Signature Shop to ask for directions. I didn't want to be late.

"Serea is just down the hall, out to the back patio and to the right," said the older woman behind the counter before her counterpart, a woman stocking inventory, chimed in.

"It is a special occasion?" she asked.

"Well...in a sense, yes. Yes, I'd say it is," I answered – once again amusing myself privately.

"I knew it," she countered with a big smile. "It's always a special occasion when someone goes to Serea."

I thanked the ladies.

"Have a special night," she said grinning as if she was now in on a secret.

I started down the hallway very much liking the idea my new friend had chosen Serea for our dinner.

The entrance to Serea is on the back, western-facing ground-level side of the Hotel Del Coronado. It was very festive on the expansive back lawn as a mix of hotel guests, tourists and attendees sat in what appeared to be a balloon-festooned celebration in the softening golden California twilight.

The restaurant appeared quiet, though, and the walkway was bathed in setting sunlight when I arrived at the white maître d stand. The 5:30 reservation she'd made was under her name but despite the fact she lived next to the hotel, she wasn't there yet. Rather than meet her empty-handed, I stepped up to the adjacent tiki bar and quickly ordered two glasses of champagne.

I tapped my toe with nervous impatience as the bartender dawdled a bit opening the bottle and funneling the bubby into the flutes. Without a second to spare I was able to present the glasses as a greeting and provoke a sublime smile as she spotted me while strolling up the sidewalk. It was a champagne moment – followed by a toast – and a table overlooking the Pacific at a gentle, sophisticated restaurant we had virtually to ourselves.

Serea Coastal Cuisine describes itself as a "sea-to-table" dining experience serving sustainable seafood from San Diego down the Baja Peninsula. Chef Jojo Ruiz, a Californian who includes a Mediterranean flair, sources ingredients from purveyors such as Pacifico Aquaculture, known for its innovative, sustainability-first farming program for ocean-raised sea bass.

Our lively, joyful dinner conversation and laughs flowed back and forth across the table without seams so eating seemed secondary, but we started with the Serea Mezze. It was perfect to pick at the marinated olives, marcona almonds, hummus tahini, salsa macha, whipped farmers cheese and grilled pita. We didn't really need to order mains, since the conversation was so satiating, but we dutifully added Pacifico striped bass to the sips of sauvignon blanc that followed the champagne.

The culinary presentations were as visually appealing as the white, blue and gray pattered skirt she wore and my somewhat sympatico white linen paisley jacket.

We strolled down the sidewalk for a margarita nightcap on the patio at the hotel's Babcock & Story Bar, where a deejay played pop-hits. The only song I recall was a Beatles tune that provoked conversation about how she'd met Paul McCartney. I had once met Billy Joel. Given our intriguing lives in travel, never once did we try to trump each other. We shared stories and sentiments of countries and continents, resorts and retreats.

She entertained with stories of her studies at The Sorbonne and life in London; her early years growing up in Mexico; her San Diego television work and her daughter's school bus schedule. Plus, her brother's participation in their wildly successful family travel advisor business founded by her mother – who she referred to as "Big Mama." (Big Mama, by the way, has a ticket to space aboard Richard Branson's Virgin Galactic when her turn comes up.)

After a margarita we walked under the stars along the Pacific to the parking lot where she put me in her personal, neighborhood golf cart – customized with doors – for a ride to my car. Since she loves Paris, we bid each other adieu.

When I got back to the valet entrance of the Westin San Diego Gaslamp Quarter Hotel, the large wall bordering the entrance was lit up by a large projected mural. It was, like the couple in the bar; the fellows who complimented my appearance; and the gift shop ladies who felt something special was in the air; yet another fun coincidence. The light-up mural read "Tonight is a good night for a good night."

The next morning, in keeping with my passion and profession, I was up early on my way back north to Anaheim to check out the latest additions to Disneyland. It was starting to get light in the Golden State at 6:30 when, as I steered my rental car north, I noticed the scenic Del Mar Race Track off to my left. The next landmark visible from the freeway would be the Mission at San Juan Capistrano – where the swallows return each year.

I was alone with my thoughts while my radio was blaring a bumping tune by 2Pac called "California Love." As I streamed past the palm trees while I grooved to the song, I also heard the alert of an early morning text message hit my I-phone.

"Ping!"

The Bluetooth screen on my dashboard spelled the message out. It was from my worldly, charming dinner companion. The text read:

"Thank you so very much. Last night was a prefect evening."

My road life and profession then took me to the Dominican Republic, Germany, Mexico, Arizona, and Cuba and beyond since our sunset dinner. Instead of texting with her I now occasionally stick a stamp on a handwritten postcard and drop it in the old-fashioned mail from places like Leipzig, Mazatlan, or Miami. She's since been to London, Scotland, and Napa Valley.

Given our globetrotting, our paths will maybe cross again somewhere out there. But only maybe. But, to use a Casablanca cliche...we'll always have Serea. "A perfect evening."

6

PAULA ABDUL ON THE HOLLYWOOD RED CARPET

The Golden State's setting sunlight streamed across the Hollywood Boulevard corridor as if it were a river of gilded glamor.

It was the fog of fame - a magical mist set further ablaze by the camera lights on the red carpet across the street from the Dolby Theater - known as the venue of gold statuettes named "Oscar."

One glance upward, behind the adjacent Loews Hotel, was the iconic Hollywood sign. But I could not see past Paula.

Paula Abdul. The pristine, preening, pretty but not pretentious, Paul Abdul.

The famed Laker girl-turned pop music sensation and "American Idol" founding judge was among the luminaires who'd accepted invitations to the premier of "Chip 'n' Dale: Rescue Rangers," the animated film that would play that evening on the silver screen of the El Capitan Theater.

John Mulaney and Adam Samberg, the voices of "Chip" and "Dale," respectively, were posing for pix and chatting on camera between the pipe-and-drape and temporary hedges that created a bigshot bubble on the red carpet covering the sidewalk under the carnival-colored marquis above the theater's box office window.

Cast members Seth Rogan and J.K. Simmons were supposed to be on their way, I was pinching myself that I was actually there. Paula Abdul was, like her hit song title, "Straight Up" (from her 7-million copy-selling, 1988 debut album "Forever Your Girl") right there before my eyes. The question was, could I manage to muster the courage to approach her? Would she be, like another of her song titles, a "Cold Hearted Snake?" I tried to read her "Vibeology" to see if maybe "Opposites Attract" and she might be "Forever My Girl."

Did I dare introduce myself to Paula Abdul? Read on...

Show biz scenes such as the one I found myself in happen frequently on Hollywood Boulevard. Loews Hollywood Hotel is baked right into Tinseltown's cake. The 20-story hotel is literally embedded into the cement footprint of the aforementioned Dolby Theater; the iconic TCL Chinese Theater; the Hollywood and Highland shopping complex; and surrounded by the Hollywood Walk of Fame. Hotel guests can see all of it, plus the Hollywood sign and the mysterious Magic Castle, from Loews guestrooms, starlight event spaces and rooftop swimming pool.

There are many, shall we say, varied tourism experiences in the hotel's vicinity. Souvenir shops sell replica Oscars and there are tours of the homes of the stars (present and past.) You can put your hands and feet into the cement spots celebs did and get selfies at the sidewalk star of your choice. Costumed characters will pose for pics for tips.

ABC's Jimmy Kimmel tapes his late-night television show weekday afternoons at 5 p.m. at the El Capitan Theater in front of a studio audience. Tickets are free at 1iota.com and it's the best entertainment value in town: Kimmel up-close; a live band; the opportunity to see how a major television show is taped and celebrity guests.

Don Barris, the Don Rickles-type comic who warms up the Kimmel audience, sometimes performs after Kimmel up on Sunset Boulevard at the famed Comedy Store.

Keep your eyes open at Loews, too. During my three nights in a fourth-floor room there was a private security person guarding the end of the hall opposite the elevator from my room. I knew better than to ask who they were guarding. Guests of shows such as Paramount's "Dr. Phil" are lodged at Loews, too.

Blocks away from Loews Hollywood Hotel, Musso and Frank Grill have been serving actors and agents since 1919 – from Charlie Chaplin to Johnny Depp (who sat in the booth next to the phone booth waiting for a studio callback for his big break.) More recently, in 2019, dynamic director Quentin Tarantino shot scenes of his "Once Upon a Time in Hollywood" in the dining room with Al Pacino, Leonardo DiCaprio and Brad Pitt.

A quick cab or ride share from Loews just past the Hollywood Bowl will put you in the Universal Studios Hollywood Theme Park, where I was surprised to find the customary studio tram tour is also part simulated, high-tech thrill ride. There are plenty of actual movie-based thrill rides, too, based on "Jurassic Park," "Transformers," "The Simpsons," "The Hulk," and "Harry Potter."

Universal's expansive, scenic park offers sweeping views of Warner Brothers and Disney's studios below in Burbank, too. Being dropped off and picked up at Universal Studios will save you time and money.

I knew my red-carpet coach would soon turn into a pumpkin when everyone went inside to take their seats. I'd already had the opportunity to stall by exchanging a quick, friendly word with John Mulaney -

but it was now or never. I noticed Paula Abdul standing alone after one of her attending entourage - a slender man in a dusty mustard-colored suit – had finished touching up her makeup so she could pose before the customary paparazzi wall.

In terms of a red-carpet designer fashion report, I can't tell you "who she was wearing," but Abdul was in arresting red from head to toe, including her lipstick, which matched the handbag she clutched, which was shaped like a pair of lips ala the Rolling Stones logo. (I later learned it was by lulu Guinness - $380, for what it's worth.) Her shoes were super-high white pumps with the same red lips on each of the toes. The big puffy, cape-like shoulders of her otherwise short, tight, mini-dress itself, evoked an image of those same red lips.

Paula Abdul's brown hair was up in a bun with bangs trailing over and around her eyes and Syrian/Californian complexion. I noticed red fingernails and rings on both pinky fingers and one on her right pointer. Long, thin, silver (or white gold?) chain earrings dangled down.

For a woman who was a Laker cheerleader, served as Janet Jackson's choreographer, and danced her way across the world stage, Paula Abdul was vibrant even when standing still.

I was surprised a bit to see her, amid the other "beautiful people," standing alone. So, like jumping into a cold pool, I sauntered (maybe stumbled) toward the solo-standing Paula Abdul. I'd suddenly gained the confidence to chat her up since I was, after all, and however I got there, a guest on the red carpet, too. It wasn't a big crowd of people I found myself mixing with. So...mix I did – without a plan of what I would say. So, I kept it spontaneous and sincere.

"Hello, Paula. Thank you for all the fun you've given us over the years, I said."

I was anticipating from Paula maybe a nod and smile, or maybe even a customary "your welcome" response from a dismissive distance. But Abdul approached me.

"Well thank you very much. That's very nice of you to say," she said.

She could not have been more gracious, warm, or friendly. She seemed genuinely appreciative that I spoke to her and offered her hand to allow me to introduce myself.

I told her my name while gently shaking her palm-down, soft, smooth, bent hand. She intimated that she wanted to know more about me. It was then I tried to get cute and drop a name I knew she was familiar with from her Laker days.

"I'm from Lansing, Michigan. Magic Johnson's hometown."

To say my statement went over like a lead balloon would imply that Abdul gave it any notice whatsoever. If she heard it, she pretended not to. I don't know why but perhaps they're not the L.A. pals I presumed they'd be.

I didn't have time to regret the comment – or even recover from it – because Abdul then extended the conversation:

"We have met before, haven't we?"

I was surprised and searched for a polite way to tell Paula Abdul that no, we hadn't met before. The last thing I wanted to do was disagree or correct her. The only time I'd been in any room with her was the front (or maybe second) row at the 20,000-seat Palace of Auburn Hills during one of her concerts in the late 80's. She did sing off the stage and high-five fans but c'mon, a sea of people in front of the lights dancing during a song? No way she was remembering that.

Before I could offer any of this as a compromise, Abdul spoke again. This time I noticed she looked directly into my eyes.

"Yes, I am certain. That's it. You and I have met before," she said.

Paula Abdul was way more interested in talking to me than I would have expected. Is it possible I was being naïve? I began to wonder whether maybe she was saying this as a way to actually extend the conversation.

So, I mustered up some Hollywood suave:

"Paula, I'm not sure if we've met before...but I'd sure like to meet you again."

Bam! LOL. I delivered the line with all the "007 schmaltz" imaginable.

Abdul was smiling and about to say...something...when, alas, out of nowhere, her handlers hustled her away! As they hurried her in those tall red heels in a "Rush Rush" toward a bank of television cameras, she turned enroute to look to me from under her bangs and bid me goodbye with a gracious smile and a wave of the lulu Guinness clutch bag. Or was it goodbye...again?

Until next time, Paula!

7

PRICELESS ENCOUNTER AT CASA DE CAMPO RESORT

 What I love about Casa de Campo Resort and Villas, near La Romana in the Dominican Republic, is the excitement of knowing that each day can be so very different from the last. I experienced this in a romantic lightning bolt that struck during an already satisfying sunny sunset. More on that in a moment.

But why is the Casa de Campo experience so varied? It's because the resort's luxury offerings are spread out and staged in not only different places but entirely different settings. And all of them open air to embrace the warm, tropical reason you came – or moved – to Casa de Campo.

These resort areas are populated by a variety of people: business titans who arrived by Lear Jet; sailors who came via cabin cruiser; golf aficionados who've made a pilgrimage to challenge the Pete Dye-designed Teeth of the Dog course; the betrothed and honeymooners; and more.

The variety of voyagers not only have the option of three completely different scenic golf courses but also to shop, dine and discover entertainment in the gardens of a Mediterranean medieval village. They can feel as if they're lost on a desert island with the comforts of a beach club.

Plus, unlike crowded beach destinations like Cancun, Rio or Miami, Casa de Campo has no high-rise buildings and in terms of population is very low-density.

Guests who don't want sand in their toes can also socialize in glamorous, designer swimming pool settings; and stroll with a Cuban cigar through a marina setting that feels closer to Portofino than Punta Cana.

There is a sense that anything can happen. And it can.

Casa de Campo, which translated from Spanish means "country house," is not your ordinary golf destination. It is 7,000 acres of homes, hotel rooms and holes of golf both along the Caribbean Sea and high above the property over the Chavon River. Everything about the resort is dramatic and chic with a thick sense of international intrigue in the air.

The homeowners, hotel guests, marina boaters and staff who populate the enclave come from around the globe to put their feet up, lace up their soft spikes, or lift a mojito to celebrate sunsets in an infinity pool looking over the beach.

You'll overhear a symphony of different languages bouncing between Spanish, Italian, Portuguese, French Canadian, German, English and more blowing in the breeze under sunny skies. The resort's staff of internationally intriguing golf professionals come from as far and wide as Canada, Argentina, Italy, Wisconsin and San Diego under the direction of Robert Birtel from New Orleans. The head caddie master is from Puerto Rico.

Polo, riding, shooting, spa-going, golf, tennis, swimming and shopping are part of the Casa de Campo experience on a gated property so expansive that hotel guests are given golf carts to maneuver between amenities. Getting some steps in on the golf courses, or laps in the pools or warm sea, is a good idea given the quality culinary choices available throughout the resort. Sometimes hotels and all-inclusive resorts, particularly properties on islands, serve substandard food or average fare. Not Casa de Campo, which serves a wide variety of international gourmet choices at restaurants with completely varied atmospheres.

Chilango Taqueria overlooks the cobblestone Plaza Chavon and its church-front fountain in the replica 16th century Medieval village of Altos de Chavon. This is a popular scenic spot for weddings and especially wedding photos. The casual restaurant serves Mexican street food in view of blanketed donkeys and artists selling their jewelry and wares.

La Piazzetta is in that ornate, Altos de Chavon setting high above the river, too. Casa de Campo's first restaurant was designed by Oscar de la Renta and embraces the major influence Italian immigrants infused in the La Romana area.

Minitas Beach Club and Restaurant is the premium spot for sunset on the sand and along the infinity pool deck. You might catch sight, through the blowing, white linen curtains of the cabanas, of an occasional ocean liner cruising by. In that sophisticated setting try the octopus carpaccio; duck confit; ossobuco; prawn and avocado salad; mango gazpacho; tropical ceviche; Iberian pizza; chicken and pork paella; or Mediterranean branzino in addition to many other unique dishes.

La Casita and SBG elegantly serve ocean-to-table seafood in seafront settings.

La Cana serves French-inspired fare with live music, hand-rolled cigars, and Dominican rums. Causa serves Peruvian food in the creole, Nikkei and Chifa style.

Breakfast at Lago allows for pre-round views of the famed Teeth of the Dog golf course or a peek at other players finishing their rounds during lunch after the round.

One is wise to keep their eyes open for celebrities, too. The likes of Jay-Z, Beyonce, A-Rod, J-Lo, Derek Jeter, the Kardashians, Drake, Rihanna, Michael Jordan, Dennis Quaid, and many others have enjoyed the stylish luxury of Casa de Campo's Minitas Beach Club; yacht-filled marina, and Altos de Chavon Mediterranean artist's colony with its coliseum amphitheater opened with a performance by Frank Sinatra. Ol' Blue Eyes was known as the Chairman of the Board, and Commanders in Chief have caucused at Casa de Campo as well including U.S. Presidents George H.W. Bush, Bill Clinton, and George W. Bush.

Stylish, swank, and sophisticated architecture throughout the resort makes everyone feel like they're on-stage in surroundings that feel like movie sets. And sometimes they are. "Apocalypse Now," starring Marlon Brando, Robert Duvall, and Martin Sheen famously filmed jungle scenes on the Chavon River in the shadows of Altos de Chavon.

Casa de Campo is a headlining resort that is a star in itself, much like hotels that make enduring appearances in television shows like Four Seasons Maui HBO's "White Lotus" or the Turtle Bay Resort in "Forgetting Sarah Marshall," or Miami's Fontainebleau Hotel in the 007 flick "Goldfinger."

Straight out of central casting is Montreal native Gilles Gagnon, the French Canadian who was a professional hockey player in the early 1970's but traded scoring goals for sinking putts by skating into the position as golf professional at Casa de Campo Resort. He now keeps all of the resort's secrets as Casa de Campo's golf professional emeritus and special golf ambassador. One of the secrets is the exact burial spot of a golf world legend.

Gagnon is loved and respected throughout the golf world as is his late friend Pete Dye who designed the famed Teeth of the Dog and the resort's other scenic golf courses including the Links Course and the dramatic Dye Fore course.

"Without proper heavy machinery to crack the coral the tireless Dominican crew used sledgehammers, pickaxes, and chisels. The result is a true masterpiece with seven holes created by God," wrote Dye in his autobiography.

Dye also created landmark PGA Tour courses such as TPC Sawgrass; Whistling Straits and Harbor Town, and chose to live, die and be buried at Casa de Campo.

The title of Dye's autobiography "Bury Me in a Pot Bunker," was fulfilled by his surviving family members and Gagnon. The latter took the ailing Dye for a sunset cart ride near the bunker in question on the golf course during his final days. "Pete looked across at the sea and I told him, 'You've really done good, my friend.' The moment provoked a smile and a tear in his eye."

I met Gagnon 17 years ago while traveling with my eight-year-old son Harrison aboard a Windstar sailing cruise bound for Casa de Campo. I was one of about 120 passengers who'd boarded the sleek, four-masted sailing ship in San Juan and made golf course and spa stops in St. Barth's and Nevis.

During a day at sea Gagnon stood on the teak deck and gave, in his French-Canadian accent, a presentation on the golf courses of the Caribbean, particularly the dynamic Dye courses created at Casa de Campo – especially the Teeth of the Dog course.

"If you dare to challenge the 'Dog' at some point in your game this Dog WILL bite you...guaranteed," Gagnon warned with a grin.

I liked him immediately, but I also came to enjoy the casual company of an intriguing French woman named Elisabeth who was cruising solo with Gagnon and his wife Merrilee. Elisabeth, and her suntanned aura, reminded me of Jacqueline Kennedy Onassis. She spoke to me with an accent from behind her ever-present designer sunglasses and her slender self was always outfitted in perfectly pressed haute couture.

Our spontaneous conversations were exclusively limited to watching the waves while standing at the ship's rail apart from the others while Elisabeth enjoyed the occasional slender cigarette. I'd like to paint the picture of the mysterious, glamorous woman drawing smoke through a long cigarette holder, but I suspect that is a supplement of my romantic, creative imagination years later.

Ours were polite conversations of convenience since we were unaccompanied adults both single, shipboard, and solo. I liked Elisabeth's edge, but she was friendly. As intrigued as I was, I remained careful to respect the space of a person who'd surely come to value the solitude of a cigarette as a moment of meditation. She was not the type of person I would normally meet, but that's what Casa de Campo is all about.

One afternoon Gagnon and I stood on deck watching the wind in the sails as the Windstar ship slipped closer to Casa de Campo. It was the home port of Gagnon and his wife Merrilee, who, of course, lived at the resort development as did Elisabeth, who owned a home there.

"You seem to be getting along with our friend Elisabeth," Gagnon mentioned to me.

"She is definitely an intriguing woman," I answered.

"You should come spend some time at Casa de Campo. Get to know her," he suggested.

"You think so?"

"Yes," Gagnon said. "You'd be good for her. What Elisabeth really needs is someone to show her that life is not all about being rich."

"Oh?"

"Yes," he said. "She's worth about one-hundred-million dollars."

I wish, to this day, I could have seen the reaction on my own face.

"Gilles," I recovered and replied, "If Elisabeth really needs what you said then we are definitely a perfect match. Opposites attract!"

We both laughed...and are still laughing about it to this day.

8

NEW BOND GIRL MAY BE UKRAINIAN

The next 007 should face a beautiful but complex "Bond girl" to seduce and challenge him. That Bond girl should be Ukrainian actress Viktoriia Lazuto. Ana de Armas lit up the screen in her limited role in the last Bond film "Tomorrow Never Dies," and went on to play Marylin Monroe.

Lazuto, who has a Marylin Monroe connection and has appeared in Playboy's Ukraine edition, has a similar glamorous international likability that can launch – or sinisterly sink – 1000 ships.

I first met her in Hollywood while she was background acting on a feature film. Between takes, I asked her name.

"Call me 'Beautiful.' You can call me that, because I am beautiful," she answered in a dramatic Eastern European accent. "Where I go, the camera goes, because I am beautiful. And famous."

There is a lot of waiting around on movie sets, so I had time, during Lazuto's energetic, entertaining steam-of-consciousness chatter, to learn she is Ukrainian. "'Now I am in the 'wild, wild west.' But I am from the 'hot, hot east' of Ukraine – the craziest part."

It was a long, chilly overnight shoot on location. "I am not cold, because I am hot," she insisted, then she snuggled close to me and said, "You keep me warm." While sitting there, she answered a quick call on her rhinestone-encrusted smartphone. "So what? When I tell you to call me, call me 10 times," she demanded of whoever was on the other end.

After Lazuto hung up, I felt Lazuto shrug while she explained: "This guy tells me he's 'not ready to be my boyfriend.' I told him I can speak to him however I want because he said I am not his girlfriend! But I also want to find real friends in the industry who are men...not just men who are trying to sleep with me."

"I think they need you on set," I told her.

"I know they do," she said.

Earlier, during a dinner break on the shoot, I saw the little-but-mighty Lazuto juggling two designer bags and a little plate of French fries. "It's Friday. After we wrap, we want to party!" she shouted.

"There is a lot going on there," I suggested to the actor seated next to her.

"Dude, it's non-stop," he replied.

On the set of a TV series, she decided I should refer to her as "Rocket" because her career has blasted off. We settled on the combination of "Beautiful Rocket." During a year in America, she's acted in enough roles to earn her Screen Actors Guild card. I listened to her giving advice to another young actress who told her she'd refused to do kissing scenes to respect her boyfriend. Lazuto was having none of it.

"No, no! Then your boyfriend must pay you for the kissing parts you turn down! If I ever have a daughter, I will teach her: 'No money – no honey!'" she lectured. "I want to have a big black truck with a driver."

Lazuto's off-camera intense, humorous performances liven up the shoots.

"It is 15 hours for me on a set as a background actor. I'm freezing and waiting in holding areas in short skirts and dresses. Sometimes I get time to eat something small. In summer you want to die because of hot weather. Sometimes I say, 'I hate Hollywood,' but then I get my paycheck and I say, 'I love Hollywood,'" she admitted. "There are lots of women who dream to be an actress in Hollywood, but it is hard and funny and amazing."

I witnessed the capricious, calculating nature of a Hollywood set when a director selected a few people from the pool of background actors to dress up a scene, but Lazuto was not among them.

"Why are you here, left behind?" I asked her. It may have been acting, but Lazuto was undeterred and refused to feel rejection in answering.

"I am here because I am preparing myself for the next set and scene when I will be the main character," she insisted and then blew me a kiss. Such optimism.

Lazuto's reality could be an episode of the old series "E True Hollywood Story."

"My story is one of hope and dreams. Hope and dreams," Lazuto repeated. "I am from a small city in the east of Ukraine. The war in 2014 caused me to look for another life by moving to the capital in Kyiv. I was studying in Kyiv, working. I had a fancy life in Kyiv...and then this recent war happened there, too, I could not believe it. It happened in my life twice. I was in shock."

Lazuto described Ukraine's struggle to survive as painful.

"Children now in Ukraine will only have known war in their lives."

The Russian invasion may have seemed like something from a movie, but it was deadly real. Her mother and nieces nearly had their house bombed.

"I am thankful to God I have amazing friends who pushed me out from Ukraine. I had four days to decide. A friend in Poland texted me to pack my bag, get on the train and come to Poland. I packed and unpacked my bag over and over. Pack...and unpack. Why? Because I understood it would be a one-way ticket. I knew I would never be back."

Lazuto said when she reached the hotel room in Poland she sat and cried for two nights.

"My family was praying I'd come back. They knew if I moved, I would probably move far away."

Moving far away, for Lazuto, meant Hollywood, California. It had been her far-off dream for years.

"Kyiv was a good place to spend lots of time learning and studying, but my plan was always to come to Hollywood. The war propelled the plan," she explained. "I always knew I had to be in America. When I was a child sitting on a couch after school watching an MTV show, I saw a video with the Red Hot Chili Peppers. It showed California with tan people and the ocean. I asked God, 'Why I was born here and not there?' I studied a lot, I worked a lot, and I always feel that I had to be in America."

It wasn't just MTV. Lazuto remembers, when she was a little girl, watching, "Some Like It Hot," a perhaps fateful movie choice that set Lazuto on a path to become a bombshell sex symbol herself like the film's star.

"Marylin Monroe is an icon. I love her with all my heart. I was inspired about how she acted and how she played with the men. She was a real girl. She understands how to treat a man," explained Lazuto who, like Monroe, found herself appearing in Playboy Magazine.

For Lazuto, it was the Ukrainian edition. "I was in the November 2021 issue. It was my protest because I worked in the business community and I wanted to show people that I am a woman, first."

Lazuto said the photos were tasteful. "I love to work with photographers who make the pictures in a way that your imagination has to work."

Later her first film job cast her naked in bed with small coverups on.

"I worked on a show where I had my clothes off. I told everyone, 'Guys, it is only for money. I don't want to be a star or be recognized.' But I came to understand that I love the camera. I need the attention! It is not only for money. It's passion."

After her initial exit from Kyiv, with one suitcase, for two nights in Poland, Lazuto said she went to stay with her cousin in Berlin, Germany for two weeks.

"I started to make a plan: A-B-C. I needed to go to America. I could not stay in Europe because I don't know any languages as well as I speak English. My English is 'MTV Level' because I watched MTV a lot. When people ask me my level of English, I tell them 'MTV Level.' Thank you, MTV for teaching me to speak English."

But she found herself unable to secure a visa.

"So, I decided I had to go to Mexico and try to cross the border into Arizona there. I took a flight to Amsterdam and then to Mexico City. My friend and I rented a car and drove to the American border," she explains. Officials at the U.S. border turned her away.

"I had spent a month crossing half a world for this – to find a new life in America – only to be turned away, so I started to cry," she admitted.

Again, though, ultimately undeterred, Lazuto, now a homeless refugee, decided to try a different border crossing at Nogales.

"They were much nicer at Nogales and asked me some questions. They asked me, 'Why did you choose to move to America and not stay in Europe? It's closer to your country.'"

With everything at stake, this is how Viktoriia told me she answered the immigration officials.

"'Guys, when I was a kid, I watched a lot of the show 'Teenage Mutant Ninja Turtles.' I remember they had pizza with a lot of cheese, so I am here to taste that pizza!'"

Lazuto said her answer made the border officials laugh.

"They thought I was so cute and kind of crazy. They looked at each other and went to find some pizza for me and water. I was starving after a month of being on the road. When I ate this pizza on the border between Mexico and the United States, I understood that I was in the right place with the right people around."

It turned out crossing the border was not life's last hurdle for Lazuto.

I didn't know what I was going to do once I got to America. I started to apply for office jobs, but they would not hire me. I couldn't work for five months because I didn't have my paperwork.

She works now, as much as she can, accepting assignments as an aspiring actor and model.

"It's so exciting. When I go on set, I turn around and see a celebrity. And I ask, 'Is it true? Or is it still on TV?' Then the celebrity turns around and says, 'Hello,'" Lazuto described. "I was only a child after school in Ukraine in a small-town watching movies, and now, when I am on a movie set, I wonder if it's true or if I am still this kid sitting on a couch watching TV!"

Lazuto enjoyed working on the HBO show "Winning Time" about the Los Angeles Lakers.

"I met Adrian Brody. He was so nice and asked me questions. These celebrities are everyday people. I find the actors talk with me with respect and it makes me realize I am in the right place with the right people. I want to do this."

I am convinced Lazuto's look – a combination of sultry and dangerous – plus her lyrical voice and wry attitude, makes her the best candidate to be the next "Bond girl" in the new era of 007. I asked her if she auditioned for a Bond girl role, how would she present the part. Being the human firework that she is, Lazuto didn't hesitate to jump into character:

"I would look at James Bond...right into his eyes with a gun in my hand and say only five words: 'Good evening, Mr. Bond. Undress.'"

9

HONEYMOON IN VENICE...ALONE

 The delicate decadence of Venice begins with arousal on arrival in Italy's Aeroporto di Venezia. Could there be an airport name that stimulates the imagination more than "Marco Polo Airport?" The historic Venetian merchant and explorer drew his last breath in 1324.

When my Alitalia flight landed in Venice on Boxing Day seven centuries later, my new marriage, having not lasted one earthly voyage around the sun, was as dead on arrival as Polo, Casanova, Michelangelo, Vivaldi, Tintoretto, or any of the other historical figures who'd breathed artistic life into what I anticipated to be the world's most romantic destinations.

During what was expected to be a romantic trip-for-two, I was slogging solo. My blonde bride had found another ride, if you know what I mean, and unceremoniously voided our voyage. She'd applied the word terminal to our marriage instead of the airport.

So, while traveling alone instead, my carry-on was a heavy heart. I expected that toting it alone to Venice would, for me, turn the frosted, wedding cake-architecture of this succulent city into cruel gruel. But I decided to, via Venice, swallow a spoonful of sugar with my split to help the breakup medicine go down.

I went on with the show because the stage had been set by IC Bellagio, the bespoke "Italian Connection" company that created a customized adventure through Venice. The detailed itinerary IC Bellagio provided read like a romance novel.

It included local Prosecco-tasting; morning Mass at Basilica di San Marco; a guided tour of the Palazzo Ducale; a visit to the skyline's striking Gallerie dell'Academia; and an artistic Venetian mask-making experience. The latter would give us an opportunity, even though we were over a month early, to feel a part of the annual pre-Lenten Carnivale di Venezia – one of the most visually mysterious and therefore sensual festivals on earth.

Knowing we were from Michigan and discerning I was a devotee of Ernest Hemingway, IC Bellagio's guest ambassadors arranged for visits to Hemingway's haunts. We would toast Papa with a Bellini in Harry's Bar and take a boat ride across the Grand Canal to the tiny island of Torcello where, in 1948, he wrote "Across the River and into the Trees" at the Locanda Cipriani Inn while sipping Campari near the fireplace in between duck hunts.

The itinerary was very detailed with historical context and thoughtful practical advice. It detailed a full schedule of private tours and insider access behind the stained-glass windows of the Venice elite. My only companions during my days in Venice, it turns out, would be the IC Bellagio tour guides.

I was fully aware my visit was scheduled to conclude days later with, of course, a twilight gondola ride under the Bridge of Sighs as a grand finale. I admit I was dreading the prospect of completing that iconic romantic experience with the gondolier singing "O Solo Mio" to me...alone.

According to the IC Bellagio itinerary I had printed and folded up in my passport pocket, our overnight scheduled stays in Venice would be at the historic Baglioni Hotel Luna. A lodging cloaked in Venetian history at a circa-1118 palazzo once frequented by the Knights Templar. A couple nights there would include an exclusive, endorphin-enhancing chocolate tasting experience amidst its Murano-glass chandeliers (glass we would actually see hand-blown at the island factory.)

During our stay we were also scheduled to lay our heads at the 53-room Hotel Londra Palace, which my itinerary said had 100 windows in suites overlooking the Vaporetto dock on the San Marco basin and the Venetian Lagoon. Even by my lonesome, an opportunity to experience these hotels intrigued me and seemed relevant to my situation.

Especially when, in the detailed IC Bellagio itinerary, I read poet Joseph Brodsky's words about Venice. He wrote of the restorative powers of waking up in Venice in the winter and flinging open the windows to "let in the damp oxygen and prayers:"

"No matter how autonomous you are, how much you've been betrayed, how thorough and dispiriting, you assume there is still hope for you...or at least a future."

Walking off the overnight flight and through Marco Polo Airport I was in a rumpled, sleepy, hazy daze. Even though it was my first time there I was not concerned about where to go. I didn't have to think much because the itinerary was very detailed. It listed a mobile phone number to an IC Bellagio guest ambassador to use at any hour if I had questions, but it gave me precise directions to the "ground transportation" which turned out to be a covered marina of docks where I would be ferried to my hotel by private water taxi. Just as I stood wondering which boat to step aboard, I heard my name spoken in English with an Italian accent.

"Mr. Shiels. I am Giulia. IC Bellagio sent me to greet you and welcome you to Venice."

I was surprised and struggled to find words to respond with. I'd practiced some Italian language but hadn't had to use it yet. Unprepared, I shrugged, shook her hand, and greeted Giulia in English.

"How did you know who I was?"

"Mr. Shiels, we have been waiting for you and are happy you are here. Is your companion nearby? We are expecting two?" she said, her voice rising at the end like a question as she looked around the dock.

"Just me, grazie," is all I answered.

"Bene. Non c'e di che," she said, immediately, dismissing the issue, I felt, diplomatically. But maybe she just wanted to get me where I was going and get on with her day. Either way I liked her energy and hoped to dispense of thoughts of my missing sidecar as easily as she did.

"You speak Italian?"

"Uh, piccolo Italiano," I answered, even fumbling for that most basic response.

She flashed me a toothy smile. I suddenly then found myself also self-conscious about my wrinkled sweater and the way my hair was sticking up after flying all night. I'm sure my eyes were puffy and, though I tried to work in some Italian words, I felt entirely awkward as Giulia, with her wavy brown hair, fresh face, and sparkling eyes, in a coat and scarf, directed me to the proper boat.

"Let's go," she said.

"Si, andiamo," I managed this time to reply, though it was only mimicking what she'd said.

Giulia smiled again and nodded - and I suspect resisted chuckling.

Two things surprised me next. While other arriving passengers were rolling their suitcases onto ferryboats, I was led aboard a smaller, private boat. She was a beauty too – like a maritime limousine. It was a long, elegant wooden boat.

My second surprise was that Giulia came along too. She explained that not only was it her job to meet and greet me but also to guide me to my hotel.

There was open-air seating in the stern, and for a bit I was excited to enjoy the sunshine and view of the expanse of water the motored across. But the morning air, while refreshing, was brisk. Giulia was cuddled in a puffy, winter coat wrapped with a scarf but still, with just a look from her warm eyes, agreed it was cold, so, without a word, we climbed into the windowed cabin of the boat.

"Simpatico," I thought to myself.

She seated herself on the upholstered bench seat across from mine and we were knee to knee. Giulia pointed out the plain causeway bridge connecting cars to Venice and explained that Venice is a collection of islands.

"But that bridge is not special," Giulia said. "Your hotel is very near Ponte de Rialto – that is a very famous bridge. You're near the fish market, too."

That was the second or maybe third time she'd mentioned the fish market, which she seemed very excited about. In between pointing out points of interest, the pointy-featured, friendly guide engaged in small talk with me.

"I fell in love with it when I moved here to Venice 20 years ago. And I fall in love with it over and over," she revealed as I looked into her brown eyes and listened. I was beginning to awaken but, at the same time, her story and the rocking of the boat soothed me.

"Just when I think I am used to it I notice the light after a thunderstorm or a higher sculpture I had never noticed before."

I nodded and let her words resonate. With difficulty I then shifted my gaze from Giulia to the canals and buildings coming into view and, while looking away, responded by asking her, "Do you find Venice to be the most romantic city in the world?"

She waited for me to look back before she answered. "I think if you are a romantic person anywhere is romantic."

I sat still for a moment, hearing only the waves lapping against the side of the wooden boat.

As we neared the hotel Giulia then pointed out the façade of a building on the Grand Canal which appeared in the 007 movie "Casino Royale."

"This is the Cannaregio district. People are always surprised to see that palazzo is standing because at the end of the James Bond movie it is seen collapsing into the lagoon," she remarked. She laughed and said, "I remind them that you cannot believe everything you see."

Her words were simple but somehow, on this morning, a reflective one for me in an inspiring destination like Venice, they were resonating at a deeper level.

"You can see this in another way if you look there, near the Palazzo Bolani Erizzo," she gestured. "There you see the Ca' da Mosto."

I nodded.

"It's Byzantine. 13th-century. The oldest in Venice. You see it, and it's striking, right?"

"Si."

"Yes, but inside it is a disaster. And then I remind people that sometimes it looks nice, but it doesn't work. It's not functional."

When our boat arrived at the Rialto Mercado landing stage, I was sorry the ride was over. I rolled my luggage only a few hundred feet along the canal, while Giulia walked beside me offering to help, from the Vaporetto dock to the contemporary Hotel L'Orologio.

Upon check-in I learned the contemporary, boutique hotel was celebrating its second anniversary. It occurred to me, that my marriage never would.

With my baggage checked and my room key in hand I walked Giulia back out front of the hotel to take a photo and say "ciao." Before we parted, as thorough and helpful as a mother dropping her child at school, Giulia listed and described areas I might like to explore there in the San Polo sestiere historical center once I was settled in.

She pointed the way to Campo San Polo; Rialto Bridge (Venice's oldest); Palazzo Santa Sofia's golden Ca' d'Oro, and once more, the fish market, which again, by her wide eyes and the tone of her voice, drew her highest level of enthusiasm, which again was charming.

As we hugged goodbye I considered, for a moment, inviting Giulia to join me on that scheduled, end-of-the-visit romantic gondola ride under the Bridge of Sighs. But I just sighed, instead, as I watched her board a boat and glide away down the Grand Canal.

10

VENICE'S RED CARPET

I first met Giulia De Carolis at Christmas of 2016 when she greeted me upon my landing at Marco Polo Airport on my first visit to Venice, Italy.

Giulia, working as a guide at the behest of the very detailed IC Bellagio tourism company, led me, with my luggage, via water taxi to my hotel – the L'Orologio, on the Grand Canal near Rialto Bridge. It was a splendid morning boat ride. But Giulia, with her big wavy hair, even bigger smile, and her happy demeanor made the little morning journey through Venice's canals "molto Bellissima."

"I fell in love with Venice when I moved here 20 years ago. And I fall in love with it over and over," she looked into my eyes and told me. "Just when I think I am used to it. I notice the light after a thunderstorm or a higher sculpture I had never noticed before."

Giulia's words were poetry, and her appearance was art, so I was inspired to pose a question.

"Do you find Venice to the most romantic city in the world?"

She answered, "I think if you are a romantic person anywhere is romantic."

Sono stato colpito dal "fulmine!" Just like Michael Corleone, I was hit by the "thunderbolt!"

We were together on that boat ride into Venice for only a short while, and I didn't know much about her, but henceforth whenever I thought of beautiful, romantic Venice, I thought of Giulia.

I returned to Venice for a short stay six years later. Once again, I collaborated with the IC Bellagio (Italian Connection Bellagio) company for the custom planning of my visit. IC Bellagio always plans and provides a descriptive, detailed itinerary via email and on an amazing app. I was happy to notice, when I checked the itinerary, that at the end of my Venetian dolce vita, Giulia de Carolis was scheduled to lead me by private water taxi, back to Marco Polo Airport...this time, six years later, for my departure as opposed to arrival.

Because of a change in my schedule, I checked with IC Bellagio guest ambassador Nicole Bellatti to see if Giulia might like to visit a bit on the afternoon I would depart? Bellatti, via email, informed me that Giulia accepted the invitation.

During my three days in Venezia, I would view masterpieces in the Gallerie dell'Accademia; peruse Peggy Guggenheim's astonishing art collection; see Tintian's large format works in the Scuola Grande di San Rocco; and celebrate Mass in the beautiful Basilica San Marco.

But best of all, as a grand finale, I would get to see Giulia again.

The search for beauty in Venice is easy. I viewed generations of astonishing art in each of the museums I mentioned above. Random churches throughout Venice, large and small, are full of frescoes, sculptures, and statues both soothing and shocking. The candles and soaring ceilings make those sacred settings even more dramatic.

Floating along the Grand Canal or walking the winding streets of Venice also reveals architecture that would never be attempted or afforded today. The dreamy doorways, arched windows, columns, pillars, gargoyles, and intricate trimming are not imagined but real in Venice.

But beauty is more than a visual vibe.

As Paris was a "moveable feast" for author Ernest Hemingway, Venice was, for me that week, a "musical feast." The melodies, movements, songs, and performances I encountered along the way served as a soundtrack to the exquisitely romantic setting Venice is.

"Venice is always special. We recently sent a guest to Venice for the twelfth time," said Andrea Grisdale, IC Bellagio's founder (IC stands for "Italian Connection.") "While Venice is geographically small, it really does have so much to offer, so people keep returning."

IC Bellagio creates custom Italian experiences for discerning travelers. Therefore, Grisdale and her expert "guest ambassadors" arrange for their clients to stay at Venice's stylish Hotel Londra Palace. Just as Guilia did for me, IC Bellagio's guests are met at Marco Polo Airport and brought to the hotel, in style, by private boat. During their stay IC Bellagio's expert guides lead guests to all of Venice's secret treasures and experiences from the Londra Palace.

Alain Bullo leads the hotel as its maître de maison/general manager.

"We work well with IC Bellagio and their nice guides," said Bullo, "Coming along the Grand Canal at night it is interesting to see inside the windows of the palazzos."

Londra Palace neighbors the Bridge of Sighs and Doge's Palace – two of the treasures next to St. Mark's Square. The hotel's 53 uniquely different rooms and 100 windows overlook the San Marco basin with sweeping views of the dramatic church on tiny Isola di San Giorgio Maggiore and the commanding dome of Chiesa della Salute.

The historical-style guestrooms are contrasted with the white, classic, contemporary lobby, restaurant and bar making the boutique hotel a well-rounded, sensory experience.

Rich tapestries and wall coverings, marble bathrooms, and stately palace-style furnishings are found in guestrooms with windows that open to balconies above the Riva degli Schiavoni. The walkway is bustling with shoppers, merchants and tourists disembarking from gondolas or vaporetto boats.

"The views are amazing," Bullo told me when we talked in an elegant meeting room off the ground floor lobby in the 170-year-old, refurbished building. "When we live here, we don't always maintain the level of emotion visitors do. But when we take guests to their rooms and open the door and they look out the windows to see the St Mark Basin and lagoon they get emotional at the sight of the Grand Canal and San Giorgio Island and the towers."

Bullo, who commutes from Lido Island, reminded me that, historically, Venice was built to impress merchants, as it if were an open-view theater.

I like Hotel Londra Palace's location among the modern merchants, shops, and restaurants in St. Mark's Square and beyond by boat or on foot. The vaporetto boats, Venice's busses, stop in front at the San Zaccaria dock.

Londra Palace offers easy access, compared to other Venice hotels, for sightseers who want to go in and out all day on foot. Or sit out front at its sidewalk café and enjoy breakfast or a refreshing spritz, whether it be made with Aperol, Campari or Select. (Prosecco and Pellegrino are the other ingredients.)

"The spritz is a tradition in Venice. Sometimes, since it is a cocktail, people expect they should pay more for it. But four or five euro is the tradition, and we honor that," Bullo insisted.

It was late morning, and Bullo had just finished gathering his entire staff in the hotel restaurant and toasting them for a successful month.

IC Bellagio, and the Hotel Londra Palace had prepared for me, later that day, a supremely successful evening.

"You sometimes get lost in Venice, even for me," said Bullo of the ant farm-feel of Venice's narrow, winding, deep, dark streets. There are no cars on the many little islands and bridges that make up Venice. "It's fun. Sometimes I try something different when walking and then must look for the yellow signs pointing to Rialto or San Marco."

IC Bellagio comes to know its clients' proclivities well. Understanding that I sometimes like to explore alone, Grisdale, Bellatti, and the team had arranged an unguided, exquisite experience for me on this, my last of three evenings in Venice. A moving, musical adventure which I could easily do on foot.

I walked from the hotel to the side entrance of the Basilica of San Marco to attend 6:30 Mass at the side altar of the Byzantine, Romanesque, Gothic and even Islamic-style church built in 1063. Attending this brief Mass, sung and said in Italian, allowed me to be with mainly locals and to see some of the inside of the basilica without waiting in line and when it was quiet with no crowds (and no photos allowed, fyi.)

I noticed one of the attendees in the congregation was a flight attendant in uniform pulling her rolling carry-on bag. She'd either made Mass her first, or last stop in Venice.

It was all a soulful start to a peaceful evening.

What turned out to be my next stop was a spontaneous surprise. It was not on the itinerary IC Bellagio had given me, but their expert guest advisors knew, based on the obvious walking path of my schedule, that I would "happen upon it."

After Mass I walked out of the basilica and right through the middle of the ancient arena-type area known as Piazza San Marco. With the ornate basilica bordering the open portion, the square is otherwise surrounded on the other three sides by a continuous, multiple-story, stately wall-type building. Under a columned colonnade there are retail and restaurants. Some of the eateries offer elegant outdoor seating in the square and stages with live orchestras.

The live band music drew me to take a table under the awninged section at the neo-Baroque, circa 1700's Caffe Florian. I came to learn Caffe Florian had served cappuccino and champagne to the likes of Claude Monet; Andy Warhol; Charles Dickens, Friedrich Nietzsche, and Casanova, among centuries of others.

Tonight, it was just me, and the 20-euro, fanciful goblet of gelato: "Coppa Pesca Melba." It's worth every penny: a work of art itself with vanilla ice cream, a peach in syrup, whipped cream, raspberry sauce, a crispy wafer and a long pirouette cookie...with an even longer spoon.

The atmosphere, though, viewing the sky and the basilica and campanile, is the most priceless part. Although the café concert Middle Europe tradition, part of Florian's heritage for more than 100 years, comes with a six-euro change. The tuxedoed orchestra members, under the direction of Cristian Pintilie, performed on violin, piano, accordion, bass, and clarinet. A two-sided menu listed the "Repertorio" of "Musica:" Venetian classics, soundtracks, standards, Opera arias, bossa nova, jazz and more.

As I sat, the orchestra was just finishing a bouncy version of 1924's "Tea for Two." By the time me gelato came, they were playing an arrangement of Billy Joel's "Just the Way You Are." It was sublime, but early on I noticed none of the patrons, drinking and talking, applauded the orchestra at the conclusion of each number. These fine, fun musicians were treated as background music.

Well, I wasn't having it.

I loudly applauded the artists, at first alone (for what seemed like an embarrassing eternity) but I kept at it. Heads turned and, eventually, some, and then the full audience joined me in clapping. The orchestra members noticed what I'd done and smiled and nodded my way. I think they were surprised by the response I'd provoked: rousing rounds of applause!

To show appreciation, the accordion player pointed to me in the crowd, nodding and gesturing at the other musicians. I looked in his eyes, pointed at myself and lifted my eyebrows to ask if he was pointing at me? He nodded emphatically, gestured again at his bandmates, and they began playing a song for me:

It was the Godfather Theme "Speak Softly Love."

I laughed out loud at what I presumed to be the implication that I'd made the audience an offer they couldn't refuse! I stood, bowing to the band, touching my heart, and applauding. (And then, of course, very visibly tipping.) I'd made an orchestra full of new friends.

There are a number of similarly sophisticated snack stops around the square, too, including Gran Caffe Chioggia facing Doge's Palace.

My evening walk continued through a passageway out the back of Piazza San Marco and reasonably directly, thanks to the map I carried and directions I was given, along a series of streets, landmarks and little bridges. This included Calle Larga; Ostreghe; Campo Santo Maurizio; and finally, Campo Santo Stefano, where I would find, among the trees between the Grand Canal and the square, Chiesa San Vidal.

The current church was created in 1696 and was where Antonio Vivaldi, the virtuoso Venetian violinist, known as "the red priest," gave birth to beloved Baroque compositions enjoyed to this day. He died in 1741 in poverty, but it was only 30-euro to attend, in the Church of

San Vidal, a performance of Vivaldi's famed concertos known as "the Four Seasons."

Every seat was taken on that warm night, so I perched on a concrete window bench along the side wall in the steamy setting and perspired. I used my program book to try to cool off, which I suppose gave a few seconds of relief, but was mostly futile.

The 13 musicians of the group, Interpreti Veneziani, dressed in black, walked up the center aisle with their instruments and took the stage on the altar. When the welcoming applause died down, there was silence. And then, as if from heaven, at full tempo and at full volume, they struck up the supremely recognizable strains of Vivaldi's Four Seasons - "Le Quattro Stagiono" - Primavera op. 8 n. 1. Even those who do not follow classical music are familiar with this piece.

I am not exaggerating when I say that hearing that music strike up, in that setting, took my breath away. Then I broke into an unstoppable smile at the heart-swelling nature of the moment. I looked up into the ceiling of the church and silently mouthed, "Grazie, God," to a spirit so generous as to lead me to this surreal, sweet moment. I savored every second of it...right on through Estate, Autunno and Inverno.

As I listened to Giovanni Agazzi, and later Anania Maritan on the violin, lead the ensemble, I was tempted to close my eyes. I couldn't help but to view the main altarpiece of San Vidal on Horseback with eight saints and the artistic works of the crucifixion; the Trinity with saints Peter and Paul; guardian angel; and the Immaculate Conception in the inspiring setting charged with history and beauty.

"A meeting of music and other muses...to create that moment of perfection born from the symbiosis of two elements which seem made for each other," the program read.

After the concert, with my heart at ease, I took a walk over the very nearby Ponte dell' Academia bridge and rode the vaporetto boat back across to the Hotel Londra Palace. As we floated toward the San Zaccaria dock, I took the advice Alain Bullo had given me to peer into the warm, lighted rooms behind the windows of the palazzos we passed.

Passing, too, like the water below us, was my time in Venice. I thought about how the next day, on that same Canal Grande, I would be floating toward the airport. I had also received word that my son Harrison had missed his flight to Venice, where he was to join me for an afternoon before we transferred to Trieste to board an exquisite cruise through Croatia and Greece on the way to Istanbul.

This news was crushing to my heart. I would leave Venice without the opportunity to show it to 25-year-old Harrison, and I was facing the prospect of taking the cruise alone. It was, in a way, reminiscent of climbing into a romantic gondola for two, alone, on my first visit to Venice, when I came solo after the unexpected end of my marriage.

I first met Giulia when she guided me into Venice from Marco Polo Airport during that bittersweet sojourn. Ironically, and graciously, she agreed to keep me company again the next day, this time on the way out of town, via the same private water taxi that was supposed to pick up Harrison from the airport and give us a floating tour before we were taken out of town. The tour was cancelled, but she agreed to meet me at the appointed time, anyway.

I sat waiting in the stylish lobby bar of the Hotel Londra Palace, after a late afternoon checkout, on the corner couch near the window with a view of the lagoon. There was a chair across the small table with two champagne glasses on it. I wore a white blazer and flowered tie while the rest of my clothing was packed to leave for the airport and stored behind the front desk. Next to me an ice bucket kept a bottle of prosecco chilling while I waited.

I'd slept late that day, still depressed by the absence of Harrison, and took it easy in the hotel's luxury on that, my departure day from Venice. Now it was my last hour in Venice. To celebrate, I was pouring prosecco into one of the glasses when, out of the corner of my eye and through my right ear, I first sensed, then heard, and then saw the early arrival of Giulia De Carolis.

"Ciao, Giulia!" I said, rising to greet her.

"Michael," she answered with a smile I appreciated.

"Principessa, Piacere! Come sta?" I asked Giulia. The bottle was in my hand so I also gestured to see if I could pour her a glass."

"Grazie," she said, (the last time she would speak Italian to me that afternoon). "But for me it is too hot for prosecco."

"Pellegrino then?"

"Yes, thank you," she answered with a shrug and in the tone of someone who doesn't want to put you to any trouble.

Giulia had maneuvered through a sunny, steamy summer day across the canal from her home near the Gallerie Accademia, Venice's 12th century monastery and art school that now displays world class masterpieces.

I secured the sparkling water with ice from the barman, while Guilia, fanning herself with her hand, sat down in a chair on the other side of the little table. She wore a long, dark blue skirt and a light blue, short-sleeved top with frills around the shoulders. Those were the pleasantly unassuming Guilia's only frills, other than tasteful diamond stud earrings and a diamond pendant plus her two wedding bands.

"Where is Harrison?" she asked.

I surmised she hadn't been told the reason the tour was cancelled.

"Allora...it's a long story."

She tilted her head and nodded with the sensitivity of someone not wishing to pry. Then I changed the subject.

"You changed your hair?" I asked, before it was too late for me to stop myself from making such a stupidly banal observation. I hadn't seen her in six years, but I nevertheless noticed her big reddish frizz was gone in favor of straight, dark long hair.

She nodded yes and smiled.

The conversation, believe it or not, eventually improved. Giulia's English is exceptional without sacrificing her entertaining, ideal Italian accent.

She'd professed her love for Venice on the boat when we'd met six years previous, but Giulia explained she is originally from Puglia.

"Giulia from Puglia," I joked.

She'd clearly heard that one before. Her mother still lives in Puglia, as does her sister with her husband and two children. Sometimes she visits Puglia – sometimes they come to Venice. Guilia from Puglia had visited some intriguing places herself. She told me as a student she'd traveled to Syria and Egypt.

"As a young woman you went to those places? Wasn't that dangerous?"

Giulia explained she'd traveled with another female student, and they handled themselves well. She also said she'd been to New York, Philadelphia, and Boston. She liked Boston best.

"I didn't care for Niagara Falls," she allowed. "It was...kitschy.

Over the hour, and throughout the bottle, Giulia and I spoke more about our lives. By listening, I found her to be even more thoughtful and sensitive than I had remembered. She gave me an understanding and interesting perspective on my son whose fear of flying prevented him from joining me that day. If she knew my heart was breaking over this development, she only showed it by comforting me that this happens to many people and most of them get over it.

I learned that her longtime husband, who also works in tourism, is not completely vegetarian, but she is. She loves to cook but they switch off duties while taking care to remember that he is allergic to garlic, and she is allergic to peach.

Giulia told me her husband likes to drink an "asparagus spritz." She shared the ingredients but kind of lost me at "asparagus" instead of Aperol. Since I had the bottle to myself, I kept pouring the prosecco.

By the time she'd cooled down, our conversation had warmed.

"Were you able to see the travel column I wrote about my last visit to Venice? Did someone show it to you? You played a starring role. I wrote about meeting you."

"Yes, yes. I read it," she demurred. "Some of it was true. Bits of it were accurate."

I laughed and pretended to be offended.

"But I realize you are a poet," she continued. "Your writing...it is to tell a story."

I took this poet comment as a compliment from an exceptional woman whose conversation with me six years previous inspired the prose.

And Giulia, herself, is actually in show business too, our conversation revealed. She manages the red carpet for the esteemed annual Venice Film Festival – the world's oldest! The International Exhibition of Cinematographic Art of the Venice Biennale.

"But I am not on the red carpet. I am nowhere near the red carpet," Giulia insisted. "I organize the red carpet from my office on Lido."

"But you are glamorous, Giulia. You should be there among the stars. You should be presented with the Golden Lion!"

"Michael, I am fifty years old."

"Fifty? Non possovere, signiorina giovane."

"Yes, fifty."

"Tu non occhio cinquanata!" I efforted further, raising the pitch of my voice into a comical singsong and gesturing with my hand that was not holding the prosecco glass. "Tu no vecchio. No...come se dici...tu non anziano!

Giulia knew what I was attempting to say. She thanked me for the sentiment, so I continued.

"Allora...mi dispiaci. Mio Italiano...bruto!"

"No, no," she disagreed kindly. "It is good."

"No, no. Lo so. Lo so."

We both laughed. Then I took a swig of the prosecco and asked, "Do you know, Giulia, what I consider the perfect age for a woman?"

"50?"

"Yes! 50!"

"Soon enough you will be saying it is 60," she shot back.

I gestured a toast to Giulia's humor with the prosecco glass.

Just as I began to further tease Giulia by asking if she could introduce me to the Italian bombshell actress Claudi Gerini - who is also 50 - Hotel Londra Palace's general manager Alain Bullo passed through the lobby. I excused myself to stand up and the timing let Giulia off of the hook on Claudia Gernini, whom she had, in fact, been with when Gerini spent nine days on the film festival jury panel.

"Mr. Bullo, perhaps you've met Giulia De Carolis?"

Their paths would have crossed as Giulia guides many IC Bellagio guests to and from the airport via water taxi. I spoke as they greeted each other.

"Mr. Bullo lives on Lido Island," I told Giulia.

"Mr. Bullo, Giulia's office is there. She organizes the red carpet for the film festival."

Mr. Bullo, in a suit and tie, recounted some of his involvement in the festival and walking between the parties near the Palazzo del

Cinema. "I recall seeing ladies watching for George Clooney in his water taxi and crying and waving! 'George, George!' they called."

"Might they similarly be calling for me when Giulia takes me on the water taxi to the airport in a bit?" I asked.

They'd probably heard that one before also, so instead, I pivoted to the topic of a most famous grand dame actresses who had earned a reputation for being notoriously impossible to please.

"It's alright, though, Giulia gently explained, dismissing, and forgiving the behavior. "It bothered her more than it bothered anyone else."

Try as I might, Giulia steadfastly refused to name her.

Both Giulia and Mr. Bullo did, however, vividly recall the storm of December 2020, when winds and floods swamped the many delicate islands of Venice.

"It gives me chills, still to think about it," said Giulia. She was leading a tour on Murano Island when the storm struck. "The boats, the lagoon...unpassable."

She recalled that one of the famed, ornate, pointy Venetian gondolas came up in the tide and smashed right through the front window of the Londra Palace.

Mr. Bullo confirmed the hotel had been swamped.

"We didn't just have water in this lobby. We actually had waves up to here," he explained, pointing to a spot next to the elevator that appeared to be three feet above the ground.

"Now with the MOSE system we are not having that high water," said Giulia, referring to the movable gates that now operate to attempt to keep the Adriatic Sea out when needed.

Mr. Bullo excused himself to take a meeting and it was time for Giulia and I to cross the avenue in front of the hotel and board the water taxi for Marco Polo Airport. Giulia had apparently cued a bellman from the hotel ahead of time, so the friendly front desk attendant informed me my big rolling suitcase was already aboard the boat.

It's a good thing I finished the bottle of prosecco because it cut the pain of leaving Venice. Even still I dragged my proverbial feet a little as we neared the dock.

"If I am late for the flight, can I stay at your house?" I joked to Giulia.

"And you can sleep with Pepita," she immediately shot back.

"Pepita?"

"Yes. 'Miss Pepe.' My dog," she laughed.

Pepita meant a lot to Giulia, I came to learn at the dock, as did her deceased sister Lolita.

"They were sister dogs, which are unusual to come by. We found them at the Venice port," she explained. Giulia showed me a photo of Pepita in her doggie stroller. She was a happy looking, cartoonish little dog with adorable pointy ears that stuck out like the wings of the airplane I'd be going to.

"Will you, yourself be traveling anywhere soon."

Giulia said she had not planned any travel because little Pepita was at an advanced age, and she needed to take care of the doggie and be there for her.

Being in Venice, of course, is hardly a bad place to be. And if one must leave Venice, the sophisticated Venetian private water taxi is the most memorable way to do it. Giulia and I stood alone in the open-air back of what's known as a "motoscafo." It's a long, low-rise, classic, beautiful boat. It's like a limousine on the water.

It was early evening and the ride first through the lagoon was very pleasant because some of the day's heat had burned off and, gliding through the narrow canals, we were often in shade.

Giulia, ever the professional guide, was kind enough to share some places of interest along the way, including the aforementioned Lido Island.

"Lido becomes a sad place in the autumn when no one goes to the beaches anymore and everything closes," she explained, again displaying the artistic sensitivity that initially drew me to her.

She pointed in the direction of peaceful, natural Torcello Island, where her wedding reception was held at the charming Locanda Cirpriani Inn, which has also hosted even Queen Elizabeth.

She denied that, during the environmental inactivity and absence of motorboats, even the vaporettos, during the pandemic lockdown, dolphins were seen swimming in the canals. "Jellyfish yes. The water was so clear," she said as our boat slid under one of Venice's tiny bridges. "But you cannot swim in the canals. If you are caught you will be expelled from Venice."

"They must be drunk and fall in?" I asked. "I was warned, if it happened to me, not to worry about drowning...but to be careful to keep my mouth closed."

Once again, she'd heard that one before.

When the boat reached the open expanse of water and its channel markers that guide water taxis beside the road and railway line leading to the airport, I asked Giulia how often she came to and from the airport guiding visitors.

"Every day."

"Do the Americans behave themselves?"

"Americans are easy. Some others are not."

Try as I might, Giulia refused to name which type she was referring to.

The boat pulled beside the dock and tied up. The boatman was lifting my suitcase up and out of the boat. It was time to go. And time to say goodbye to Italy and Giulia.

"Will you always be here in Venice?"

"If I were to live anywhere else, it would be Paris," she answered. "But I love it here. I don't even have a driver's license. I like life with no cars: only walking and boats."

I first met my friend Guilia De Carolis when she guided me into Venice on water taxi.

Six years later we parted, again, by boat.

Both times she had a face that could launch a thousand ships.

11

PUPPY LOVE IN VENICE AND A FASHION FIND IN FLORENCE

"I am happy in Venice, but it is happy with an aftertaste, perhaps because of the accumulated past, the excess of beauty, because it is too much happiness."

-Cees Nooteboom

Fate gave me the great fortune of visiting Venice, Italy for a second time in four months.

This meant, because she is gracious, I would get to re-visit my favorite Venetian friend, Giulia De Carolis. We'd met twice in our lives, both times in Venice, where she lives and assists visitors to Venice by greeting them and showing them how to navigate the "streets of water" from the Marco Polo Airport or the train station to their hotels. This is more complicated than it sounds because Venice is actually made up of 117 small islands, countless little bridges and tiny, windy streets and narrow passageways.

Life's events, for me, happened to also be a touch complicated both times I met Giulia. On the two occasions I'd met her, I was, due to dramatic, unforeseen personal circumstances, forced, at the last minute, to travel to dreamy Venice alone. Both times she diplomatically inquired as to where my scheduled traveling companion was.

One was a soon-to-be-former wife; the other was my college-aged son; each of which had bailed at literally the 11th hour.

Giulia's brief company, to this lone wanderer, was a welcoming, calming, positive presence. I considered her unsinkable attitude and buoyant advice, in a watery town, to be a timely life raft from the angels. She's a bright light of joy.

IC Bellagio.com, Italy's premier and revered custom travel advisor company, contracts Giulia to steer their clients to the private water taxis to take the vacationers, and their luggage, up the Grand Canal and to their hotel docks. Along the way, like a proud professor, she points out the virtues and values of Venice's vistas, while insisting, modestly, that she is not an official guide.

Giulia's husband Alberto Venerandi is in the travel and hospitality industry, as well, owning and operating a guest house called Corte Loredana. The casual property, popular with backpackers, is full of rentable, ensuite rooms in the chic, authentic Jewish Ghetto area of Venice. I look forward to staying there someday.

Giulia's full-time job is to assist in the management of the annual, historic, Venice Film Festival, and though she's dealt with some of show businesses' most glittering people, Giulia, who has movie star looks and poise herself, is unassuming.

I was charmed at the way she once hesitated, and looked to gage my reaction when, during this visit, she began to spontaneously refer to me as...a friend. It was a reference she posed in the tone one would ask a question.

"I am honored you would say that." I told her. "Anyone you'd consider to be a friend is blessed."

I have come to know Giulia downplays flattery, even when it is sincere, in the same way she eschews the famed Italian luxury labels on her elegant scarves, clothes and accessories. Gucci? Nah. Max Mara? Si.

Giulia, who is worldly, elegant, and wise, is also diplomatic. Early in her life, after growing up in Puglia, she studied and worked in Syria and Egypt. She can speak and write Arabic.

In the days leading up to my two-hour train trip from Florence to Venice, I was filled with appreciative anticipation to see Giulia again. As I wandered about Florence, I wondered how I could show her my admiration when she welcomed me back to Venice in a few days. I searched the streets and shops for the perfect gift. And because Giulia has perfected her English, I thought it would be courteous to come up with an amazing greeting to surprise her with by delivering it in Italian.

Unlike Venice, Florence has one river – the Arno – which divides the city. But being able to center ones'self with the Ponte Vecchio, the "old bridge" full of gold shops that survived even the Second World War, doesn't make Florence any less tricky to navigate than Venice.

Even my famous and historic hotel, The Brunelleschi, can be tricky to find. Stefano Lodi, the hotel's general manager, told me its tucked-away spot is an advantage.

"Our great location is the best in Florence. We're just a few steps from the cathedral."

Lodi was referring to the Renaissance-era Santa Maria del Flore, known as "The Duomo," which presents an elaborate exterior by Brunelleschi himself. It kidnaps your eyes and when its' cathedral's bells toll, your ears, too. Respectfully attending Mass, by the way, is the easiest way to avoid crowds, lines, and fees, if you don't take a guided tour.

"We're very close to the hustle and bustle and people-watching of Florence," Lodi continued, "but also in a quiet square. Our guests can get both experiences."

My IC Bellagio.com-assigned driver, a most-amiable fellow, knew just how to get me from the airport to the Hotel Brunelleschi, so I didn't have to worry. One never does when their trips are planned by IC Bellagio.

"We tend to work with partners, such as IC Bellagio, that have the same mentality and morals and transparency. They want to make sure their clients have the best experience," Lodi revealed. "IC Bellagio helps us to have as much information as possible about our guests. It's teamwork. The guest experience starts long before they arrive and doesn't end until well after they are gone."

The Hotel Brunelleschi is the oldest building in Florence, its Pagliazza Tower having been built by the Byzantines 1,500 years ago. "Even by Italian standards, that's old," said Lodi, who explained the hotel even has a museum detailing that there was always some level of luxury: the building was originally a Roman spa and baths.

"Italy and Italians have historically had this charm to the rest of the world. Our way of life is very attractive to many. It's a little bit slower than other cultures. Our ability to enjoy life has to do with the fact that we are surrounded by history and art and amazing food."

As we spoke in the Hotel Brunelleschi, Lodi became philosophical.

"Richness is not necessarily in the wallet. Wealth is in experiences and memories and things you can tell your friends about seeing new worlds and new cultures and history. The world is beautiful," he said.

I was even more grateful IC Bellagio had planned my visit to the Brunelleschi and given me the opportunity to meet its partners, guides, and providers such as Stefano Lodi and Giulia De Carolis.

Most of the hotels I saw in Florence's city center were stylish and provided a historical sense of place, as opposed to being cookie-cutter.

The newly renovated NH Collection Firenze Porta Rossa, with 70 rooms, boasts a 13th-century Torre Monalda tower and ancient frescoes. The former Palazzo Bartolini and Palazzo Salimbeni now also features modern contemporary design pieces embracing the color red (rosso.) The cozy, eclectic NH Collection Porta Rossa is close to the train station.

Still searching for a gift for Giulia and a catchy Italian phrase to greet her with, I floundered about Florence, which is an entirely walkable maze of small streets. I was often joyfully lost, turning a corner to encounter yet again the unique Gucci Garden Museum I'd passed only moments before! But in my search, I did find this about Florence:

-The butter chicken and steak Florentine – with a tortellini antipasto – at Trattoria Sostanza, are culinary masterpieces in the little restaurant's food-centric, family atmosphere.

-It's widely accepted that the greatest gelateria in Florence is La Carraia, along the Arno River. Try the white chocolate with pistachio sauce; ricotta cheese and pear; and Tuscan cookie flavors.

-The twilight, panoramic view of Florence from the 19th-century Piazzale Michelangelo is worth the 12-Euro each way cab ride. You'll find musicians, snacks, and souvenirs up there so you can linger in the light and festive atmosphere.

-If you're going dancing at Space Nightclub, the crowds don't come in until well after midnight.

-When taking a VIP daytrip to Tuscan wineries such as Casa Emma in the Chianti region or Podere le Ripi in Montalcino - with a stop in Siena - be certain to pay your respects at the stunning Florence American Cemetery, where 4,400 WWII American servicemen and women are laid to rest.

Back in Florence's city center, I'd seen the graves of Michelangelo, Galileo, and Machiavelli at the Basilica of Santa Croce, and I moved over, according to my IC Bellagio itinerary, to the Hotel L'Orologio, on the Piazza Santa Maria Novella. I would tell you the Hotel L'Orologio is in a different part of town, and it technically is, but it's a misleading statement because one can easily walk from the Brunellecshi to the L'Orologio while just looking for a slice of pizza.

Translated, "L'Orologio" means "clock" or "wristwatch," and there are plenty of ornate, impressive clocks around the stylish property. Mass time, I found out, was 8 am at the Basilica Santa Maria Novella, the striking white church which is viewed across the piazza from the front of the hotel. During morning Mass, I saw that the inside is even prettier and more ornate than the outside. And guess what, I found inspiration inside, and outside the basilica.

While wandering the piazza between the hotel and the church, I stepped upon an engraved stone in the far corner near and an as yet unopened gelato shop. The big, square stone read:

"Tutti I passi che ho fatto; nella mia vita, mi hanno portato qui, ora = Every step I have taken in my life has led me here, now."

As a travel writer myself, the message moved me.

As a romantic, I came up with an idea.

Giulia had once, kindly, referred to me as a "poet" due to my colorful enhancement of times and tales in my travel stories. So, for my friend Giulia, I decided to memorize the saying on the stone in Italian and deliver it to her as a greeting. I snapped a photo of the stone and spent the next 24 hours endlessly repeating it over and over and over, or, to borrow at Latin phrase, ad nauseum.

I recited it in my mind 100 times while walking, shopping, touring Florence's famed museums, in the hotel elevator, and in the shower, day and night. Knowing, though, that I might choke under pressure with stage fright when the time came to deliver the line to Giulia, I'd need to practice verbalizing it out loud in front of another person.

I chose the bartender at the L'Orologio. While pouring prosecco, he was patient enough to tolerate me and correct my pronunciation. And he suggested I adjust the ending.

"Instead of 'qui ora,' say 'da te.'"

"Si?"

"Si," he explained. "Instead of saying 'here now,' tell her 'to you.' All your steps brought you to her."

"Dolce!" I proclaimed.

The other bit of inspiration that morning, with the orologio ticking, came from Andrea Grisdale, the founder and CEO of IC Bellagio, the custom travel company that planned my Italian spree. Grisdale, a compulsive connector of people, had suggested I meet her friend Simone Fammone, the founder of EMMA Firenze, at his atelier studio.

"'Made in Italy,' when it comes to fashion, means the finest craftsmanship and materials," Grisdale explained. "Simone, with his EMMA Firenze, is designing and manufacturing the world's finest fashions...for dogs."

The penny dropped for me! The last time I'd seen Giulia, four months earlier, she showed me photos of her cute little doggie Pepita.

"I hold Pepita's head in my lap like a little baby," she admitted.

I recalled Pepita meant a lot to Giulia, I came to learn at the dock, as did Pepita's deceased sister dog, Lolita.

"They were sister dogs, which are unusual to come by. We found them at the Venice port," she explained. Giulia also, at the time, said she had not planned any travel because little Pepita was at an age at which she needed to take care of the doggie and be there for her.

Some haute couture for Pepita from EMMA Firenze would be the perfect gift to give Giulia!

I texted Nicole Bellatti, my on-call guest ambassador with IC Bellagio, who quickly arranged a late morning visit with Fammone and his partner, who would translate for us. I hurried across town to meet the maker of dog designer duds.

Fammone's Emma Firenze is the Gucci, Prada, Versace, or Ferragamo of dog fashions. In touring their studio, I saw, firsthand, their fashions were not cutesy canine costumes. This was serious stuff.

"We have a huge variety of textiles from which you can choose. Any breed can be satisfied, and the clothes are all reversable to adapt to the climate – double-faced with one face being cashmere and wool. The other side, which is lighter but waterproof, acts as a raincoat," Fammone explained as he showed me the quilted coats, hooded sweatshirts, and accessories EMMA Firenze has been customizing for customers from all over the world who have been ordering online.

"Clients can choose on the web. They get the final choice, he said.

I asked Fammone if it would be a fashion faux pas to order a striped sweater for a spotted dalmatian?

"Maybe the contrast could be really trendy," he answered, laughing with a shrug.

Emma Firenze is also starting to create dog fashions for the traditional luxury clothing labels as they begin to market products for dogs. Fammone said EMMA Firenze is about to collaborate with Italian and English car companies to create dog accessories in their luxury vehicles.

Then we got down to business.

"Do you know the size of the dog you'd like to buy a gift for?" Fammone asked me. "We do custom measurements, of which there are three: the circumference of the neck; the chest; and the length between the neck and the tail. It can be a miniature dog or a huge dog. We can do anything."

"Pepita," translated, means "nugget." But I already knew Pepita was tiny because Giulia had shown me a photo of Pepita, with her big ears pointing like the wings of an airplane from her head while being pushed in a stroller. I pulled out my phone and showed Fammone and his partner two photos of the Giulia's "baby."

"Hard to tell size from a photo, but the dog is named 'Pepita?'" Fammone asked.

"Si. 'Pepita.'"

Fammone and his partner both smiled broadly at the photos and the cute name. Then they pulled out tiny tops and a big variety of items for me to choose from. Dog fashions in all forms were flying at me from their shelves and racks and hangers and adorable displays.

With their assistance, I selected, for Giulia and Pepita, a little hooded sweatshirt with thin red and gray stripes, evocative, in a subtle manner, of the uniforms of the Venetian gondoliers. I purchased another small, designer doggie-related item to accompany it, which they carefully, and with deliberate precision, packaged in tissue paper and placed in a fanciful, ribboned box worthy of Tiffany's that also included a certificate of designer authenticity.

"Perfetto!"

After a brief stop in Bologna, my train from Florence pulled in, on a sunny morning, at Venice. One last time, I rehearsed the line I'd studied so hard. Then I straightened my tie before disembarking.

"Michael," I heard her voice call, and there was Giulia, on the train platform, dressed for the crisp Autumn morning, in a navy-blue coat and pattered scarf. It occurred to me that the last time I saw Giulia was during Venice's sweltering summer July humidity and heat that reached 90-degrees Fahrenheit. She truly is a woman for all seasons.

I welcomed her in the traditional Italian manner, with air kisses on both cheeks, and then nervously tried to look at her and roll out the line: "Tutti I passi che ho fatto; nella mia vita.....uh......uh......um...... mi hanno portato da, te."

It was a clumsy, epic fail, and I wondered, as she looked at me, if Giulia understood my meaning.

"Capisci?" I asked.

"Si," she answered, "but it's not true," thereby dismissing my romantic phrase, with the wave of a hand, as she would a teasing brother.

I grinned and we both laughed as we walked up the platform. Then I secretly sighed.

Once through the train terminal, Giulia led me through the crowds and over to the dock for the transfer to the hotel. She tried to help with my luggage, a gesture, of course, I refused. I was toting a duffel bag since I was in for only one night, but I kept the EMMA Firenze bag with the wrapped doggie gifts out of the duffel and ready to give to Giulia as soon as we got settled.

Aboard the elegant water taxi, which is more akin to a limousine, we sat underneath in the warmth on the benches on opposite sides of the small, windowed cabin, knee to knee, cruising up the canal. I secretly put the elaborate gift bag right next to my feet and kept my hand on its handle.

As the boat motored along, it rolled through the currents and slapped against the waves.

"The water is high now," Giulia explained.

In fact, I noticed a gondolier having to duck – no easy task as he stands with a pole on the back of his long, sleek craft – to maneuver the boat and its cooing passengers under one of Venice's hundreds of little bridges.

We made small talk about whether there had been any of the serious alta acqua flooding Venice had experienced in past Novembers, which thankfully there had not. There was also a little small talk about how, after I'd left in the summer, two men had illegally surfed on motorized foils between the gondolas in the canals. This drew the ire of Venice's mayor Luigi Brugnaro, who tweeted they were "overbearing idiots."

Giulia also pointed out the mayor's office, Ca' Loredon, as we passed it on the Grand Canal, and explained there was some level of controversy about holiday lighting, which was already blazing, at City Hall and in Piazza San Marco.

Giulia also shared she'd had an unpleasant, three-week bout with Coronavirus in October, and only recently, thankfully, had fully recovered. She allowed that her husband's symptoms had been less severe and shorter.

Hearing this, I sensed the timing was right to present my cheery gift. So, I asked brightly, "How is Pepita?"

But Giulia then stopped speaking entirely.

Her head tilted a little and her chin drooped.

"Oh...," she said, looking into my eyes.

"Pepita passed away."

She'd said it as gently as she could, in a tone of regret.

Regret for me asking.

Regret for having to tell me;

and regret for it being true.

"I thought that I had told you."

Giulia's eyes welled and I felt the pain of her heartbreak.

Unless one can hear a broken heart beating, the only sound now was the boat bouncing though the water and the suddenly noticeable drone of its engine. The otherwise moment of silence sat before I said, "I am so sorry" and briefly placed my hand atop her gloved hand.

It is an acute ache when someone you care about is hurting. I wished I could have eliminated Giulia's pain. All I could do was, as subtly and quickly as possible, slide the gift bag under the boat bench behind my knees and out of her view. Thank God I hadn't given the gift to Giulia for her to open before she shared the sad news.

Giulia, who had inadvertently been a strong source of inspiration, comfort, and counsel on my two previous melancholy visits to Venice, did not really need my counsel in return. She is an independent woman of great pose and presence. But she certainly had my sympathy. And when she returned the conversation to pointing out palazzos of interest along the canal, I understood why.

Navigating from the train station to a private water taxi is very convenient, especially with Giulia guiding and when IC Bellagio.com puts you in a luxury hotel. I would be staying at The Centurion Palace, right on the Grand Canal – between the Gallerie dell'Accademia Museum and the big Baroque, Basilica Santa Maria della Salute – circa 1687, built as a votive offering for a terrible plague.

The basilica, and its' convenient vaporetto (water bus) dock, are just across from Piazza San Marco and one block and bridge away from the Centurion. The Centurion Palace's lobby areas and sitting rooms are like art galleries. Of course, the view out the windows, even from your guestroom, is picture-pretty. And the sound of the water lapping on the walls of the canal is a constant reminder Venice's "streets" are filled with water.

The Centurion's courtyard is divided by a floor-to-ceiling, glassed-in breezeway connecting two parts of the renovated and modernized palazzo. Beyond the glass is the patio and dock, with its colorful striped poles. Day or night it is a world class setting facing, across the canal, the old Gritti Palace. The Centurion Palace is a fun place to come home to whether by boat or on foot.

The gothic-style Centurion Palace Hotel was once known as Palazzo Genovese. It is located in what once was the neighborhood of the billionaire heiress Peggy Guggenheim, who donated her home to become the Peggy Guggenheim Collection. Her home, the 18th-century Palazzo Venier dei Leon, which hosted so many glamorous gatherings, is now a canal-front museum full of works of Surrealism and abstract expressionism. Guggenheim herself was a gas, apparently. The billionaire heiress unabashedly claimed to have slept with 1,000 men - often artists and writers - while she lived in Europe. When asked how many husbands Guggenheim had, she replied, "You mean my own, or other people's?"

Guggenheim's father went down with the Titanic. Guggenheim herself died in 1979. Her ashes are buried in the museum courtyard, resting beside the remains of her prized pooches.

Giulia and I, along with some friends, sipped a bottle of prosecco in Piazza San Marco in front of an orchestra that evening at Quadri Gran Caffe. She also led us to taste designer Spritz drinks at Amo in the T Fondaco dei Tedeschi mall near the Rialto Bridge – the area she'd shown me when I first met her on Boxing Day, 2016.

Giulia will be using the time this winter to travel away from Venice. She'd recently taken a trip to Nice, France, and was planning to take a long-awaited trip to Japan with her husband – Tokyo and beyond. I suggested her employers at the Venice Film Festival send her on "research and observation trips" to the Academy Awards in Hollywood; the Cannes Film Festival in the South of France; and the Toronto Film Festival. Of course, the modest Giulia laughed and dismissed my sentiment. "Those types of trips are for my director," she demurred.

The next afternoon it was time for my trip away train. Giulia guided me, via water taxi again, to the train station and dutifully, but thoughtfully walked me right onto the train car and to my seat. She probably wanted to make certain I actually left town! Safely tucked on the train, it was time to once again bid Giulia "Ciao, bella."

But before the train pulled away, she presented me with a gift – a book – entitled Venice- the Lion, the City, and the Water, by Cees Nooteboom. When I read the book on the train later, one phrase resonated with me: "I am happy in Venice, but it is happy with an aftertaste, perhaps because of the accumulated past, the excess of beauty, because it is too much happiness."

After Giulia presented me with the book, as she climbed the steps back down onto the train platform, I handed over a partial, curated version of the gift I had originally intended for her. It was a wrapped up "goodbye" present for her.

Inside the fanciful gift bag, Giulia, when she opened it later, would find some candies and a tiny, decorative, stuffed dog, of orange-colored cloth – a hand-made accessory from Emma Firenze. She'd also find a very personal note expressing my condolences and appreciation for her friendship, dignity and elegance.

Just before I left, I handed it to her. "Ciao, e la mi cara amica," I managed to warble out.

"Why did you bring me a gift?"

"Because I love you," I said. "And I know how much you loved Pepita and Lolita."

Giulia's "neighbor," the late Peggy Guggenheim, is a billionaire buried next to her dogs. And though I'd only seen photos of Lolita and Pepita, I saluted Giulia's priceless devotion to the dear dogs – her babies who will always live in her heart, if not on her lap.

12

VENICE DAN BROWN STYLE

 "Da Vinci Code" author Dan Brown sent his protagonist researcher Robert Langdon, played by Tom Hanks, on a clue hunt through Venice in his book and film "Inferno." Piazza San Marco; Aeroporto Marco Polo; the Grand Canal; Ponte di Rialto; Venezia Santa Lucia railway station; and Ponte degli Scalzi are among the locations which serve as the settings.

It wasn't quite as intricate, but I would soon set out on a Dan Brown-style clue hunt of my own through Venezia.

Sometimes Venice comes to you...as it did when I received a gift. Amy Spagnuolo and her family own Spagnuolo's Italian Restaurant in Michigan. The restaurant is decorated with actual family photos of Sant' Ippolito, in the municipality of Cosenza, in Italy's Calabria region. This is the home village of her parents, family patriarch and matriarch Vincenzo and Silvana. In addition, firsthand photos Amy snapped when she visited Italy during college in 1988, including Venice, also hang in Spagnuolos.

As her teenage son "Giuseppe" neared college age in 2022, she took him to visit Venice. It was Amy's first time back in 30 years. So, as a gift, I secured an expert guide from Italian Connection Bellagio (IC Bellagio) to meet them at their hotel - famed Londra Palace, which has a sweeping view overlooking the lagoon.

The connected and educated IC Bellagio guide enabled them to avoid any lines to see and learn of the artistry of Piazza San Marco, Doges Palazzo, the Bridge of Sighs and other historical treasures. All topped off with a traditional gondola ride through the canals.

My travel tip, though somewhat historical in nature, was less sophisticated.

"Drink a Bellini at Harry's Bar," I suggested. "It was invented there. You can drink where Hemingway drank."

Apparently, it was on Amy's walk to hydrate at Harry's after their tour that she came across a street artist. There are several of them along the lagoon in front of the Hotel Londra Palace and all the way down near Harry's where the Grand Canal begins.

Amy bought a painting, brought it back from Italy, and presented it to me. It was an elegant, vertical sepia-style painting of browns and tans depicting a gondola floating in front of what appeared to be a church, belltower and bridge. The windows had subtly colorful flashes of burnt orange in them, as did the gondola seats.

I loved it.

I'd only been to Venice once myself, so I did not recognize the scene depicted. It was not the typical Saint Mark's Square or Rialto Bridge scene seen in so many paintings and pictures. I wondered if the painting was a true spot in Venice or perhaps just an amalgamation of Venice-inspired elements?

When I learned I, myself, was destined to travel to Venice a few months later, I decided to find out. Since I would view this painting on the wall each day in my home, I felt it was worth learning its backstory. I also wanted to honor this "dolce" gift by seeking out the spot of the painting and taking a photo there. And while I was at it, I thought it might be fun to find the artist.

I fancied it a "Robert Langdon-style" clue hunt through Venice worthy of a Dan Brown novel.

My search for the genesis and inspiration of the painting among Venice's treasure trove of architecture and artisans began immediately upon departing Marco Polo Airport by private water taxi.

Upon arrival, I didn't even get up the stairs to the reception desk of the Venice Venice Hotel – an avant-garde new property built inside a 13th-century Byzantine-style palazzo that describes itself as "postvenetian" - before I encountered (and I do mean "encountered") a startling work of art:

The dock-floor entrance of the hotel led to a parceled, cement-square walkway over water. At the front of the foyer, a life-sized sculpture splayed out on his back over a stone cube, was the crucified Christ.

I stopped in my tracks as I'd seen a sculpture like that before, but in a very different setting. Not on a cold stone slab, but in the warm lap of love. The hair on my neck stood as I looked across the vestibule. Steps away, as I continued, was a sculpture of the Blessed Mother, looking down into her lap where her dead Savior son usually lays. It was a replica of Michelangelo's Pieta with Jesus separated from the Madonna!

I learned the artist, Fabio Viale, named it "Souvenir Pieta." It had been shown for years around Italy but this now permanent showing of his two-piece work is the first time both sculptures had ever been displayed in the same town let alone the same building.

Prepare to be overstimulated at Venice Venice Hotel. The sensual EROSE (eros?) logo is everywhere...on everything from the black grand piano to the cans of shampoo.

Visual treats reveal themselves around each corner. Once you make your way down the dark, draped hallways and into your room (mine was two stories tall), you'll find even more sculptures and books. A simple hunk of naturally chiseled sandstone-colored rock on the shelf beside the bed vexed me during my entire stay. At times it appeared to resemble the head of a dog, yet in other moments I saw in it a human face. Art is subjective, as when a Yeti cooler with wheels is used as a piece of furniture.

Ambience meets modern convenience in the rooms of Venice Venice. A switch panel at both the door and bed turns on lights, mood lighting and music – and has a USB charging port. (Otherwise, there was only one power outlet in the room – it is a 13-century building, after all.

A candle was lit nightly by a housekeeper during turn down service and the "dream-builders team" leaves a hand-written card with the next days' weather forecast. On my last night there, the card noted directions to my local vaporetto waterbus stop, instructions about which line to take and that I should get off at the San Zaccaria dock. The card was signed, "We rose you."

In addition, the coffeemaker was preloaded each day with water and grounds so only the push of one button was needed, and everything in the minibar was mine to drink.

The hotel's Venice Bitter Club bar has tapestry-covered walls juxtaposed with a scrolling electronic sign and overlooks the Grand Canal. Several cocktails included Erose handmade vermouth, including The Blood and Sand, with whiskey, cherry and orange.

I typically was the first to breakfast in the hotel's Venice M'art. Like everything in the Venice Venice Hotel, it is done uniquely and in a "postvenetian" manner.

Because of its location near the Rialto Bridge on the Grand Canal, the palazzo's waterside level historically was a connection between the boats and the charming Campo Santi Apostoli square. The open, airy thoroughfare has a bazar-type feel for shopping, dining and art. (You can even buy the Yeti coolers there, and Erose-labeled merch.)

Sitting at a linen-covered table under an arch on the dock, the morning light gave the canal an aquamarine color. Though the temperature was already warm, the spot was still shaded. Boats made deliveries all along the canal and suddenly my server delivered a pile of pastries to my table with butter and jam and fruit.

The waitress wore a black and white-striped shirt like the ones traditionally worn by Venetian gondoliers and a long apron. She was little with a big smile, dark hair and dark features.

"Buongiorno," I ventured. "Come sta?"

"Bene. Grazie," she answered and then, in English, asked my room number for her ledger.

"Two-forty. Mi chiamo Michele Patrick Shiels."

"Grazie."

"Como ti chaima?"

"Ana."

"Piacere di conoscerti, Ana."

"Okay," she offered in return.

Ana, who spoke very little English, smiled and patiently tilted her head forward each time I attempted to speak in Italian. Sometimes she seemed to laugh a little, too. To be completely frank, had she been a waiter and not a waitress, I may have been more embarrassed. One time I even saw Ana pricelessly trying to guard a grin and shaking her head after she walked away from the table.

Allora...I was in such a festive state that, with the brioche, muffins and croissants, I requested a glass of prosecco. (Anna definitely had to double check my Italian and intention on that one.) An elegant presentation of eggs benedict with lobster followed. Then, hot chocolate with the decadent consistency of pourable pudding.

A whimsical, silent chess game of sorts ensued with Ana. As a travel writer, I was staging everything on the elegant table, including the silverware and small flower vase, in the right light and beautiful background so that I could take a nice, concise photo to publish with my story. But before I could take the snap, each time Anna passed the little table, she quickly, and I suppose impulsively, returned the butter and spoons and other items to their proper position.

As soon as she walked away, she would watch me start moving the saltshaker and prosecco glass and plates once more. Again, the sparkling-eyed server was left to shake her head and laugh. She probably thought I was an ill-mannered, unrefined American tourist.

Allora.

My table at Venice Venice Hotel's Venice M'art, was, in such a noble, ancient place, as sublime a spot as I had ever eaten breakfast.

But it was time to get busy.

While Ana had been enchanting, it was an efficient, yet charming woman named Claudia, at the Venice Venice Hotel front desk, who literally got my sophisticated scavenger hunt off on the right step. In the maze of Venice's canals and equally narrow, serpentine streets, I knew it was best to ask for advice – and to do so in English. So, I showed Claudia a photo on my smartphone I'd taken of the painting and asked her, "Do you recognize this place? Is it a real place?"

Claudia nodded immediately.

"That is San Geremia, near the train station," she said while already pulling out a map.

"Is it far from here?"

"No. Not far," Claudia said, while circling the location along the Grand Canal. She also circled the location of "Ca da Mostra," the name of the ancient palazzo in which the hotel is located, that is how it is still labeled on the map.

"Grazie," I said. "I might not have found my way back, otherwise."

"Prego," she said, while circling another spot on the map, and tapped her pen on it and looking me in the eye to give me a warning me. "If you want to see San Geremia from this perspective you must go to the other side of the canal. This view is from across the river."

Had Claudia not told me this, I would have set out behind the hotel, on a 90-degree day, over the small bridge across the little canal, through Campo dei Santi Apostoli, and up the shop-lined Strada Nuova past Ca d' Ora, Casino Venezia and the Nino Chocolate store to reach Chiesa San Geremia and the bell tower and bridge. Once there, if I recognized it, I would have wandered another mile back and forth around it trying, likely unsuccessfully, to find the perspective in the painting.

Just like Langdon's educated sidekick in "Inferno," Dr. Sienna Brooks, Claudia saved me hours of searching.

Following the map, I walked well past San Geremia and almost to the Santa Lucia train station. I then crossed from Santa Croce into Cannaregio via the Ponte degli Scalzi – the "Bridge of the Barefoot Monks" Brown included in "Inferno."

Santa Lucia train station is also in the "Inferno." The saint's bones are nearby in the San Geremia Church in the painting, where they have laid since 1861. Brown, who feasts on sometimes sinister historical intrigue, must have relished the relatively recent story of "Saint Lucy."

In 1955 a Venetian future Pope had a silver mask put on the saint's face to protect the corpse from dust.

The head was the only thing left behind when, in 1981, the rest of Saint Lucy's 1,700-year-old body vanished from the church after thieves broke into her glass and marble coffin. Gunmen bagged her body but her head, with the silver mask, broke off and rolled down the aisle.

Police eventually discovered her bones in a bag at a hunting lodge 25 miles outside Venice...on her feast day! Eerie!

Santa Lucia is the protectress of eyesight, and from the barefoot bridge, you can look back to see diners enjoying dishes under the awnings of canal-side restaurants with mounds of flowers lining the railings.

What I could not see from the other side of the canal as I back-tracked is when exactly I was across from San Geremia. The placement of some of the buildings directly on the canal does not allow one to walk uninterrupted along it. This forced me to walk "inland" through little passageways occasionally, to check my position, wending my way back on side streets back to the canal until I found the painter's perspective.

"How did that artist even find this spot in the first place?" I wondered as I wandered in the non-descript neighborhood.

The payoff, though, was priceless, when I did hit the street that presented the panorama of the painter's perspective. I checked the photo of the painting saved on my phone and stood in the spot at the water which recreated the exact angle.

I took in the treasure hunt view and enjoyed the mystical feeling of finding it. It was as if a dreamy setting had come true. Like seeing a magazine model in the flesh. All of it was there across the canal: the brown, brick belltower, the arched windows which appeared orange in the painting, the delicate bridge over the side canal and the church.

"Bravissimo," I said aloud in salute.

After admiring the moment – and sitting down to rest – I stood in a shaded spot to frame a photograph that would match the artwork. There was no Anna here to reposition the elements of my photo – in fact the current edifice of San Geremia has been there since 1753. But there was one thing that crept into my photo frame: to my amazement, just as I lined up the shot, a gondolier happened to steer his boat by pole right through the frame, across the watery scene, matching the one the painter depicted! The photo I then snapped matched the painting precisely.

And if the gondolier wasn't singing "Santa Lucia" as he passed the church in which she was laid to rest, he should have been!

My next step was to meet the man who sought out such a unique spot to put brush to canvas. His card, with his name, was taped to the back of the painting: Luciano Santangelo Virgilio.

Robert Langdon-style, I did a little triangulation. I considered the footprint of Amy and Giuseppe's visit to Venice: Their IC Bellagio tour focused on the Piazza San Marco-area sights; they stayed at the Hotel Londra Palace; and they took my advice to have a Bellini at Harry's. Those are all places lined up along the lagoon.

Souvenir sunglasses, artwork and keychain kiosks are also lined up along the water. Surely it would be there that I would likely locate Luciano Santangelo Virgilio.

I set out on foot to find him. Brown's character Robert Langdon, and any of IC Bellagio's expert guides, would laugh if they were to see the route to reach San Marco I took throughout that day. To walk or boat straight "as the crow flies" in Venice is never possible, but a bird bombed on Bellinis would have gone more directly than I did.

The countless little streets, though, were so small on the map and I certainly did not want my experience walking through ancient Venice to be guided by Google maps and having my phone chirp at me every turn.

My initial idea was to follow along the Grand Canal, but there is no continuous Malecon in Venice and so I quickly lost sight of the serpentine waterway.

So, like Langdon might have, I was left to look for directional clues along the way. These clues came mainly in the manner of occasional little yellow arrow signs, placed or painted on buildings randomly above eye level, that pointed to either "San Marco" or "Rialto." They were almost never uniform.

I also tended to follow where crowds seemed to be flowing instead of down the countless narrow passageways that sometimes led to dead end courtyards. (Though there weren't many tourists most of the way I went.)

In letting myself get a little lost, I saw much of Venice I would not have otherwise. I wanted to get my steps in and didn't mind the sense of wonderment and wandering because it revealed many scenes of intrigue and surprises.

For the challenge of it I tried not to ask anyone for directions. It did cross my mind that I might need to board a vaporetto bus-like boat at some point to cross the canal, and to do so I might need a protective surgical mask. I ducked into a tiny trinket shop to see if they might sell souvenir masks.

Just as a friendly man behind the counter was shaking his head and explaining that he didn't sell them, I noticed other "protective" items on display beside the counter. I did my best, with a smile, to point out to him the irony.

"Tu soldi condoms; no facia?" was my best try in Italian. My point was his store offered souvenir condoms...but no masks.

"Is better, no?" he queried in response while laughing.

I crossed countless little bridges and spotted political graffiti messages in some spots:

"No Mafia! Venezia e' Sacra" next to Rialto Bridge.

"Basta Fare Schifo (scusa mamma)" next to a little canal further on.

Since it was sunny and steamy, occasionally I would stop for a drink and find some shade to sit for a bit. I walked through an opening in a wall to find benches in a small, deserted university courtyard. A sign indicated "no picnics," but I figured my Coke Zero didn't constitute a violation.

There was a woman on the other bench for me to commiserate with even it was just with a look, a pantomimed wiping of my brow and a sympathetic shrug.

I felt rewarded when I stumbled across Chiesa San Rocco – circa 1771. The Renaissance-style church with its sculpted Biblical scenes and stately Scuola Grande di San Rocco next to it were ornate and beautiful from the outside. However, I stepped inside to view the altar in the church and the large-scale works of Tintoretto and Titian.

My walk had turned into a sort of "art crawl."

Venice, if you look from above or on a map, is shaped like a fish. I think I was as wet as one during my "art crawl" through steamy summer Venice in search of the painter. It was a worthy walk, though, because in addition to the fanciful architecture my fancy footwork led me through two of the world's greatest art museums: the Peggy Guggenheim Collection and Gallerie dell 'Academia di Venezia.

I also took a peek at the dramatic dome and intricate interior of Basilica di Santa Maria della Salute. It was warm inside the 1681 church, and I almost fell asleep on a stone bench staring up into the basilica's inspiring rotunda. Woozy, I went to chill outside and people-watch on the stone steps of "Saint Mary of Health."

From that watery perch I had a sweeping view across canal to the towering, pencil-like pointy campanile of St. Mark's Square. It was time to complete my search. I hopped a vaporetto water bus to get across the Grand Canal to the Zaccaria dock in front of the Hotel Londra Palace. From there I could stroll to survey the sales on the street along the piazza toward Harry's in search of a merchant selling art resembling the painting I possessed.

Near the piazza, after perusing and passing by the souvenir trinkets, and seeing a couple of painters with works that did not match mine, I reached the reached a row of artist kiosks set up between the Royal Gardens along the lagoon. Like Langdon, I spoke, again in my "pico Italiano," to the first artist I saw.

"Scuzi, signior. Come ti chiamo?"

"Cosa?"

"Tu Signior Luciano Santangelo Virgilio?"

"No."

A man standing with him overheard (and apparently, despite all odds, understood) our conversation so he got my attention the pointed to a man about forty feet further along the sidewalk.

"Si?"

"Si."

And there was Luciano Santangelo Virgilio, with his unmistakable vertically oriented paintings on display, sitting at his easel under a tent-type tarp. He was near the base of a tree and facing the Royal Gardens with his back to the water.

I walked over and introduced myself. He corrected me on my pronunciation of his name but did so in a friendly manner...and in English.

Luciano had about 30 paintings on display, including a larger, full color version of my sepia San Geremia painting. Naturally he had depictions of the Bridge of Sighs and other Venetian scenes.

I explained to him that someone had given me one of his paintings as a gift. And I told Luciano how much I admired his work.

"Complimenti, signior. Bellisimo!" I said in Italiano, out of respect.

"Grazie, grazie. Where are you from?" he asked.

I told him I was from America...Michigan, specifically.

"Ah. I often wonder where the paintings I sell go. Where in the world to they end up," he shared.

I pulled up the photos on my phone to show him the picture of his painting I'd been given.

Amazingly, though it had been four months earlier, Luciano told me he remembered parting with that particular painting.

"Yes. I recall this. It was a woman, yes? With a boy."

It struck me as special. And it occurred to me that Luciano must feel a connection to his creations as if they were his children.

"Luciano, how many paintings have you created?"

"50 years' worth. Venice my whole life. I am 70 years old."

"Occhio non anziano!" I exclaimed, gesturing to his white sneakers, shorts, blue t-shirt with a Hollister teen skateboard logo, and full head of wavy, brown hair.

"Grazie," he said with a smile.

I then showed him the shot I'd taken of the actual San Geremia location that inspired it. Luciano nodded and noticed that I'd even caught the gondolier going through the scene.

"I had to include the gondolier in the painting, you see, because the gondolier is the original actor of Venice. People want the gondoliers," he explained.

Luciano told me that he lived outside Venice and commutes in daily.

"How often do you paint?"

"Every day. I paint every day," he answered.

After my warm conversation I asked a passerby, with Luciano's permission, to snap a photograph of us. We posed, smiled...and parted.

My quest across Venezia didn't save the world as Robert Langdon did in the novels and movies. But I did enjoy a feeling of Dan Brown-style, mystery-solving accomplishment. And more palpably a sense of human connection and an opportunity to show appreciation to a Venetian painter who'd dedicated his life to the arts. He now knew where in the world at least one of his paintings hung...and that it was greatly appreciated. I would think of him, and Amy, every time it caught my eye.

I continued to Harry's Bar to celebrate with a Bellini.

As I walked, I texted Amy, who had gifted me the work, a few pictures. I sent shots of the painting she gave me; the actual setting I visited; me with the painter...and my gratitude and love.

13

MEMORABLE MEETING ON VENICE'S RIALTO BRIDGE

A novelist or film director would have relished the romantic sound of it all – we were to meet at noon on Venice's Rialto Bridge.

But first...

I emerged from Harry's Bar after a noonday Bellini. The Bellini was unavoidable, really, since the San Marco Vallaresso vaporetto water bus docks directly outside the door of Venice, Italy's historic, classic watering hole. I had ridden the vaporetto only one stop across the Grand Canal from the Salute vaporetto dock, in front of the iconic Basilica di Santa Maria della Salute. It was the nearest stop to my hotel, the swank, waterfront Sina Centurion Palace Hotel.

I was bound for the Hotel Londra Palace, where I planned to look in on Alain Bullo, the luxury hotel's general manager, whom I'd met during a summer stay there in Venice four months earlier. The Londra Palace has 100 windows overlooking St. Mark's basin and the island of San Giorgio Maggiore. Furthermore, Londra Palace is neighbors to the touristic, historic Bridge of Sighs and Doge's Palace.

If you know Venice, you are aware I could have more conveniently ridden the vaporetto boat all the way to the San Zaccaria dock, which is just steps from Londra Palace Hotel and its Vittorio Emmanuele II monument out front. But what fun would it have been to skip Harry's Bar? Also, to have missed the opportunity to walk the Riva degli Schiavoni promenade and pass by the sight of the ornate Basilica San Marco, its lively piazza, and Venice's iconic campanile tower on the way?

After two little left turns out the door of Harry's and at the little corner of Calle Vallaresso it occupies across from the vaporetto dock, I crossed over one of Venice's 300 little bridges. I then strolled between the canal to the right and the trees of the Palazzo del Magistrato's Royal Gardens on the left. Spots of shade there had been prized when I'd last passed through in July. This time, since it was November, slivers of sunshine were welcomed.

I received a warm smile when I spotted Luciano Santangelo Virgilio, the painter I'd sought in the summer, selling his artwork in the same spot at which we'd met in the summer. This time, instead of shielding his works with a tent-type tarp, he was hustling, with his back to the water, to keep the breezes from taking them.

"Michele," he called out, surprised to see me again. I was surprised, also, to be back in Venice again after only four months.

"Signior Virgilio. Come stai?" I responded as we embraced.

We assured each other we were each "bene" and once again I complimented his compelling paintings. He spoke about my radio show and a column I'd written about him and the Venice Venice Hotel at which I'd stayed. Amazingly, as if on cue while we talked, my mobile phone rang. The readout on the phone indicated the call was coming from "Ana Lazari," a Venetian woman I'd also met four months earlier during my summer visit to Venice.

Venice Venice Hotel's Venice M'Art Restaurant location was waterside near the Rialto Bridge on the Grand Canal. It was during breakfast at a linen-covered table along the aquamarine-colored water that I met a server named Ana, who, along with her smile, wore a black and white-striped shirt and a long apron. Ana spoke very little English and pricelessly grinned each time I tried to speak Italian.

I enjoyed the back-and-forth banter and the setting so much that I requested a prosecco, even though it was early morning, to toast the delightful, dark-haired Ana and the beautiful breakfast of brioche, muffins, croissants, lobster and eggs benedict.

Since I am a travel writer, I staged each of those items on the table, including the silverware and a small vase, in order to take nice photographs of the food to publish. But Ana, before I could take the snaps, would quickly and dutifully reset the table and return the butter and spoons and other items to their proper positions on the table.

Then, as soon as she walked away, Ana would watch me reposition the saltshaker and prosecco glass and plates again. The sparkling-eyed server was left to shake her head and laugh. She probably thought I was an unrefined, stubborn American tourist.

Ana and I took a photo and, after the article was published, stayed in touch from afar.

Four months later, after that breakfast in July, I stood back in Venice, with the artist I'd met on that same summer day and answered a phone call from Ana. I had let her know, via text message, that I'd be in town if she had time to meet for a spritz, Venice's most popular drink.

"Pronto, Ana. Buongiorno, Ana," I said, in my best Italian, knowing, from past experience, she'd be laughing at my Italian.

Ana's voice then burst through the phone loudly, clearly, and in a colorful spree of rolling, bouncing Italian. Instead of Ana laughing at my language, I was the one smiling at the sound of her colorful, enthusiastic voice. I could make out the words "domani" and "Rialto," which I knew to mean "tomorrow" and Rialto, the area of Venice near the Rialto Bridge where we first met.

Luciano Santangelo Virgilio, the painter, could overhear Ana's voice and smiled with me. Since he spoke Italian and English, I got the idea he could translate the call for me!

"Ana? Un momento, per favore, cara," I said into the telephone, before handing it to an only slightly befuddled Luciano.

"Parlare Italiano Englese, per favore, Signior?" I asked. "Possible for you to translate the conversation?"

After the discussion and negotiation, Ana asked me to meet her at noon the following day at Rialto Bridge, which was in sight, along the Grand Canal, of the hotel veranda on which we first met. This is when a novelist or film director would have relished the romantic sound of it all – noon on Rialto Bridge.

Hotel Londra Palace; Venice Venice Hotel; and Sina Centurion Palace, were each recommended to me by IC Bellagio, the leading "Italian Connection" custom tour company based in Bellagio, on Lake Como, Italy. IC Bellagio is a member of Virtuoso Travel, the U.S.-based international network of worldwide travel advisors and providers. IC Bellagio arranges exquisite experiences, accommodations, tours, logistics, guides, meal reservations and access for visitors to Venice and all of Italy's treasured destinations from the Dolomites to Sicily.

Sina Centurion Palace Hotel has 50 bold-colored, contemporary, artsy rooms. Common areas include a courtyard on one side of a

glassed-in breezeway and a terrace overlooking the Grand Canal –
where guests arrive by boat – on the other.

The centralized location makes all of Venice, including many of the
treasured museums, landmarks, restaurants, shops, gondola rides, and
churches, accessible by water taxi, vaporetto, and even by foot.

After a cappuccino on the Sina Centurion Plaza veranda the next
morning, , I strolled, in a blue pinstriped blazer, up the narrow street
and climbed, again, aboard the vaporetto boat to cross the canal and
over to Mass at the Basilica San Marco.

Historians say construction of the church likely began in 1063.
The design, as well as some of the actual columns and sculptures were
plundered from churches and palaces in Constantinople, including
the four bronze horses over the entry. The result is Middle-Byzantine,
Romanesque, Islamic and Gothic influenced architecture. St. Mark's
bones, also stolen, but from Alexandria, are behind the main altar.

The easiest way to get into the Basilica is by respectfully attending
one of the scheduled Masses. This will allow you to avoid any lines or
fees, and, if you open your spirit, you might even receive some grace
and peace. No photos are allowed, though, and you may be limited to
only the side altar. but, if you're on a time crunch, and checking off
Venice's boxes, you can see most of the basilica from there.

On this particular morning, there was a touch of Venice's "acqua
alta," when water temporarily flowed up and flooded the side of Piazza
San Marco closest to the basilica and Doge's Palace. Authorities placed
narrow, wooden platforms for people to walk on just above the water.
It's a little like walking on six-foot banquet tables.

After Mass I avoided putting my Pradas in the puddles and set out,
on foot, for the Rialto area through the maze of narrow streets. You
can find your way to Rialto or San Marco by following the (mainly)
yellow arrows above window level at the corners and on the walls along

the way. A GPS app also works but it's a shame to miss all the scenery, people-watching and window-shopping along the way.

I was shopping along the way – enjoying looking for a gift to give to Ana at our noon meeting. World famous Murano Glass is made on one of Venice's islands of the same name (IC Bellagio can arrange intriguing factory glass blowing tours). In a delicate, tiny shop, I chose a small, glass heart pendant and necklace chain. And, for a laugh, I bought a glass brooch pin of Disney's Snow White because I felt the cartoon character's dark hair and fair facial features resembled Ana's.

I reached Rialto half an hour early, for a few reasons. One is that I really like the area (sestiere) around Rialto Bridge. The canal bends after running under the bridge, which makes for a scenic panorama when surveying the area while standing on the bridge, alongside it, or even below it aboard one of the water taxis, vaporettos, industrial barges, or romantic gondolas that slip underneath amidst the stream of aquatic traffic.

There is lots of foot traffic, too. People bustle back and forth, snapping selfies, shopping for souvenirs, buying oversized cannoli, dining on margherita pizzas, and drinking Aperol spritzes.

Rialto Bridge, itself, an architectural icon was built in 1591. There are shops on the white, stone bridge and all around the banks on both sides of it, including the nearby fish market. From the top of the bridge, I spied a location I thought would be nice to enjoy – a table along the sunny side of canal among the cafes and restaurants just a few storefronts from the foot of the bridge.

I walked down and secured the sidewalk table at what turned out to be Ristorante Caffe Saraceno and was early enough to enjoy a pre-meeting drink amongst the colorful crowds celebrating Saturday morning. I cut my nervousness and warmed myself up for the meeting by sitting in the sun, sipping a spritz, and chatting up a couple from France at the next table.

The woman was drinking a nice, warm cappuccino topped by a heart drawn with milk across the top. The man had a great glass mug of lager so big it would be an effort to lift. They were each dressed in all-white, warm clothes that made them appear they had just come off the ski hill at St Moritz. But they seemed happy as clams, which set a pleasant tone as the clock ticked toward noon.

"At Rialto," read the text from Ana I received at noon.

I quickly straightened my tie and straightened up the table, which struck me as an ironic callback to the breakfast chess four months earlier at nearby Venice Venice Hotel. I then peered up at the bridge looking for her, but not seeing her. I responded to Ana's text by sending her the name and location of the café.

Coming out from behind the table, I stood on the sidewalk waiting for her. It wasn't long before, amidst the wandering crowds, Ana appeared, wearing a warm winter coat and big, glamorous, starlet sunglasses.

"Ciao, Ana," I called out as she approached. Hers was as sweet as a smile could be, and we greeted with the three quick, customary air kisses.

I started to attempt to speak more of my rudimentary Italian greetings: "Come stai?" "Piacere di conoscerti."

But Ana, properly, moved the conversation over to introduce someone standing behind her – her 16-year-old son Elia Lazari. Elia was taller than both of us – nearly 6'1, I figured - and fit with a dark head of wavy hair. Elia greeted me politely – in English.

It was all happening fast and suddenly I remembered my manners and gestured for us to get out of the crowd and be seated at the table.

I suggested Ana and Elia take the seats offering the view of the bridge and canal while I sat across the table facing them.

Ana managed to speak enough English to explain that she lived outside Venice and had come in with her son to accompany him to a job interview which was scheduled just before our meeting. Whatever gaps she had in speaking English to me were filled in by Elia, who said he'd learned the language in school.

Believe me, Elia had to translate more of the gaps in my attempts to speak Italiano than he did with Ana's English. I was glad he was there to translate, but even more, I was very flattered that Ana would bring her son to meet me at our visit. I told her so – through his translation, of course.

"Grazie, mi cara amica. Es accoglienti," I told Ana, gesturing toward Elia. "Tu famiglia bene bambino." Ana nodded and I was hoping what I said, in my bruto Italiano, conveyed something close to "Thank you, my dear friend, for being comfortable to being your family, your good son, today."

What I thought to myself was, "Poor Elia. The young guy is stuck sitting with a stranger on a Saturday afternoon!"

Furthermore, I thought he might look at me with suspicion or trepidation, but Elia, instead, was friendly and he engaged easily in the conversation, which was great fun.

I signaled the always preoccupied server and, when he came to the table, Ana asked for a cappuccino, but I don't recall what Elia drank. I sipped a spritz and we caught up with small talk.

At some point the vibrant French couple at the next table interrupted to kindly say goodbye and that they'd enjoyed meeting me before they departed into the growing throngs of passersby who walked in each direction between our table and the canal.

Remembering the gift I'd brought, Ana seemed surprised as I placed the little bag on the table in front of her, along with a card I'd written out in carefully translated Italian. She opened the card first and read it, in which I basically thanked her for meeting me and told her how much I enjoyed her personality and getting to know her a little while keeping in touch since our first meeting in July.

She looked up when she finished and expressed that she was touched by placing her hand on her heart and verbalizing, "Awww." She made the same sound after opening the box with the Murano glass gifts.

"Grazie. Grazie," Ana said a few times, while immediately putting the necklace with the heart pendant around her neck under the fur around the hood of her black puffy coat.

As for the cartoon brooch pin, to be honest, after Ana unwrapped it, I sensed she either didn't agree with, or didn't like, the comparison I made to her look and the visage of Snow White. Maybe the humor was lost in the translation, but Ana just nodded that she understood my point and took a sip of cappuccino.

We eventually got into a functional language rhythm of trying and translation. Ana explained she was no longer a server at Venice Venice Hotel's restaurant. She now worked at the Hilton but, in February, would be employed by the Hotel Metropole, which she was pleased about.

I asked Elia how he felt his morning job interview, which was also at a hotel, went. The question opened up a very engaging exchange about his life.

"My real dream is to go to America and be a Mixed Martial Arts champion," he revealed with total conviction.

"Mama!" I cried out to Ana, gesturing at Elia.

"Yeah, 'Mama,'" she said back to me with a humorous shrug. It was comical, but the more Elia shared with me the more I saw her looking at him with affection and admiration.

"I notice you say you will be an MMA champion, not just an MMA fighter," I said to Elia. "Complimenti!"

"Thank you," he responded, speaking purposely in English to me. "If I am going to fight, I am going to win. And when I win, I will win until I am a champion."

Elia, at 16 years-old, spoke with the complete conviction of a seasoned motivational speaker.

"This is my dream now, but my dream with be a reality in the future."

He was focused purely on his goal, not any hurdles potentially in his way.

"I must do this on my own. And I understand what it will take. It will take training and discipline."

"Mama!" I said again to Ana, wide-eyed to convey how impressed I was with Elia's words.

"Yeah, 'Mama,'" she replied again, trying not to grin. Ana, behind those big, blocky sunglasses, was displaying, yet again, the mischievous charm I noticed in the summer at the breakfast table. She was a sassy Sophia Loren.

Elia then told me all about a Muslim MMA fighter named Khabib Nurmagomedo, a Russian who defeated the Irish star Conor MacGregor on the way to being inducted into the Ultimate Fighting Championship Hall of Fame.

"While Conor McGregor was partying, Khabib was working out and training five times every day. Khabib respects his opponents," Elia explained. 'I will have this choice, as well. When my friends are going out for drinks in the evening, I will go to train."

Hearing this, as I sat sipping a spritz, made me feel a little inadequate.

"You're inspiring me," I told Elia.

"America is inspiring," he countered. "In America anything is possible. Americans have the attitude they can do anything. I will go to America and I will be a champion."

"Mama!"

"Si, 'Mama.'"

I toasted Ana's cappuccino with my spritz.

"Salute, Mama. Salute, Elia," I proclaimed.

I admit that while sitting in the shadow of the Rialto Bridge with a beautiful Venetian woman, this was not a conversation I would ever have anticipated having. But it was an experience I thoroughly enjoyed. Ana, who had clearly been a very successful parent to Elia, treated me sweetly. And the discussion allowed me to learn about MMA and UFC, a popular sport I had known nothing about.

Elia's enthusiasm was encouraging and exciting. The young man's admiration for America was touching, especially since so many from the USA desire, conversely, Italy's dolce vita lifestyle. But the Italian art of "far niente" (doing nothing) didn't seem to fit Elia or his hard-working mother, the very active Ana. Elia even intimated that when it came to courting Ana, couch potatoes need not apply.

I invited Ana and Elia, if they come to America, to stay with me.

"Mi casa accoglienti tu," I attempted, again in my "male Italiano."

"Do you mean it?" Elia asked me in a serious tone.

"Si. Vero," I answered him.

"Do you mean it?" he asked again.

"Si, si. Molto Vero."

When he found out I lived in Michigan and Los Angeles, Elia spoke of his admiration for Detroit-born music star Eminem, who also made it in Hollywood.

"I love Eminem. And I embrace his lyrics. 'You only get one shot, do not miss your chance to blow this opportunity knocks once in a lifetime...'"

I turned the conversation back to Ana, who'd finished her cappuccino. We talked lightly, but openly, about our private lives in terms of past romantic relationships, personal situations, and current status.

Elia, involved in the conversation as a translator but also a participant, chimed in.

"You must respect my mother. She is a wonderful person," he said, looking me in the eyes.

Ana touched her heart again. But it was my heart Ana and Elia touched.

"Si. Io molto rispetto tu Mama," I responded. "Ana tu Mama bellisimo persona."

14

HAVANA'S LADIES IN RED

"I am a sincere man
From where the palm trees grow
And before I die, I want to let my verses out of my soul..."

Anyone who visits Havana, Cuba swoons at the sound of the ever-present tune "Guantanamera," a melody they recognize whether they hear the lyrics sung or not.

The Cuban ballad transcended the island and wafted into pop culture through films and television as the anthem of the island long before the American military and its' naval base made people more aware of that remote location called Guantanamo – the area from which the man in the song hails.

It's almost impossible to eat a meal or drink a mojito in Havana without the dining experience being accompanied by live musical acts. If you are hearing music in Havana, you will undoubtedly, in a short amount of time, hear "Guantanamera" if you didn't already hear it in your head.

The song makes visitors settle back, breathe, draw on a cigar, and imagine they, themselves are a musician, fisherman, artist, or Ernest Hemingway himself.

And while they're at ease in touch with their artistic side in a calmed state, do they see elegant, mysterious ladies in red dresses emerging from the shadows and sweeping over to attend to their needs...or is it their imaginations?

Relax for a moment, let go, and let's find out.

Havana, Cuba entices and seduces the imaginations of people who visit. Also, those who will never set foot on the shore and walk the seven-mile Malecon walkway to see the sea smash and soar over the fishermen and all the way across the tops of the taxis motoring along the road.

Turning through the pages of the tales of Hemingway, the sensitive but macho outdoorsman and literary giant who, while living in Cuba, penned the prize-winning novella "Old Man the Sea," one can feel the heartbeat and heartbreak of Cuba's people and their culture.

To physically visit and explore the plazas and streets of Havana is to be physically transported to a city that, with its old-fashioned classic cars and simpler pace of life, may seem forgotten by time.

But Havana's ornate, fanciful buildings and infrastructure have not been ignored by the erosion of the tropical elements and the challenges of a trade embargo against the governing political system.

It is the lack of overly commercial encroachment, due to the block-ade or otherwise, that maintains the timeless, cultural uniqueness of Havana.

Unlike, for instance, Dublin, Ireland, where visitors to once tra-ditional Grafton Street can still see and hear the buskers perform, but they are amidst an M.A.C. makeup shop and Disney Store, for instance.

I'd like to think that even if the U.S. embargo ended, this portion of Havana would be spared the capitalistic invasion of Starbucks and McDonalds.

The dichotomy of the candy-colored classic Cadillacs and beautiful, but sometimes crumbling buildings is all part of Havana's very visible story. But despair which, nevertheless, is not visible on the faces of the Cuban people, who, outside the tourist areas, endure gas shortages, supply chain issues, and power outages.

They project a warmth, even as they gaze over the Malecon into the turbulent ocean and swear they can spot the lights of the South Beach high-rises in Miami.

The most remarkable "high rise" in Havana is the seemingly, especially at night, bejeweled capitol dome. Ironically, it is nearly identical to the United States Capitol building in Washington D.C. (but slightly, by purposeful design, taller.)

The best birds-eye view of the capital and Havana's historic city center, including its central park, is from the sixth-floor, rooftop swimming pool deck of the Gran Hotel Manzana Kempinski La Habana. The luxury hotel, now Havana's finest, is located inside the historic, early 20th-century Manzana de Gomez building.

After first serving as a school, this building expanded to become Cuba's first shopping mall. Shopping for fashions, shoes, perfumes, and art is still available to tourists in the hotel courtyard and breezeways.

Kempinski Hotels deserves the praise and loyalty the company receives for its record of renovating and preserving historic buildings around the globe. They do this by turning them into vibrant, luxury hotels which become landmark destinations and social hubs.

A courthouse in Yangon, Myanmar; an 1858 Bavarian royal guest-house in Munich; the neoclassical Central Telegraph Building in Vil-nius, Lithuania; Singapore's Capitol Building – a former theater; and an Ottoman imperial palace on the Bosphorus in Istanbul; plus cur-rent renovations in the Dresden, in Germany's Saxony region, to name just a few.

Kempinski opened the Gran Hotel Manzana La Habana's 246 rooms with 50 suites in 2017 and did a magnificent job of maintaining the buildings' subtle, stately, authentic, Old Havana exterior appear-ance. In fact, a museum in the hotel basement displays photos of the original construction and building as well an entire wall of the original, rocky foundation.

Stepping inside, though, a new experience for Havana hotels pre-sents itself. It begins with the lobby's contemporary, modern, stylish luxury animated by doormen, a greeter, front desk staff, concierge and yes, the aforementioned, striking "ladies in red." (More on them to come.)

Let's continue at the top, via one of the hotel's glass elevators. On the roof of Gran Hotel Manzana Kempinski, lunch, dinner and drinks can be enjoyed poolside, known as Bella Habana, as well as in the shaded open air of Bar Surtidor. Or indoors in the windowed, panoramic San Cristobal Restaurant and Bar.

Bites and meals such as slow-cooked lamb; steamed lobsters, suck-ling pig with pumpkin puree, and beef "Ropa Vieja, Cuban pork chops, pasta and other culinary treats are presented by servers in white linen dresses all day and night. According to the male bartender, it's never too late, or too early, to request a drink. Diners can be as casual or as formal as they choose.

Lounging on cushioned chaises on the hotel's roof can intoxicate guests via sweeping skyline views all the way to the Malecon and the sea; the intricate panorama of Havana Vieja's ornate and sometimes crumbling buildings below; the very warm water of the swimming pool and heat of the sunshine; and perhaps the mojitos and Cuba Libres. You are in the center of a UNESCO World Heritage site forbidden to some and fascinating to all.

In your ethereal, dazed condition of bliss, you can ramp up the Zen even more by stumbling to the hotel's same-level Albear Spa – one of the 10-best in Latin America, to be further pampered. The surprisingly expansive fitness center and extensive spa seduce all the senses.

This includes the eyes because its treatment rooms, daybeds and peaceful relaxation areas are presented in an art-gallery-style setting with both darkened spots of solace and lots of natural light from even more sweeping views.

Between the Gran Hotel Manzana Kempinski's rooftop paradise and the lobby are levels of guestrooms and a second floor of fun. All this surrounds an artsy lounge that can serve as an indoor reception area.

Gicela Diaz Viera, the hotel's public relations manager, walked me through every hallway and corner of the hotel so I could view its varied charms and functions. She was well-versed in the history of the building and all its features.

"Many of our guests the Gran Hotel Manzana Kempinski's guests come from Spain and Switzerland," Gicela told me when I noticed various languages being spoken during our elevator ride.

Gicela was leading me toward the location of the daily breakfast buffet, which is included when I thought I saw two brunette ladies in red dresses sweep past the elevators through the lounge area.

But the doors to the breakfast restaurant closed behind me. So, I continued with the tour and viewed the restaurant with its' large, white-curtained windows behind which was a view of the park.

Next to the restaurant was an expansive, elegant cigar lounge called Evocacion, which housed a walk-in humidor overseen by the award-winning Juan Jesus Machin Gonzalez. He is known as a "master of masters" in pairing prized cigars with Cuban rum, and I was honored to meet briefly as he prepared for the day.

While the cigar lounge is sumptuous, dark and masculine, I found its counterpart, at the other end of the hall, to be the complete opposite in style: Bar Constante, with its turquoise-colored walls, arched passageways, tropical artwork, tiled floor and white marble bar is fanciful eye-candy.

As the sun streamed through its floor-to-ceiling balcony windows, Gicela explained why the lounge and bar had its name with a little game of show and tell. Beside the bar, outside the open window, and below on the corner of Calle Obispo and Monserrate streets, I spotted the famed dusty pink exterior and neon sign of the El Floridita bar. Gicela knew I would notice it.

"El Floridita's bartender in 1914 was Constante Ribalaigua Vert. He went on to become the owner of the bar and invented the daiquiri," Gicela explained.

Since the hotel's bar had such an undeniably special view of "la cuna del daiquiri," Gran Hotel Manzana decided to name its bar in honor of Constante.

I decided to linger, that late afternoon, in Constante. The place was mine, other than the bartender, who busied himself cleaning glasses until they sparkled. I opened the tall door to the tiny balcony overlooking the street and posted up at a high-top table with a stool.

A ceiling fan cooled Constante. In addition, a little breeze seemed to occasionally kiss the balcony as it wandered down the street through the twilight glow that cast dramatic shadows on Havana's intricate buildings. The smoke of my cigar mixed with the breeze, and I could not have been more contented or at ease.

I was not passing time...I was savoring my time smoking the cigar and sipping a fresh mojito.

I found myself enraptured in that moment. With no place to be, I was happy where I was. I enjoyed the languid ability to notice every detail and take an interest in it as if I were on a stakeout.

As colorful as the interior of Constante was, I let my eyes cast down onto the Calle Obispo corner where El Floridita was both visible and audible. The live music from the bar's band was pleasantly muffled but clearer each time a customer went in and out of the door.

The Latin tunes accompanied by the shaking maracas were as colorful as the classic pastel-flavored Buicks, Thunderbirds, Chevrolets and yellow tuk-tuk taxis lined up out front. There was a horse and carriage driver ready for a rider on the plaza-like street in the space between the Gran Hotel Manzana and El Floridita.

Ernest Hemingway has been revered at El Floridita since the days he lived and wrote at his lovely Finca Vigia estate outside Havana and drank in town. Hemingway's boat, the Pilar, which he piloted from the nearby fishing village of Cojimar, remains on display on the grounds, which is now a museum.

El Floridita is just as important a pilgrimage sight for Hemingway aficionados. The waiters in red tuxedo jackets serve daiquiris named after him. There is a photo of the writer, known affectionately by Cubans as "Papa" and Fidel Castro on the wall. And I can only imagine what Hemingway would think of the life-sized statue of him standing at the end of the bar. (Hemingway often wrote, and drank, standing up.)

That statue is in the front corner of the bar, to the left, when you walk through the door. Papa would have seen all the goings on from that corner. In fact, everyone in the bar can view anyone who walks into what's been dubbed "the greatest bar on earth" because the door is right next to the little, floor-level stage where a live band is always performing.

Having been in El Floridita and knowing all this about Hemingway, and now looking at the door of the establishment from the window above in Gran Hotel Manzana's Constante bar, my mind wandered, in a relaxed fashion, to a tale I once heard of Papa's close writing friend F. Scott Fitzgerald.

Fitzgerald frequented the Grove Park Inn Hotel in Asheville, North Carolina. Naturally the author of "The Great Gatsby" could have stayed in one of the hotel rooms with views overlooking the city below and the Great Smoky Mountains on the horizon.

Instead, Hemingway's pal preferred a less-desirable room on the opposite, parking lot side of the hotel. His reason? So that all day long, while he sat by the window writing, he would have a bird's eye view of the hotel's entrance and scout the arrivals of any women coming into the Grove Park Inn.

As I sat in Constante's window watching the streetscape and El Floridita's door, I smiled and lifted my mojito to Fitzgerald. I also saluted the other notable writers who deigned to down a daiquiri at El Floridita, including Ezra Pound and Graham Greene, who penned the book "Our Man in Havana."

As a writer myself, I indulged myself in the Havana hubris of accompanying them in the drink.

My mind was on writers as the sun was about to set to my right over Havana's Capitol building and its neighboring, old, four-story Hotel Inglaterra, which had live music playing on its patio.

Milking my moment, my pop-culture imagination ran reels of 007 stories in which Ian Flemming cast his James Bond spy in Havana; and how Mario Puzo had Fredo Corleone struggle with ordering a banana daiquiri in "Godfather II."

The previous night I'd walked Havana Viejo's narrow streets around the Kempinski Hotel, which is in the middle of so many intriguing landmarks. Including the strikingly angular vertical architecture of the neighboring building that was formerly Bacardi Rum's headquarters.

And just a block or two beyond that is the reason why the building is no longer Bacardi's HQ: Cuba's Museum of the Revolution in the former presidential palace.

Some museum exhibits – including Castro's bullet-riddled jeep; the Granma yacht; a downed spy plane, a missile, and an Eternal Heroes of the Motherland Memorial Flame – are presented in the outdoor garden area and visible from the sidewalk.

As I walked along the fence in the dark, I noticed a Cuban military guard, in his intimidating olive-green uniform and red beret, keeping his post by standing straight all tall on a small cement platform.

Because I was transfixed by his imposing visage, I watched him for a while in the shadows, without making eye contact. And because I was watching him for a while, I got to see something I considered revealing and special: Every few minutes this Cuban soldier, presumably to break up the monotony, would look around to see that no one was watching, and dance on the platform.

I am not connoisseur enough to know if it was salsa or soft shoe. But as incongruent as it was with the uniform and the military setting, it was delightful to see. So I stuck around to watch him do it a number of times – each time not believing my eyes. (I admit I was nervous about photographing a Cuban soldier, though.)

Just a few doors from the Museum of the Revolution I entered a lively, two-story restaurant called El Carbon. Once again, the band was positioned in the front of the restaurant near the door, so patrons stepped immediately into the festive fun.

El Carbon was a colorful, well-decorated dining experience with a menu full of traditional, delicious dishes of all types at moderate prices. The upstairs section, reachable by a spiral staircase, was partly open-air and full of fauna.

It was there I spoke with a Cuban server who astonished me with her command of the Spanish and English languages. She could start a sentence in Spanish and finish it in English with no transition whatsoever. It was like a party trick!

She was as entertaining as the band was and said she was studying to be a psychologist. She'd hoped to work with children and gave me a fascinating explanation of how seeing what children draw, including the colors they use and the pressure with which they put crayons to paper, can tell a lot about their psyche.

Then she showed me one of the restaurants' more unusual, exotic items when she pulled out a tray of broiled pigs heads. Like I'd seen 007 do in the movies, I tried not to flinch.

I took a taxi to what I was told is Havana's hottest nightclub - Bar 2.45. It is owned in part by Javier Sotomayor, the greatest high jumper in Cuba's history (thus, the name). He set two world records during Barcelona's 1992 Olympic Games in Salamanca, Spain, which is the name of the attached restaurant.

Inside the bumping club, with bottle service, dancing to DJ music, and then a late-night live superstar salsa performance, you would never believe the story the taxi driver told me on the short drive there. He'd come to Havana from Ukraine with his parents when he was a little boy.

"Russia and Cuba were close, then," he explained.

But now he planned to emigrate to Canada, where he said the Canadian government provides immigrants with 15 free hotel nights and $3,000 Canadian dollars.

I asked him where in Canada.

"Anywhere," he answered. "I don't care where."

The last straw for him was waiting 30 hours in line to buy gas for his taxi, which he said, compared to other countries, was an inexpensive $1.50 per gallon.

"You sat in your car in line for 30 hours?" I asked.

"Not exactly," he explained. "Think of social media. Our social media was getting out of our cars and talking. Then getting back in to move the car. Sometimes we'd share a bite to eat while we waited."

His car was not a classic antique, but rather a boxy little Soviet-made model.

Mind you, there was no talk of any transportation issues by the drivers who took me to and from central Havana from Jose Marti International Airport. Kempinski's Gran Hotel Manzana can arrange that efficient transportation in advance.

One need only wander Havana to experience the dichotomy of disparity...coupled with the resilience of spirit and culture of the people.

I sat still contemplating on Constante's balcony, enjoying my Gran Hotel Manzana moment after all of this. Chilling at Constantine had given me the time to reflect on my days in Havana as if my life was a movie and I was on set.

Then my ears were tickled. Was that, from El Floridita's band below, the melody of Guantanamera I heard wafting up to the window scoring my scene? Of course, it was.

The forbidden fantasy of Havana had become real...but felt surreal.

But the next sound I heard over my shoulder was very real.

"Hello, sir. How are you?"

Since I was the only one in the bar, I knew the voice had to be speaking to me, so I turned around to find two "Ladies in Red" right before my eyes. They stood, with perfect posture, in striking, perfectly pressed, knee-length, solid red dresses with impeccable hair and make-up.

They smiled with knowing expressions on their faces. The brunette, peaceful "Ladies in Red" had an ethereal quality about them.

It was the most gentle and greatest interruption ever.

All the Ladies in Red wanted was to know that I was happy, on behalf of the hotel.

I stood and introduced myself and explained who I was.

"We know who you are," one of the ladies said, smiling. "We are the Ladies in Red."

I came to learn the "all-knowing" Ladies in Red specialize in curating wisdom about the hotel's guests and subtly make themselves available to intuitively ensure guests have a memorable and comfortable time.

"We are the 'Ladies in Red,' we are powerful," Ariana said, with a gleam and the confidence Cuban woman culturally command. It was cute and charming.

As I did, guests will occasionally catch glimpses of the Ladies in Red throughout the hotel. They don't lurk – it's more like they float or sashay.

"You ladies are like celebrities," I told them.

"Really?"

"Si," I said. "Encountering you has a magical quality to it. It is like seeing Mickey Mouse at Disney World." The ladies laughed, but it is true. They are ambassadorial.

Kempinski created the position at each of its illustrious properties to not only welcome guests but to share their unrivaled local knowledge and expertise about the hotel and local area. When casual conversation moves into that realm, I noticed they become all business and take the dialogue seriously.

I observed them, with other guests at the pool and in the lobby, anticipating needs and requests, and even encouraging them to ask for them.

As for their "powers," they can plan surprises, organize last-minute requests, and lead guests to experiences, even on-property, they might not have known about.

I salute the dreamy Ladies in Red at Kempinski Gran Hotel Manzana la Habana: Ariana, Ana, Iris, Amanda, Leslie, and Melanie.

15

IN PRAISE OF DANGEROUS WOMEN FROM LONDON TO THAILAND

 London's Langham Hotel is a central character in three of my more memorable romantic travel stories. The historic, luxury hotel located in the West End's Portland Place, was once owned by the BBC, which built its Broadcasting House across the street. That was magic to me since I am a radio host.

Major movies have been filmed at Langham. To me, the most thrilling of which was the 007 movie Goldeneye, when Pierce Brosnan, playing James Bond, emerged from the hotel's ornate front entrance.

I was put up at The Langham by ITV. The British television network brought me in to recreate the "runaway bride" situation I had experienced in Dingle, Ireland, for its documentary show "Weddings from Hell."

The storybook wedding, after only a few hours of "matrimonial bliss" dissolved into the shortest marriage in Irish history, so it made lots of news in the tabloids and in the media on both sides of "the pond," including the Doctor Phil Show. Dr. Phil's team, which had seen my story on Inside Edition, flew me to Los Angeles and put me up at Loews Hollywood Hotel to appear on the show at Paramount Studios

ITV flew me to London for a couple nights at The Langham to get acclimated. Then the production team and I flew over to romantic, sea-smashed Dingle to recreate some of the scenes. It was all very dramatic.

Whilst at the hotel, I met Englishwoman, Diana Moxon, who, at the time, was Langham's Director of Public Relations. She was a very vibrant woman. Since I was a travel writer, we hit it off professionally and kept in touch.

We will return to The Langham in a few pages, but first, take an exotic journey of digression with me.

When Moxon, an adventurous traveler, took a new position representing Anantara Hotels in Thailand, she invited me to Hua Hin to experience that resort and, as a journalist, cover the King's Cup Elephant Polo Matches. She promised the King of Thailand would be there. (I swear, I am not making any of this up.)

I was a long way from "Jolly Old" when Moxon took me to the matches. There I noticed the international elephant polo teams were sponsored by up-market champagne, Scotch whisky, and beer companies, along with automakers and banks. Plus, there was a fanciful throne and royal viewing box set up for the King.

During the competition, a mahout rides atop the elephant and guides him while the player, also on top, uses his mallet to move the ball. The official rules stated: "Sugar cane or rice balls packed with vitamins (molasses and rock salt) shall be given to the elephants at the end of each match and a cold beer, or soft drink, to the elephant drivers...and not vice versa."

Hua Hin, a three-hour drive southwest of Bangkok, is also the King's home city. It is peaceful with beach resorts along the Gulf of Thailand, shopping, golf, and dining. Thailand is best known as "The Land of Smiles", which is very true. However, another marketing slogan for the country is "Mysterious, Sensuous, Thailand." There is good reason for that, too.

Moxon was not the only Brit who looked after me in Hua Hin. Richard Catska, an English golf photographer living in Hong Kong, whom I had met in South Korea, connected me with Frank Gilbride, when he heard I was going to be in Thailand. Gilbride was an English ex-pat operating a golf tour operation in Hua Hin. Got all that? Small world, eh?

Gilbride told me by telephone he would come to the Anantara Resort at noon to pick me up and give me a tour of Hua Hin. Imagine my surprise when Gilbride showed up to fetch me on a moped. Fourteen hours later, at 2 a.m., I was returned to the resort in the back of a tuk-tuk: a motorized, three-wheeled rickshaw.

"I came to Thailand on a two-week trip but stayed forever," Gilbride told me over our first frosty beer with ice-water-soaked wash-cloths around our necks.

After our day on the town, I could see why he stayed:

Whiskey was about $4 a bottle. You and your mates could drink all night on a $20 bill.

Hotel rooms in snazzy, oceanfront resorts with swimming pools and manicured gardens could be had for $70 a night!

A 90-minute, beachfront Thai massage cost $5!

I picked out the fabrics and was fitted for three suits, three dress shirts, and two pairs of shorts, all custom-tailored for a grand total of $400.

New-release, bootlegged DVDs of films currently showing in theaters were $1.

Designer-brand clothing, or knockoffs of the same, were abundant and so inexpensive that you could sweat through them one night, throw them away, and buy new duds the next day.

Hua Hin also boasted a bunch of open-air bars. Many of these watering holes also featured pool tables and were full of festive "bar girls" offering hospitality, shall we say to tourists. Gilbride pointed out the licensed ladies playfully populating the bars, shooting pool, having drinks and chatting with customers. You would never know they were anything but out for a night of fun until they ask the question, "You want to go hotel?"

Gilbride, a bald Brit with a bold sense of humor, let me swim on my own when a particularly stylish and striking bar girl in a glamorous red gown and equally ruby lipstick slinked up next to me. She set the old board game "Connect Four" on the bar between us. You remember the stand-up grid in which you drop red or black checkers down the slots hoping to line up four of them before your opponent does?

Since she spoke almost no English, the game was a way for her to break the ice and communicate. The gorgeous woman had perfectly straight, long, dark hair spilling down over her tight, red evening dress and her perfume scented the humid, night air.

The woman defeated me in every game of Connect Four with deadly efficiency...and always seemed pleased with herself – but not surprised – when she won. After each win the woman then gave me a charmingly sympathetic look beckoning me to: "Try again?"

It was fun. It was flirty. I was feeling tipsy and worldly as my "James Bond 007 alter-ego" kicked in. The woman and I got into a rhythm of dropping the checkers into the slots, but sometimes I would pause when it was my turn and stare into her eyes, lifting an eyebrow to play up the drama and try to read her strategy. She looked straight back into my eyes, tossing her hair, pursing her lips or winking, coyly.

Gilbride watched in silence from his barstool behind me as I bought her a glass of champagne. I admit I was enjoying the losing streak, though I became intent on winning at least one game of "Connect Four."

Whether or not the lady in red let me win is unimportant. The fact is I won a game, at last. When my winning checker fell into the slot, she stared at the board, squinted, and pretended to be miffed she lost to me. And then she broke into a broad smile and nodded to magnanimously acknowledge my victory. I smiled back.

It was all romantic, right?

It sure was when she then reached around the game and gently placed her soft hand, with her perfectly polished red fingernails, on my hand. This time, with no checkers between us, then looked deep into my eyes.

"We go hotel?" she asked, quietly.

"You'd like me to take you to my hotel room?" I asked, channeling my inner 007.

"Yes," she said, in a seductive tone, still lightly caressing the top of my hand.

"That would be very nice," I admitted. "You're very sexy."

She smiled and lightly, with her nails, tickled my hand.

"But let me ask you something first?" I continued.

Without breaking our gaze, she nodded. Then I continued.

"Are you...'one-hundred percent?'"

She tilted her head and tried to smile playfully. But I could see her becoming crestfallen when I waited for an answer.

"'One hundred percent? Or no?'" I asked again.

She stared into my eyes for a few seconds, and then, resigned, answered, "Not 'one hundred percent.'"

I shrugged my shoulders, smiled, and removed my hand from under hers so I could extend a parting handshake.

"No hotel. Only 'one hundred percent,'" I said, in a respectful, apologetic tone. "Thank you, though, for the games. You are very sweet."

She smiled. "You...worthy opponent," the Thai "girl" said before nodding and slipping away into the night after I clinked my glass with her one last time.

I then finally turned back to Gilbride. He had ordered us two more cold Singha beers, which sat on the bar in front of him.

"Jolly good, Shiels. Well done, 007," Gilbride said, playing up his British accent. "But how did you know? I wondered where it was all going. How did you know she was really a 'lady boy?'"

"No Adams Apple," I answered in a matter-of-fact fashion. I concealed the fact that I did not immediately realize the gender bender I had been matching wits with over game of Connect Four. In truth, it took me a while. "I was disappointed but relieved I did not find out the hard way, pardon the pun, old boy!"

Gilbride later introduced me to another dazzling, brunette "lady boy" he knew well while he played a game of billiards with her. They teased each other between shots in the same way I'd flirted while playing Connect Four. Gilbride's friend was a very good pool player, even in her low-cut black, bejeweled evening gown. The brunette was also in the midst of months of surgical procedures to physically transition into a woman.

"Gildbride sunk a striped ball and then, with a smile, told his opponent, "Remember, when your procedures are finished, I want to be the first."

"Of course, darling," she responded in broken English.

Back at The Langham, during my original visit, I once again felt like James Bond when I walked back into the hotel, after a night out, through the front entrance, which was seen in the "Goldeneye" movie. As if passing through that entrance in my jacket and tie wasn't enough, when I decided to slip into the Langham's lush cocktail lounge for a nightcap, I felt even more like I had a license to kill when I heard the piano player, totally by chance, plinking out the 007 theme music in a medley of soundtrack songs from the series of movies: You Only Live Twice; From Russia with Love; Nobody Does it Better; Live and Let Die...

Naturally, I embraced the moment by ordering a vodka martini: shaken, not stirred.

This random, late-night diversion would lead from the Langham to yet another totally unexpected world destination.

That destination was prison.

A prison visit, that is.

I noticed a few of Britain's famed tabloid newspapers folded over a mahogany stand in the Langham's bar while I heard my martini being shaken. I plucked one of the more respectable among the print publications and paged, casually, through it, as I lounged on the leather seat of a broad barstool. It was not the infamous, topless "Page 3 Girls" of the Daily Star newspaper that caught my eye, but rather, an elegant photo of a fashionable English socialite.

The blonde, British beauty had been caught up in a spot of bother, it seemed, in the Palm Beaches of Florida. Here she cavorted in the champagne lifestyle via luxury vehicles at glamorous soirees on yachts in designer clothing. Chantal Watts, of Slough, England, became Chantal McCorkle when she married an older, American man named William whom she met at an Orlando nightclub while working as a 20-year-old nanny.

William had become high-profile by appearing in television infomercials offering to teach people how to get rich – like he was – by buying foreclosures at government auctions.

The infomercials turned out to be all showbiz. The testimonials given on the tube by McCorkle's happy customers tuned out to be paid actors; and the helicopters, yachts, horses, and Porsches seen in the spots were...rented and misrepresented. Even with superstar attorney F. Lee Bailey representing McCorkle, the fraud resulted in a 24-year, mandatory minimum federal prison sentence, a term the court also invited, in fact insisted, Chantal McCorkle serve as an accomplice.

Goodbye brunch on the beach at The Breakers; hello penitentiary.

Chantal, in the newspaper article, claimed to be an unwitting accomplice. I, as a tipsy, martini-drinking man, was inclined to believe her. I was quick to cast her as a doe-eyed damsel in distress dragged down by a dastardly con man.

I sipped my martini and read in the newspaper article that the British government also saw Chantal's sentence as excessive. In the United Kingdom, being swept up in such an offense may have been punished by merely a suspended sentence. International intrigue surrounded this fall-from-grace tale.

I wanted in.

I mailed the newspaper clipping and a letter to Chantal McCorkle in care of her current address: FCI Tallahassee, the low-security federal correctional institution for female inmates in Florida's capital.

Not long after I sent it, I received, in the mail, a hand-written response from inmate Chantal McCorkle. It was a very pleasant note. She was grateful for the newspaper clipping and, in addition to telling me about her situation, asked polite questions about me. She also included her prison inmate number in case I wanted to write to her again.

This initial exchange triggered a year or more of pen-palling back and forth with letters to and from Chantal McCorkle. Sometimes her letters would have sentences or parts of paragraphs precisely clipped out – censored by the prison officials who read her letters before they were put in the post. She wrote about occasional unpleasant situations, such as when she did not get along with another inmate, which led to trouble with her supervisor, and perhaps sanctions of some sort. But mainly Chantal was very positive and bright. Her handwriting was impeccable.

Chantal started sending me, almost every time, a greeting card she'd handmade out of construction paper and photos from magazines of flowers or sunsets or beautiful scenes. The 32-year-old obviously had time on her hands, but I was touched she would take the time to meticulously create these little works of art.

I always mailed back elaborate (store bought) greeting cards, magazine articles, and sometimes photos of me. In each return note, she mentioned how she appreciated the photos, and drew plenty of hearts, smiley faces, and "xoxo's," signing, "Love, Chantal."

It was all sweet and I simply hoped that in some way it brightened her existence.

At some stage, while working on the book "Good Bounces and Bad Lies," with British golf commentator Ben Wright, I decided it might be interesting to visit Chantal. I was staying with Wright who lived near Asheville, North Carolina – about seven hours from the prison in Tallahassee. As a travel writer, I had never been to Tallahassee, so I could turn the trip into a weekend getaway and explore. I had also never been to a women's prison, and being a curious type, figured this would likely be my only opportunity to see inside the walls.

"If I am ever going to be in a prison, it might as well be a women's prison," I explained to Wright, who erupted in agreement with a Churchillian chortle.

The visit took a while to arrange since it was planned back and forth via U.S. Mail. Chantal, who was happy I wanted to visit her, had to grant her permission and file the paperwork formality of adding me to a list of approved visitors. I presume I was, to some degree, vetted by the prison officials.

As I recall, prisoners were allowed only two visitors on any given weekend, so we picked a free weekend - January 25 of 2003, and I took both available visits: one on Saturday and one on Sunday. Then I drove to Florida, put on a blue shirt and tie, and entered Tallahassee Federal Correctional Institute. Sure, I was a little nervous.

I stood in a line at 10 a.m. when the visiting hours began in a security room where guests were processed by confirming their name was on the list, checking ID, going through a metal detector and a hand search. I recall signing some sort of waiver, and I think I brought a flower to give Chantal, but as I recall, visitors were not allowed to take anything into the prison. It was all rather strict.

In the holding area, which has tables and stools fixed to the floor, I observed the other visitors: various combinations of families, sometimes with children, who had come to visit their incarcerated loved ones. It was not lost on me that their visits, maybe even weekly, were much more serious and somber than my "first date" with my pen-pal paramour.

For this I felt a little guilty.

I scanned the room for Chantal as the prisoners streamed in to meet and sit with their visitors. Chantel spotted me and, looking as lovely as possible in her tan prison khaki clothing, came over to greet me. Instinctively, I reached to hug her. Chantal quickly, but politely, reminded me there is no touching between the inmates and the visitors.

"They're watching," she said, in her charming English accent, which, of course, I adored.

Chantal then suggested we go outside. I was happy to move to the open-air courtyard area. Unlike the "prison yards" I had seen in the movies, it was, of course, a fenced area, but there were trees and grass and a covered pavilion with picnic tables, which is where we sat and settled in the shade.

Chantal and I talked about things you would expect, though I tried to delay asking about her prison lifestyle. Instead, I directed the conversation toward her upbringing, family, and her interests. I did not want to make her feel bad by talking about my life traveling the world as a media person, but she insisted, because she was gracious, in asking about my life in return.

Sometimes we just sat quietly. Sometimes for brief moments, she would lightly put her hand atop mine, but then slide it away.

"They are watching," she said with a shrug.

I smiled.

I learned there was one courtesy I was able to extend: I was allowed to buy us a drink: two cans of Mountain Dew from the vending machine.

It was a far cry from the vodka martini I sipped at the Langham when I had first seen Chantal's photo. But we clinked the cans and the little ritual of sipping on them while we talked made the situation a bit more normal.

I was a welcoming listener, in part because I enjoyed her accent and her deep, warm eyes. I imagined that her eyes would have been brighter back in Britain, or even Palm Beach, when she was not a caged bird.

"I sleep in a bunk bed in a room with 22 other women," she revealed.

Each time she gave me details of her life among terrorists, including a roommate who murdered her parents, I tried to be sympathetic without visibly reacting or recoiling.

"We are fed breakfast at 6:30 – always starchy things to keep lethargic."

Having enjoyed a proper English breakfast, especially at The Langham, I could only imagine how much she, as thin and shapely as she was, missed the bacon, sausages, eggs, tomatoes, mushrooms, beans, and toast of a fry up.

"I miss Cornish pasties and chips," Chantal offered without prompting, as if she had read my mind.

We could speak freely in the open air at a table near the edge of the pavilion, but still, we did not speak loudly. She told me after breakfast she typically spends over three hours cleaning the sleeping area.

"It is one of the better jobs," she insisted.

I could not help but to silently think about the posh babysitting job for rich Floridians that led her to washing floors for criminals. Even the dichotomy of Palm Beach vs. Tallahassee – two very different cities in vastly different parts of the Sunshine State – served as a metaphor.

Chantal told me after lunch she would run in the exercise yard before being locked in her cell for a couple hours before dinner.

"After dinner I take a shower and read. I am learning Spanish," she said.

"I'd love to hear you speak Spanish with a British accent," I teased.

"Back into the cell at 9:30. Then the lights go out at 11," she said.

Chantal spoke of William, who would soon be her ex-husband. He was in a different prison and the last time she had seen him was in a courtroom.

"I was not involved in his business, yet he refused to tell the court that," she said of William.

Since Chantal had opened the door on the topic, I felt able to ask some questions about the case. She did not have much good to say about the famed attorney F. Lee Bailey, either.

Without much expertise, I gathered that Chantal was out of appeals. Time and time again her applications for a commutation of her sentence had been refused. She was, instead, pinning her hopes on a pardon or that Britain would come through with a treaty transfer to return her to the United Kingdom.

"My mother tells me not to worry about her, but I do," she said.

I wondered to myself whether Chantal expected me to stay for the entire visiting hours period...or whether she was hoping I would not. I played it by ear.

At one point one of the other inmates came over with a camera.

"She can take our photo," Chantal explained. "It is her job."

Since visitors could not bring cameras in, for $20 we would receive each receive two photos of two different poses she would take. Chantal would eventually have to mail them to me. I gladly paid, and we walked over under a tree to find a nice backdrop that did not include fencing or other prison features.

The inmate photographer was very friendly and took her job seriously, working to pose us in a photo in the best light and in which our faces were not shaded. I suppose, for a prisoner, the opportunity to be outside taking photos and meeting new people might be the highlight of the week. It was also the only time Chantal and I, as we posed, were able to stand close together and almost embrace.

I stayed very close to the end of the visiting time and told Chantal I would be back the next day, in the morning for a bit, to say goodbye before I drove out of town.

I confess to being tired and a little bit emotionally spent, so I spent the evening on my very nondescript Quality Inn hotel bed eating pizza and watching television.

Again, it was a far cry from the luxury of The Langham; but far more comfortable than the evening Chantal was having back at the prison.

And for this, too, I felt a little guilty. Somewhere along the line, I lost touch with Chantal after she was moved to prisons in California and Texas. Chantal was also bounced to lock-ups in Oklahoma City and then New York before finally being transferred back to England for a short, minimum-security stay and finally release in 2010 on June 25 – my birthday.

16

UNBUTTONING HUGH HEFNER'S LEGACY

Walking through the Golden Triangle of Beverly Hills on my way to cocktails at the Four Seasons Beverly Wilshire, I felt my blazer lose its' button.

I was in the middle of one of the most couture-conscious, fashion retail areas in the world: a Rodeo Drive-anchored, snazzy canyon of Gucci, Prada, Versace, Canali, Burberry, Armani, and House of Bijan, which has clothed U.S. Presidents, British Royals and billionaires.

This, to me, meant two things:

One: I could not hobnob among the glitterati with an unbuttoned blazer – especially one with a missing button.

Two: Surely, I could find someone with a needle and thread to reattach it.

I used Google Maps on my smartphone, which revealed a "tailor shop" 200 feet away on Brighton Way, the street on which I was walking.

"Perfetto," I exclaimed.

But less than 10 seconds after walking into Gary Gagossian's small shop, I realized I was committing a major faux pas. Any shop that uses the phrase "bespoke" is more atelier than tailor. The few "off the rack" articles on display for sale were handcrafted and haute with luxurious linens and fabrics.

I was the only "customer" in the store and a man, who I presumed to be Mr. Gagossian, was behind the tiny counter in the sewing area customizing something exquisite for someone superior.

The only reason I was in there alone was because someone like Mr. Gagossian surely meets by appointment only. It was as if I walked in on Oscar de le Renta (who I actually once met at a party.)

I began to step softly, backward, attempting to retreat out of the silent shop without disturbing the master at work.

"How can I help you?" he asked, without looking up.

"Oh, sorry. I am in the wrong place," I shrugged. "I am just looking for a place to get this button reattached."

"Give it to me," he said, reaching out his hand.

"No, really I couldn't..."

"It is okay. Give it to me."

Handing him the blazer, I prayed he would not look at the inferior, down-market label as he turned back to work with it. I likened this action to a world-class surgeon in his operating room reattaching the nose of a teddy bear. I was wracked with guilt for bothering him with such a thing.

The guilt was then followed by fear as I looked around.

"Holy Christ," I thought, "I cannot imagine what this going to cost me?"

I then noticed the only framed photo on display in the shop. Walking closer, I could see it was a picture of Playboy Magazine mogul Hugh Hefner. He was standing, in a stylish, tailored suit, next to a wax figure of himself wearing Hef's trademark burgundy robe.

Both images of Hefner were posed in the center(fold) of a bevy of bunny beauties, perhaps taken at his infamous Playboy Mansion a mile or so away in Holmby Hills. The photo was autographed, in gold pen, with the message:

"To Gary, Best Wishes, Hugh Hefner."

Instantly I no longer regretted my awkward interruption of Gagossian, whatever the potential price:

"I can now say I have the same tailor as Hugh Hefner!" I thought to myself. The irony that Hef made his fortune based on the absence of clothing was not lost on me.

Gagossian emerged at the counter and handed me the blazer.

"Thank you – and sorry for such a silly job," I said, though he seemed unbothered. I pulled out my billfold and asked Gagossain the fee.

"No, no. It is okay. No charge," he said, in a dignified manner, without being a bit condescending or dismissive.

Having my moment with Hugh Hefner's tailor would turn out to be only one of my brushes with Hugh Hefner and his Playboy legacy in the Beverly Hills area. Three of them, in fact, were at the Beverly Hills Hotel's Polo Lounge.

I shared the restaurant's famed chocolate souffle there one evening with Elizabeth Meza, who spent part of her media career as a producer for the XM/Sirius Playboy Radio channel. She spoke of events she attended at the Playboy Mansion.

In particular, a festive Fourth of July picnic Hefner threw on the back lawn for family, friends and some staff including an elaborate fireworks display.

Viktoriia Lazuto is a Ukrainian immigrant who found her way to Hollywood when the war with Russia interrupted her successful business career in Kyiv.

Lazuto told me, when we met for espresso at the Hollywood golden age Polo Lounge, that she appeared in Playboy Magazine's Ukrainian edition.

"I was in the November 2021 issue. It was my protest because I worked in the business community and I wanted to show people that I am a woman, first," she explained. Then she said the photos were tasteful. "I love to work with photographers who make the pictures in a way that your imagination has to work."

Lazuto proved it to me by showing me the magazine pages, which she had stored on her mobile phone.

I drove Lazuto over to the Westwood Village Memorial Park, a couple of miles up Wilshire Boulevard, to visit Hugh Hefner's crypt, where his body has been entombed next to that of Marylin Monroe since he died in 2017.

"There's your former boss," I pointed out.

"And hers, too," Lazuto pointed out, reminding me that Marylin Monroe, who died in 1962, was the cover girl and centerfold model for Hefner's very first Playboy issue in 1953.

Another past Playboy bunny also once, very quickly after striking up a conversation, showed me Polaroid photos of her magazine modeling shoot off her phone. This, with her husband sitting right there next to us at the Polo Lounge's tiny bar.

This time it was after dark, and it can be presumed following the consumption of potions more potent than espresso. But only a little because she was drinking an Aperol Spritz, which is, by alcohol percentage, a tame concoction.

"These photos were taken when 'these' were real," she revealed, gesturing toward her bosom under her fashionable winter white wool coat, which she then removed and tossed onto a chair next to the one at which her show-biz-handsome husband had taken a seat.

Titillating as the conversation was, I kept politely trying to bounce the banter with this extremely beautiful woman to her husband. But the former bunny playfully pivoted back to me.

"You give off a vibe. I can tell you are very sensual," she said. "I was drawn to you as soon as you walked in."

If only I could have seen my own face.

"Honey," the woman told her husband, "I want to marry him."

"I will be the priest," he offered, non-plussed.

Then she smelled my Gucci scarf by deeply inhaling as she cuddled it against her cheek. "I want to take this with me," she insisted, looking me in the eye and tickling my nose with the end of the scarf.

"Am I on Candid Camera? Or is it Punked?" I asked.

She stayed playful and told me she and her husband lived near the hotel and this was their first time out in the new year. She was sophisticated and elegantly dressed in haute couture from head to toe.

We then shared a very entertaining and wide-ranging conversation. I was all ears, and admittedly eyes, as the explained that part of her youth was spent outside of America and then getting roughed up in one of L.A.'s tougher neighborhoods.

Her pumpkin transformed into a coach when she became a successful model and enjoyed the life of being very popular in Hollywood's celebrity social scene. I told her I had come from seeing Jay Leno perform his stand-up act at Flappers Comedy Club in Burbank, that night.

"I don't really care for Jay Leno," she said in a tone that implied she, at some stage, had met the late-night talk show host. As I heard more of her story, I learned why: she dated two of Hollywood's most famous funnymen – very successful stars of both the big screen and television.

"He drove me around naked in his luxury sportscar," she said of the more manic of the two courting comic actors. She admitted she left one of the suitors for the other. "He treated me so well. But I was conflicted."

The woman conceded now, as a wife and mother, she was now concerned about society's cultural decline.

"I want to move to Hawaii," she said.

We exchanged information and took a photo together. As a model, of course, she checked the photo on my phone and wanted to re-pose for "take two," one which better flattered her fabulous figure.

I did not mind one bit.

The next time I posed for a photo with a model it was a step beyond Playboy and into the adult entertainment world, the stars of which I learned are now also social media influencers.

I stood with a tall, friendly, dirty blonde with her hair in a ponytail whose widely seen body was squeezed into a t-shirt and shorts. She was 44-year-old Cherie DeVille, who has starred in thousands of, shall we say, short films. I met her while working as a background actor on the set of a PG-rated TV comedy series being shot in Van Nuys.

"Well," I told her as we posed for a photo between takes, "I can honestly say I never thought I would be on set in a scene with Cherie DeVille!"

DeVille understood my joke, laughed, and hugged me.

Still waiting for the next scene, she told me a story of how she and an actor were about to shoot an "action scene" after the script called for her to throw a drink in the actor's face.

"I accidentally threw it in my face and then we had to stop for me to get my hair and makeup all over again," she laughed.

DeVille was exceedingly friendly, as were the rest of the all-star adult stars I met over two days on that set.

"Do you mind having been dubbed the 'Meryl Streep of Adult Entertainment?'" I asked Angela White at the craft service table during a lunch break.

"I am neutral on it, really. The Daily Beast named me that," she answered. The Australian brunette laughed and decisively shook her head "no" when I teased her about looking for vegemite on the buffet. I am not sure why, as a grown man, I was nervous talking to her, but I was.

It was all laughs when the zany, red-haired, "Fitness Nala Ray," posed for a whimsical picture with me – a photo graciously shot with my phone by Kazumi, who I learned has millions of online subscriber fans. Ray had the stars smiling all the time with her colorful costumes, bright make-up, and endless screwball enthusiasm.

Riley Reid saw us taking the photo and chimed in. "You are a bad boy. You want us to chastise you!" A subsequent Google search revealed tiny Riley Reid is a huge star after a 13-year, hall-of-fame career that has yielded countless academy award "equivalents," most of which I hesitate to specifically name on this page.

Just before rolling on a take, one of the performers, a curvy, straight-haired brunette called "Lena the Plug," came over and plopped her bottom in front of me on the table at which I was sitting. She wanted to improvise something for the scene.

"Is it okay to flirt with you?" she asked, tugging off my glasses.

I smiled and nodded. Then told her, "That is the biggest diamond wedding ring I have ever seen!"

"You're the one wearing a Gucci scarf," she countered.

"Touche!"

"Amouranth" in a green bikini was literally set dressing for the entire project. I spoke briefly with her, but she was a little more reserved and intimidating. The flaming redhead (as opposed to Nala Ray's red hair) is on record as saying she earns $2 million a month letting people watch her sleep on streaming platforms.

These industrious women have crafted their individual brands and, though competitors, by collaborating and mentoring each other, have created entertainment empires. They are like super friends like the "adult Avengers!"

The funny frolicking in Van Nuys reminded me of a midsummer night's dream.

Social media Influencers in bikinis cover all categories, it turns out.

Vanderbilt Beach, on the Gulf of Mexico in North Naples, is one of Florida's most pleasant stretches of sand. Seven miles of shoreline stretches in front of hotels, private housing, and state park property.

One 85-degree, Sunday afternoon, like many others, after a beer, I was stretched out in the sun on a beach towel listening to the lapping of the waves, laughter of children and bleating of the birds.

The bliss got a little blue when I heard two women behind me talking. Their conversational language included words with "f's" and "s's." They were talking about some dramatic events involving boyfriends or husbands, as I suppose many women do. These tales were peppered with salty language.

After a while, I could not resist the temptation to take a gander at the women propelling this prose. From behind my sunglasses, I twisted my head back to take a sneak peek at the chatty Cathys turning out the truck driver talk.

What a surprise when I saw two supermodel-style, bikini-clad, platinum blondes in all their fairer-sex femininity. So much for typecasting.

Their lewd language was not really bothering me, and I am not one to judge, but just for the fun of it, I sat up and turned around.

"Ladies," I started. "Please, excuse me ladies..."

When they turned from each other to look at me, I continued.

"It is Sunday afternoon. Would you mind watching your language?"

I think both of their jaws hit the sand at the time before the longer haired, one in the pretty pink bikini finally spoke.

"Are you f-ing kidding me?!"

They were both seated on the sand but took a defensive posture.

I sat perfectly still, straight-faced, and stared silently at them for about five beats.

"Yes!" I laughed with a big smile.

"Oh, F you!" The other one cried out as we all started laughing.

This trick triggered an afternoon of spicy storytelling and, if I remember correctly, less swearing. The pretty-in-pink, blonde told me she had served in the military, which maybe explained her vibrant vocabulary.

And it turned out the other woman was Mariah Medina, a major Instagram influencer in the recreational fishing industry, so now I understand

17

DAY OF THE DEAD IN MAZATLAN

 I didn't know it would become a golden moment. I just knew she had golden hair.

The sunlight was strong that afternoon in El Quelite – a village outpost 40 minutes by car from Mazatlan in the Mexican state of Sinaloa along a river. There was some shade in the square plaza plateaued in the middle of town. But otherwise, the cobblestone streets were steamy and the colorful, tile-roofed houses, historic buildings with pre-revolutionary porticoes and colonial churches, galleries and shops appeared brilliantly lit even though squinted eyes.

It was my understanding that buses drop tourists and cruise ship passengers to wander and shop amidst the 1,800 inhabitants of this farming town literally named after vegetables, but it was quiet on this weekday afternoon.

I, along with some other writers, had been driven from the breezy beach, Banda music, bikinis and swimming pools of the Pueblo Bonito Mazatlan Beach Resort. We were taken through the cock farms and cattle fields to sightsee in this town which may or may not be the birthplace of Pancho Villa, depending on who you ask.

If Pancho Villa was born in El Quelite on a day like this one, I hope they kept the infant covered and cool. But the heat – dry and dusty - didn't seem to deter the pre-teen boys I saw vigorously playing traditional Ulama, which is something like soccer with a heavy rubber ball. I got thirsty just watching them, so, I decided to procure a Pacifica.

Suds or shade were tied for the top priority when I saw the long, dark, covered porch of an abode across the narrow street. I could hear my footsteps on the wood as I walked up onto the empty space and sat down in a rocking chair. I recall being contented to be out of the noonday sun. But I do not remember if I was rocking or just sitting still in the seat when my eyelids drooped down like wilting lettuce leaves in a left-behind botana.

Still soaking in some sweat, I found myself swaddled in the solace of a shady siesta. In my somnolence I swam in the dreamy blue pool back at the Pueblo Bonita Mazatlan Beach Resort. In some level of REM, I was floating under the footbridge that spanned the swimming pool like a dogpaddling troll. In my dream a poolside waiter was waving me over for a frozen margarita I'd managed to order over the marching band-style sound of the traditional, brassy Banda music being played live on the beach.

When I swam, in pool water not perspiration, over to the waiter, he handed me my margarita. But when I looked down, it was actually a goblet full of ice cream just like the bowls I'd actually eaten at the resort's Los Palomas breakfast buffet. I spooned up the vanilla and chocolate soft-serve-yourself right out of the machine...as much as you want! It was like being left alone after hours in a Dairy Queen speakeasy, which was a dream in itself.

The memorable Los Palomas breakfast buffet bursts with cultural cuisine: sopes de papa chorizo; chilaquiles verdes and rojos; marlin ala Mexicana; chicharron salsa verde and frijoles. I usually added a tequila sunrise...before the sundaes.

But the nonsensical incongruence of a poolside margarita-turned-sundae, along with the next part of the dream in which a bonita seniorita in a bikini actually spoke to me, proved preposterous enough to force me awake in the rocking chair.

In reality I was parched, and it was time for lunch with the other traveling sightseers.

The Meson de los Laureanos is the type of establishment one might expect to find the leader of a band of stagecoach robbers, which is who the timeless restaurant is named for: Jose Laureano. I wandered through the series of dark, small rooms and bars at different levels until I came to an open-air, partially covered courtyard. The intricate, brightly colored room with its shelves, artwork, and even trees had the feel of a bazaar in which the heisted merchandise and minerals might have been fenced.

Little did I know it was about to play a major role in my experience.

Since I'd been snoozing, I was the last of about 10 of us to get to the long table near the side wall full of photos, shelves, and a heath. The only seat was at the far end of the table near the banos. The remote spot was suitable for me since I was woozy and not likely to provide compelling conversation.

Once seated, to my left across the colorful tablecloth was a couple from Carlsbad, California. To my right was a woman with blonde hair a bit frizzy from the heat. She told me she'd just moved with her daughter and dogs from Denver to Puerta Vallarta. Heather was solo, like me, and I liked her because she didn't seem to need to talk or impress anyone. She glistened after an afternoon in the steamy sun and yet was and completely at ease.

After I bit, I didn't mind talking so much.

As thirsty as I was, I hesitated to drink water poured from the pitcher out of caution and instead, out of habitual indulgence, had a big margarita like the one I'd just dreamed about.

Between sips, or maybe they were slugs, I tried to seem non-plussed about some of the Sinaloan local menu choices of our host, the genial, enthusiastic, Marcos Gabriel Osuna Tirado, who is an ambassador for the area. A read over an English translation which included Ranchero liver; Chilorio; Beef head in its own juice; Chicharron; and Slight - a soup with seasonings prepared with corn grains and the stomach of the beef.

I nibbled on some soft tortillas and morsels of conversation with soft, subtle Heather, who genuinely seemed as non-plussed about her intriguing life as I attempted to be about some of the unique menu items. She shared she was recently divorced after a long marriage.

"I've been down the aisle so many times when I'm asked if I am married, I answer "occasionally,'" I told Heather in an attempt to show shared empathy and yes, amuse her with some lightness. Maybe I could manage some charm, but she was the compelling conversationalist.

Heather told me how she'd bought a home, sight unseen, in Puerta Vallarta. She didn't have a car, but her daughter had driven all the way to PV from Denver. It's a 30-hour journey if it could be done non-stop and if Mexico's roads were not so narrow, windy, and bumpy. That trip also, according to Heather, meant delays due to occasional stops by both the Federales and the cartel, something she maintained was an inevitable part of the trip and both had happened to her daughter.

"The way you know the difference is the Federales pull you over. The cartel runs your car off the road," she explained. "They just want money and any guns you might have."

She said she, as a newly single woman, had not been going out much or socializing yet in Puerta Vallarta. I don't know what possessed me to ask the next question, but I was curious to know whether Mexico had a 911 system to call in emergencies.

When Heather told me she didn't know and hadn't thought about it, I encouraged her to find out as soon as possible.

"You've been living here nine months without knowing who to call in an emergency?" I asked.

She shrugged. "I guess I should find out."

"I am going figure out how to contact you so I can check on you to make sure you do," I told her in a comical way. But I secretly admired how Heather seemed to just be rolling with life as it came. With my empty stomach, dehydration, and margarita, I told her so.

"You should try it sometime," she said flatly. Her eyes were piercing but she was not as insistent with her advice as I was in imploring her to find out the Mexican emergency phone number.

The Carlsbad couple, particularly the wife, chimed into our conversation some, but only occasionally. I was too busy asking questions.

"How did you choose to leave snowy Denver to move to Puerta Vallarta?"

"I had vacationed in P.V. once. And after the divorce I felt I needed a fresh start," Heather answered.

I nodded and again mentioned that I could relate and that I'd been struggling with the compelling idea of a fresh start myself. Then she continued.

"For my fresh start I decided I was going to either start a small business in Denver or move to Puerta Vallarta. Honestly, I would have been happy with either."

I didn't ask her what the small business would have been, but I did ask Heather what her determining factor was. Again, she answered plainly as if her answer was obvious and universal.

"I flipped a coin."

She assured me she wasn't joking. She left her life's direction to the 50-50 prospect of a coin flip.

"I still have the coin," she said.

In the midst of a series of resulting questions I ended with a revealing one.

"Heather...what if the coin had come up the other way? What if the flip had determined you'd stay in Denver?"

She looked at me, thought about it, and gave me her first smile of the conversation. It was the smile of someone who'd been busted. "Then I would have flipped again."

"Maybe two out of three?"

"Something like that," she admitted. "I guess down deep I knew what I really wanted. It was kind of a 'bucket list' thing and the time was right."

I suggested to Heather that nothing has to be forever and that she can always move back if she ever wants to. Once again, I was spouting advice to someone who clearly had the confidence to not need it. So, she turned the tables and challenged me.

"What about you?" she asked. "If what you said is true what's holding you back from your fresh start? You told me you were having trouble with a decision."

Stumped, I wasn't sure how to answer. Inside I was asking myself the question in the face of someone who'd exhibited the courage to take a big, international, cultural leap of faith. As such, she didn't wait any longer for my answer.

"I am going to lend you my coin," Heather stated definitively. "I will send it to you."

She promised, just as I'd said I'd be checking on her about the 911 service, she'd also be checking on me about my coin flip to a fresh start.

Gulp!

18

IRISH PUBS, WARM HEARTS & COLD FEET

 The late U.S. Senator Daniel Patrick Moynihan was surely not speaking of romance when he stated: "To be Irish is to know that in the end the world will break your heart." But he, like many of Irish descent, had a love affair with the Emerald Isle and its people, anyway.

Each visit to Eire is a love story of its own.

I was once married in Dingle. The storybook-style, traditional noon wedding under the soaring ceiling of beautiful St. Mary's Catholic Church was on the sunniest Saturday in the history of Ireland. But no forecast could have foretold the marriage would be the shortest in Irish history. Literally hours after we emerged as newlyweds on the church steps my new wife had an inexplicable change of heart, changed into all-black, and would not sit next to me at the dinner let alone join me in our honeymoon suite.

It turned out to be a destination wedding with a dead end, which was big news in a little Irish village. Tabloid media dubbed it a "Real

Life Runaway Bride" story in outlets as wide ranging as the Irish
Independent; Good Morning America; Dr. Phil; and Inside Edition.

My lady friend Rose and I were Americans who adored Irish culture and heritage. Her young daughter was on the way to becoming
an international Irish dance champion. Therefore, we'd been on a
collision course with the Emerald Isle from the moment we met in
Michigan...and became engaged:

"Thursday is my birthday," Rose told me. "Is that when you're
going to give me my ring?"

I pulled Rose closer and kissed her. My small bedroom was warm
on that summer afternoon and her black hair felt damp.

"Well, are you?" She left her face touching mine.

"Maybe."

"Oh Michael, you! You are!"

Her eyes were wide.

"What does it look like?"

"You want to see it?"

She leapt up onto her hands and knees.

"You have it?"

"Maybe."

"It's already here isn't it? It's right here in your house!"

"Rose, I can't tell you that."

I was careful not to look up to the top of the bookshelf at the foot
of the bed. It was there in a gift bag, beyond her five-foot-five reach.
Instead, I focused on her brown eyes.

"Oh my God it is! It's somewhere in this house," she said.

Rose held the wrinkled black sheet to her bare chest and tugged
it from the bed when she jumped up and ran from the room. She
wrapped it around her slender, olive-skinned body as she searched my

little house. I could hear her rapid footsteps and the sound of her opening and closing closet doors and dresser drawers.

"You won't find it," I called to her.

Then she returned to the room and threw herself back onto the bed. She wrestled with me – the black sheet between us.

"Where? Where, Michael? Where is it?"

"I hope you realize it's a toe ring, I said."

She stared at me and then tossed her head back in laughter. Then she squeezed my chin with her little hand. "Now...where is it?"

"Be a good girl, Rose."

"Tell me, lover."

"Thursday."

She groaned and shook me by the shoulders. Then we kissed. Our lips parted long enough for her to say it again: "Thursday?"

"Thursday."

On Thursday it rained all day, and I didn't know what to do with myself. I watched the clock though the afternoon hours.

It was still drizzling at six o'clock when I put on a gray suit and light blue tie. I drove to Rose's house to pick her up. When I pulled the car into her driveway, I could already see her through the rainwater on the windshield. She was sitting on her porch swing waiting under the awning, smoking a cigarette in a satin, seawater blue dress held up by thin shoulder straps.

I fumbled with a wrapped gift box and a single flower, and tried to manage an umbrella too, as I walked up the concrete steps. The ring was in my pocket in a little mahogany box. The pitter-patter of my heart was drowned out by the sound of the rain pelting the aluminum awning.

"Can you believe my hands are shaking?" I asked her, smiling and shaking my head.

But Rose didn't laugh at all. She stood still and, with her warm, brown eyes, stared into my eyes, knowing I had come for her. She anticipated a serious night.

"You look like a princess," I said.

She tilted her head and smiled.

I gave her a long kiss on the cheek and handed her the single white rose.

"Happy birthday, Rose."

"Are we going out to dinner right now, Michael?"

"Why don't we go inside first and have a drink?"

Rose put out her cigarette. It was dark inside and quiet. Her young children were away.

"What will you drink? I'm thinking about a gin and tonic. Maybe you want a Jameson? Will you pour them?"

"Why don't you open this first?" I suggested handing her the gift box.

"It's heavy. And why is the box so cold?"

"Open it. You'll see," I said, watching her peel off the wrapping and then examine the green box with the gold embossed writing. "It's just a little birthday present."

"Dom Perignon champagne," she said.

"Chilled all day," I explained.

"While wrapped in the gift box?" she asked, pushing aside the paper and opening the box.

"In the refrigerator, yes. Why not?"

"It has two champagne glasses with it," she noticed. "Finally, we have some champagne glasses in this house!"

From time to time during our courtship, I would show up at Rose's house in the evening with a surprise bottle of Moet & Chandon White Star.

"Champagne. What are we celebrating?" she would ask on those occasions, setting water glasses out to pour it into after I uncorked the bottle over the sink.

"We're celebrating...Wednesday, I guess. Why not?"

"Oh, you!"

Rose and I would then sit at her dining room table and drink the White Star after dinner. By then her young children were in their pajamas and occupied by cartoons on the living room television.

On this Thursday night, though, Rose's living room was ours alone. No children. No cartoons.

Rose lit an Irish cream-scented Yankee Candle I'd given her on the end table next to the couch. It warmed the damp day with its light and scent. The other memorable scent was the Charlie perfume she always wore. It was the kind of perfume you'd find at Walgreens rather than Neimann Marcus.

"I know it's cheap, but I seem to always get compliments on it," she once told me.

I opened the champagne and sat down next to her on the couch. We clinked the new flutes and drank the Dom.

"I like your suit," she said between sips, tugging at my lapel.

"Thank you."

"I've never had Dom Perignon before."

"It's nice, huh?"

"Very nice," she said, after swallowing a sip.

I spilled a touch of the bubbly on my pants topping-off her glass. She excused herself to get a towel.

When I heard Rose's feet hit the linoleum of the kitchen floor, I switched off the lamp leaving only the candle's glow. I pulled a custom-made cassette tape from my pocket and inserted it into her stereo system. Then I stood with my finger on the "play" button waiting for

Rose to come back up the hall. As I waited, I thought about the fact that I was in my last moments as a single man.

Finally, I heard the sound of her satin dress sliding across her nylon stockings as she walked back toward the living room. Taking that as my cue and pushed the "play" button on the stereo.

By the time she reached me, music filled the room: "All the Way," – the duet version by Frank Sinatra with Celine Dion.

"Would you like to dance?"

Without a word, she put her little hand in mine, and I took it. My hand was firm on the small of her back. We didn't speak.

The first song blended into the dramatic orchestral opening of the second: "Ebb Tide," performed solo by Sinatra.

"First the tide rushes in...so I rush to your side, like the oncoming tide..."

I swept Rose back to the couch and sat her down. Then I dropped to a knee. Before I could speak, she leaned forward and wrapped both of her arms down around my neck and began to cry.

"Rose."

She couldn't answer out loud, but I felt her head nodding. Her long, dark curly hair smothered her face. Rose didn't let go. The music played on.

I pulled the mahogany box from my pocket and put it into her hand. She squeezed it.

"Rose, will you marry me?"

She embraced me harder, sobbing and nodding as the song swelled:

"And as we kiss through an embrace...in the rain, in the dark, in the sun...I'm at peace in the web of your arms."

"Yes," I finally heard.

"Yes," I responded.

This woman, this 39-year-old divorced mother of two, this creative coffeehouse owner with the raven black hair and dark complexion who was going to be my wife, finally looked up...laughing.

"Why did you ask me the 'big question' at the beginning of the night? My makeup is running all over now!"

"I wanted this to happen right here in your living room. Not in some restaurant," I said to my newly engaged fiancée.

"Michael. I want you to know this is your home now, too. When will you start moving in?"

"Rose, aren't you forgetting something?"

"What, honey?"

I looked down at her hand. It still clutched the ring box.

"Oh my gosh! My ring!"

She opened the mahogany box and saw it for the first time: a heart-shaped diamond placed between the gold carving of two extended hands under a crown. It was a traditional Irish Claddagh ring, symbolizing love, loyalty and friendship, customized by the diamond.

Rose began to cry again. "Where did you get this?"

"I had it made."

"How could you think to create special something like this? I cannot believe it. I can't stop looking at it."

"Let me slip it on."

It fit.

"Let's have the wedding in Ireland," I suggested.

"Let's! Going to Ireland will also be a first for me, like the Dom," Rose responded, reaching for her glass with her now sparkling left hand.

She turned back to me and we clinked the flutes.

"To Ireland," I toasted.

"To Ireland," she answered.

Little did we know we were drinking to our demise.

After the "wedding gone wild," I have gone back to Dingle, Ireland, many times – initially to drown my sorrows and reflect.

One of those nights had been a filling mix of music, drink, and now, air. Four hours earlier I'd filled a bowl of lobster bisque with soda bread at the Half Door restaurant on John Street.

The entire front of the Half Door is painted dark green. It is in the middle of the block next to Doyle's, the entire front of which is painted red. I ate at the bar and read through the Kerry's Eye newspaper. After, I walked out into the near dark, turned right, and headed up the hill, past An Droicead Beag, beyond James G. Ashe's, and Banc na hEireann. Past Paul Geaney's on the right and the Benner's Hotel, with Mrs. Benner's Bar, on the left. Just next door, Patrick Hennessy was closing up his Fado antique shop. We waved to each other, and I kept on through the dusk in Dingle, County Kerry, Ireland.

At the top of the hill, I turned left onto Green Street, which runs back downhill in front of the church on the right and then on down to the marina.

Dick Mack's Pub is on the left, across the narrow street from the church. The pub itself is a stubborn antique that retains its character through seemingly zero maintenance. Dick Mack's occupies a space that first sold dairy products. It then became a leatherworks and shoe store during the day; and a public house after dark. No food or trappings. Just whiskey and porter.

If any paint had been applied to Dick Mack's Pub in the last quarter-century, it was Oliver's bit of memorable prose on the alley gate next to the pub: "Where is Dick Mack's? Opposite the church. Where is the church? Opposite Dick Mack's."

The tiny nature of the pub and its local regulars can be intimidating. Unsuspecting travelers will come through the door, immediately sense the silence, and feel the gaze of the regulars. It can seem as though they might be walking into a classroom or interrupting an IRA meeting. Some visitors turn heel before they get in the door.

On this night there was a black-and-white dog curled up on the cement floor. And there was a woman across from me at the workbench that I'd known to be a regular but had never spoken to. She was tall and thin with angular features and a crazy, curly bush of midnight black hair exploding from her head. Her eyes were dark and her teeth uneven and shaded. Her clothing was nondescript and dowdy, and she clutched a pint glass of Bulmer's cider with ice in it.

The brunette had a large black Celtic tattoo encircling one of her biceps. Her English was barely discernable through her brogue and yet it was English she spoke to everyone around her. She laughed often with exaggerated expression. Even though the drinkers in the pub created a rumbling din, I could hear her sometimes screeching cackle as she tossed her head back and threw her hair around from side to side as if she were chained to the stool.

"What is her story?" I asked a local to my left. He was a truck driver who drove fish from Dingle over the Conor Pass and onto Cork where it could be shipped to Spain. Sometimes he ran computer parts from Holland to Ireland via ferry.

"What's her story?" he repeated to me. "Where does it begin and where does it end?"

We laughed and shrugged, but still I was curious about her. "An rud is annamh is iontach": What is strange is wonderful.

She wore no jewelry, and she was difficult to make eye contact with even though I sat right across the workbench from her.

But after a gulp of Guinness, I managed to catch her attention by telling her, "Good evening."

She was polite enough and gave a cursory nod before I attempted to extend the conversation.

"I'm Michael."

"Hello, Michael."

"What's your name?" I asked.

"What's your name?" she asked me back.

"Michael."

"Well, that's all you need to know then Michael."

I looked away and drank to the bottom of my porter, which took a minute or so. Then I tried again.

"That cider will make you crazy, you know."

"And why not?" she replied.

"I know your name anyway. The truck driver told me what it is."

Her dark eyes examined me.

"What is my name then?"

"Agnes," I joked.

She shook her head.

"Delores."

"No."

"Bernice."

Then she tired of the game.

"I am Mary. It is nice to meet you, Michael." She extended her hand, and I took the gesture to mean that she admired the way I sustained her previous smack down and volleyed back.

"Nice to meet you, too, Mary."

This time she extended the conversation.

"Our children are at home with the minder. That's me husband there," she said with a tilt of her head.

"I see," I said, nodding and then looked across the room. He was tall and thin and pointy with matted black hair. His eyes were dark, too, and some of his teeth were absent. I heard him, in his work clothing, speak in a heavy accent while flashing a crazed wild smile most of the time.

This coupling was a reminder that I was in the far reaches of County Kerry and it might be best to stay in my lane. Or head to the next pub.

After I left Dick Mack's I walked down the rest of Green Street, past Beginish and the photo shop and the chemist and the florist. At the bottom of the road, I turned right and went two blocks further. I ducked into John Benny's Pub. John Benny's, like seemingly everything in Dingle, is in the middle of a block. I leaned on the bar.

"Hiya, Shortie," I said to the tall blonde girl behind the bar.

She turned around and smiled at me. "Crested Ten?"

"Right. You've got it."

"You've come for the Craic, have you?" she asked while pouring the whiskey.

I nodded.

The tall bartender was anything but short. The owner John Benny kept a close eye on her.

"I told you I was going to work at my brother's pub in Australia?" she asked as she set the small glass of Jameson on the bar in front of me.

"You did. Going soon?"

"In two weeks. For five months. Longer if I can get the visa worked out."

I took a sip. "And if not?"

"Back home to South Africa."

"Either way you won't miss this cold."

"No, I won't, she admitted."

"Does John know yet?"

"No."

"I'll say nothing."

"Thank you, Michael."

"Good luck, Shortie."

She smiled.

I could see through the doorway to the other room that Peadar was now among the musicians playing a traditional session. I reasoned that Peadar must have mended his feud with John Benny. The feud began when Peadar was playing a session one night in the pub but was made to pay for his pint. Benny had been playing the squeezebox with the musicians at the time, and this was his excuse when Peadar confronted him after the session.

"You put a microphone in front of me and your man won't spare me a porter?"

"I cannot oversee everything when I'm playing a session like," Benny explained.

"Bollix."

"Is drink your only motivation for playing, Peadar? For fuck's sake."

To end the argument, Benny poured Peadar a Guinness. Peadar accepted it, left it untouched on the bar, and walked out.

The group, along with Peadar, played a mighty session this night. The talking was kept to a minimum in the back room in which they performed. I'd had learned some of the melodies the traditional musicians played. Many of them were of a baleful nature. As such they were still calming. I sipped the Crested Ten while a woman stood and sang a traditional song alone while the musicians rested and listened to her. Only John Benny on his squeezebox gave her light chords to serve as a little backup. Her voice pierced the pub:

"Black is the color of my true love's hair

Her lips are like some roses fair

She's the sweetest smile and the gentlest hands.

I love the ground whereon she stands

I love my love - and well she knows

I love the grass whereon she goes.

But I know the day it never will come

When she and I will be as one."

I held on tightly to my little glass of whiskey and listened hard until she was finished. Both the liquid and those lyrics were tough medicine.

Many Irish ballads don't need vocals, for the individual instruments serve as the voices of the songs. The messages of these songs hit people in different ways. They are the kind of melodies that make one take a deep breath. My heart slowed when the musicians resumed by piping the light but solemn whistle tune Innisheer. My mind replayed, with nostalgia, a bit of writing I had completed earlier that afternoon.

"You're a picture of concentration today, Mr. Shiels," said the young, English barman wearing a white shirt and dark tie as he passed through the lobby at Benner's Hotel. He was looking, through his round spectacles, for empty pint glasses amongst the antique easy chairs and mahogany coffee tables.

"Thank you, David. Don't let me take a drink until you see me turn off this laptop computer."

"Right then - at your insistence. But may I say, sir, that is not at all like you."

"You may and you just did. It was very cheeky of you."

He smiled.

"You have taken good care of me, David. I'll finish this chapter in less than an hour and come into the bar. We'll drink Veuvre Cliquot."

"I'll organize the champagne."

"Thank you, David."

"Finish the chapter for today, you mean to say?"

"Finished for good."

"This is why the champagne, then. We are celebrating, Mr. Shiels?"

"In a manner of speaking, we are. I'd say it is finally finished. Today it is finished."

"Good on you then. The finish has been a long time in coming sir, hasn't it?"

"Longer than you know. And three months ago, I told you not to call me 'sir,' so knock it off, limey."

"Was it difficult to finish?"

"Aren't all endings difficult, David? And aren't all beginnings brilliant?"

"I shall keep that in mind, sir."

David picked up two teacups and spoons from the coffee table near the leather loveseat. The loveseat was near the front window, which was framed by heavy yellow drapes. A crystal chandelier hung over the table. I sat in an easy chair in the corner next to the fireplace along the bookshelves. The old books gave the lobby warmth, but they were never borrowed from the shelves. English titles like The Cloud Above the Green, In Field and Hedgerow, Kindred of the Dust, and Off With His Head were relegated to serve as decorations. On one of the days I spent writing in the lobby, I noticed a book on the shelf entitled An Impossible Marriage by Pamela Hansford Johnson, published - 1955. I never read it, but I kept it on the shelf near me each day that I wrote in the lobby at Benner's.

My computer sat in front of me on what seemed to be a tiny, old receptionist's desk. It served as an end table otherwise. The manager of Benner's, Muirean, didn't mind the curiosity of having me as "writer in-residence" in the hotel lobby, even though I stayed just west of town in room number five at the Tower View Inn, a guesthouse owned by Robbie and Mary Griffin.

"What will you do now?" David asked. "Now that it is finished."

I looked at him.

"I shall drink champagne."

Back at John Benny's, Peadar and the boys finished playing Innisheer. I should not refer to them as "the boys" because they were each older than I and there was one woman playing with them. Peadar waved from across John Benny's between songs. I lifted my glass to him. It was empty, except for the melting ice. Peadar swiveled back on his stool and the group began to play an up-tempo instrumental called The King of the Fairies, with the squeezebox leading. A large, ungainly woman, whom I suspected to be German, sprang to her feet and began to dance around in the middle of the floor. She was trying to mimic traditional Irish Step Dancing except her arms were flailing about.

I noticed John Benny watching from behind the bar.

"You have insurance?" I asked him.

"Not for that."

I slapped a five Euro note on the bar and left. It was going to half-eleven and I didn't want to be drawn into hearing late night conversation or taken to the chip shop for grub.

Standing outside John Benny's Pub I breathed in fresh air. A brisk wind blew in from the harbor across the street. A tall ship was moored over there, and the mast flags were flapping. If I smoked cigarettes, I suppose I would have had one right then. As it was, I listened to the muffled sound of voices and music coming from inside the pub. It was dark and the Strand was empty.

I looked to my left down the street past the Betting Office in the general direction of O'Flaherty's Pub and the roundabout that leads either through Inch to Killarney or over the Conor Pass to Tralee. To the right I looked past the alley and up toward the Slea Head Drive roundabout. I'd need to walk back up to the top of town to get the Nissan Micra, which was parked in front of Geany's Pub. Some nights it was a long walk. Some nights it wasn't.

I looked again down the Strand and saw a heavy brown wooden door. The door was closed, but it was the door to James Flahive, and it was always closed. I'd never been inside, but a bald-headed Englishman once told me about the place and implored that I make it a point to go in sometime. I asked Peadar and the locals about it. They told me that the James Flahive Bar was permanently closed down. Looked like it tonight. But the Englishman told me that if you knocked on the door most nights after 10, Flahive would open the door.

I knocked.

I didn't expect the door to open, but I knocked again, and read the words painted on the window above the door:

Licensed to deal in wine, beer, spirits and tobacco for consumption on and off the premises 7 days.

The only other indication that it was a pub at all were the script letters painted on the stone above the transom: James Flahive Bar.

"Oh me God it's you," the bald-headed Englishman said after he opened the door. "You finally took me advice, did'ya? Come in! Come in and meet James."

I shook the Englishman's hand and went inside. He closed the door behind us.

"I'm relieved you are here to show me the place," I told the English-man. I am not sure he heard me as he was rushing me in.

"Yank, look at this place. Is it as I described to you or what? It's a place where you look around and say to yourself, 'What the bloody hell am I doing here?'"

James Flahive's Bar was much like Dick Mack's Pub but smaller and, believe it or not, brighter. There were four wooded stools along the counter and no other seats. Crates and boxes – four cases of Club Orange soda were piled on the floor at either end of the room. Old pictures of Gregory Peck, who starred in Ryan's Daughter - a movie shot in Dingle long before a Star Wars sequel was filmed there - adorned the walls.

The bar was no bigger than a living room and there was a drain in the middle of the concrete floor. Pulled, heavy drapes foiled any window peeps.

Only in looking around did I notice a plain looking fellow sleeping on a stool in the corner with his elbow propped on the countertop. Behind the counter there was draught Guinness and the man-himself.

"This is James Flahive," the Englishman pronounced.

The unhurried white-haired man didn't rise when I shook his hand, which was wide and smooth. He wore a gray jumper with an unbut-toned dress shirt underneath. I couldn't see his shoes. I surmised he was about 85 years old.

"I'm Michael Patrick Shiels, sir. It is nice to meet you. Thank you for allowing me in."

"Failte. Welcome...Michael Patrick Shiels," Flahive stated in a grumble that was as gruff and low as a voice could be. "Where are you from?"

"Michigan, in the United States," I answered.

The Englishman laughed at me as the corners of Flahive's mouth rose a bit.

"'Michigan...in the United States,' he says," the Englishman mocked. "...as opposed to Michigan in Italy or Michigan, China, right, James? This one he's from Michigan in the U-S-of-A."

Flahive nodded at him and cast his molasses gaze back over at me.

"Well, there is a Georgia in Russia," I said, in my defense, to the Englishman.

"Aye."

James Flahive didn't ask me if I wanted a drink, and I didn't ask him for one.

"It's a pity you didn't get here sooner," said the Englishman, buttoning up his denim jacket. "I was just telling James about the time I drank so much after a football match in Dublin I missed me flight home to London on Sunday morning."

"There are plenty of cheap flights," I said.

"Yes, but when I left for the match on Friday, I didn't tell me wife the game was in Ireland. I didn't tell her I would be gone for the weekend," he explained. "When I did finally get back home, she was gone. She'd left me."

"That's too bad," I said.

"I was unlucky," he rationalized.

I looked over at James Flahive. He had been looking at me.

"I was unlucky, wasn't I, James?" the Englishman repeated. "Yes, I was unlucky."

James Flahive looked at him and instead of answering, smiled a smile that looked as if it caused him some pain.

The Englishman told us another story about how he was once arrested for possession of marijuana. Since he'd had no other violations or citations on his record, he asked the officers if they might drive off, throw the bag of cannabis out the window and forget about the whole matter.

"The Bobbies told me they might be more inclined to consider such an idea if I was willing to tell them who the supplier was," he explained. "I thought about that for a minute. Then I agreed to tell them: 'Marijuana is a plant, you see. So as near as I can figure, God is the supplier.'"

"And?"

"And I was unlucky again."

He then took a drink of his beer.

"We've known each other a long time, my friend," James Flahive said to the Englishman.

"We have, James. We love each other don't we, James? Yes, we love each other."

Ireland's pubs are not open late. "Half-eleven" is usually closing time. It was past then but not midnight. James Flahive, the proprietor, made his point by rising from his stool. But he took his time doing it. The Englishman took note.

"May I buy the American a drink before we go, James? Now that he's entered such a rarefied establishment it'd be proper to welcome him to the club, wouldn't it, James? Would you pour something for your man at this late hour, James?"

Flahive, standing, looked straight at me from under his eyebrows.

"Uh, thank you. Yes," I said. "Any chance of a Crested Ten over ice, sir, if you wouldn't mind?"

The Englishman began poking through his handful of Euro coins. James Flahive began poking through his dusty whiskey bottles.

"Shiels is your name?" Flahive asked, but not in the tone of a question. He was reaching as high as he could to the top shelf from which he pulled down not a bottle of Crested Ten but rather the green bottle of standard Jamieson Irish Whiskey. I didn't object.

James Flahive's back was to me when I heard the sound of him scooping ice from a plastic bowl and putting it into a glass. I also heard the Englishman.

"Goodnight, James," he said. "I've left the quid for his whiskey on the counter. I'll be seeing you tomorrow night...if you open, James."

Without turning around, Flahive waved the Englishman off with one hand while pouring the Jamieson with the other. The Englishman patted me on the back and then kicked the chair of his sleeping friend, who awakened with a start. With some help he got up and they made for the door. The Englishman opened it just a crack, stuck his bald head out, and turned it both ways again to look for the Garda. Only when he saw no police did he make his way into the night, closing the door behind him.

19

AUTHOR AT SCOTLAND'S ST ANDREWS OLD COURSE

Golfers from around the world make pilgrimages to St. Andrews, Scotland, because it is recognized as the birthplace of golf. Recognizable, too, is the golf course, because the treeless, links-style layout hosts Open Championship (British Open) every five years on international television.

Its holes begin, and end, right in the corner of the medieval town, which is dominated by golf tourism and the university which educated, among others, Prince William, who will one day be king. Accomplished American golf course architect Arthur Hills allowed me to shadow him for a walk around the links on a grey summer day in 2005 along with some of his designers and his public relations man Quentin Lutz. I was observing Hills because I was, as a golf writer, in the process of collaborating on his autobiography: "The Works of Art," which included descriptions of his more than 200 golf course designs around the world.

I previously authored the autobiography of CBS Sports television golf commentator Ben Wright, the British voice of the Emmy Award-winning telecasts of The Masters and other televised PGA Tour events. That book, which received a lot of media attention and great reviews, was called "Good Bounces and Bad Lies."

A round of golf on the Old Course at St. Andrews, for anyone who plays it or even gets near it, includes souvenir selfies and photo-taking at the Swilcan Bridge. A stone's throw from the Old Course Hotel and Jigger Inn, the Swilcan Bridge is a little, ancient, stone stairway that bumps across the burn which intersects the first and 18th holes.

This would not be the only bridge which would come into play on our day.

The grey hair of Arthur Hills matched the sky color when stopped, with a professional photographer in tow, to pose for photos at the Swilcan Bridge. He was a golf design potentate who, at age 75, invested considerable financial resources ($85,000) and spent valuable time sharing his wisdom with his younger design team staffers. He was patient as the photographer, and I sought to chronicle and document his every step and utterance.

As Hills stood on the bridge, his sweater was blue but his mood was not. He knew, as everyone in golf and media does, that world famous, aging golfers making their last appearances in the Open Championship at St. Andrews, traditionally stop for photos symbolically waving "goodbye" from atop its tiny span.

"I guess this is my last 'hurrah,'" Hills said quietly.

He was very fit and in good health but allowed that he could not imagine a return to Scotland as his international travel from his Toledo, Ohio home was becoming very infrequent. His younger partner

Steve Forrest still relished the road, and Hills seemed content with that collaboration.

Upon hearing Hills, the small, gathered group let the moment sit in quiet. Hills peered across the links and out to the sea where a sliver of sky on the horizon had turned to a glowing orange as the sun sunk. We were in the gloaming and Hills was in his glory.

After a customary post-round pint at the Dunvegan Pub behind the Old Course's 18th green, Hills headed to bed back at our boutique inn just around the corner.

Lutz, the public relations man for Hills and the firm, joined me as we walked the town for some after dark nightlife.

Tennents is Scotland's favorite beer, but, drinking with the very tall Lutz, who had previously served in the Navy and then been a procurement executive in the auto industry, meant we moved on to single malt whiskys. We walked down into the seemingly subterranean Ma Bell's bar, which was lively still as midnight neared.

In the British Isles a gathering of women is sometimes called a "Hen Party," which is exactly what Lutz and I stumbled into. A gathering of "birds," as the British might also say. In addition to being much taller and fitter, Lutz was, by traditional standards, the more handsome of the two of us. He was married, though, so he did not mind playfully birddogging for me with women, especially because he knew while he had me on looks, I was far, far funnier than him. So, Lutz and I ham-and-egged it for amusement while in the pubs.

By sheer proximity in the crowded, lively bar, we began talking to a group of four middle-aged Scottish women who were dressed up for a night on the town. I don't recall if there was any occasion beyond that, but a woman named Lynne with a strong Fife accent seemed to be the group's "Horatio" and chief spokesperson.

We quipped along in the smallest of talk, which I imagine the ladies tolerated if not engaged in because of our American accents. The women had surely, though, endured their share of American golf groups bussing into town to plunder the area's many high-profile golf courses, including, now, the two courses up at the Fairmont Hotel and the newest – Dumbarnie Links. Scotties can spot the tourist Yanks a mile away by their logoed golf apparel.

Perhaps that's why Lutz decided to set us apart some by enticing the ladies with a little hyperbole.

"This guy here," he told them while throwing his arm around my neck, "is a famous American author."

The women reacted very positively and enthusiastically to what was, in truth, a highly exaggerated claim. A couple of niche golf books did not deserve such a description. Maybe more than anything, the women were relieved they might have something to talk about with these two golfers as opposed to listening to Lutz and I recount the shots we hit and scores we made that day on the course. Their ears perked up because perhaps there was possibly something novel about me, pardon the pun.

"A famous American author?" Lynne asked.

I visibly shrugged and demurred.

"Now, now, don't be shy," Lutz insisted, patting my shoulder. "You know you're an acclaimed, bestselling author."

Now the ladies were all atwitter.

"Really?"

Again, I winced.

"Really," Lutz answered them. "He's being modest."

I took a sip of my whisky.

"Would I have read your book? Is it in the shoppe?" one of the women asked.

"Maybe. I don't know," I answered.

Then Lynne, who was pretty in pink, took over the questioning in a direct fashion. "Aw come on now. What is your book about?"

I looked into her deep eyes and answered, "Oh, I doubt you would have heard about it over here in Scotland," I replied.

"Tell us. Maybe we have read it," she insisted as the others listened. I saw Lutz taking a swig of scotch and awaiting my answer, also.

"Eh, well, it is a book about these people who find some photos in a trunk after their mother dies," I said.

"Go on," Lynne said.

"She's Italian, but she lived in middle America."

"And?"

"They are surprised, when the look at the pictures, to learn their mother had befriended a man."

Lynne was listening.

"She met the man when he traveled through their remote, rural town," I continued.

Now Lynne was nodding, and the other women were wide-eyed, so I kept going.

"The man was a photographer, and they had a brief, secret romance..."

"'THE BRIDGES OF MADISON COUNTY!'" Lynne screamed out as her friends cooed and giggled. "You are the author of the 'Bridges of Madison County?'"

"Oh my god," another of the women shrieked.

I saw Lutz almost spit out his scotch.

"Of course we have heard of it," Lynne said. "Wow! 'Bridges of Madison County' is your book. You are the author?"

"Well...maybe," I said quietly with another modest, vague shrug. And another sip.

It would have broken the ladies' hearts to dampen their ardor and tell them I was pulling their collective legs. So, Lutz and I let the con play out and let them have a story to tell when they went home that night.

I don't know if author Robert James Waller ever made it to St. Andrews, Scotland, for a book-signing of his "The Bridges of Madison County" before he died in 2017. But if he did, he, and those lassies, were in for a big surprise.

20

PRINCE ALI - MY AMSTERDAM AIRPORT FRIEND

 It was a less than pleasant morning which became a memorable one thanks to some royal hospitality by a fabulous fellow.

We had flown on a cramped overnighter from Detroit to Amsterdam's Schiphol Airport. From there, after a three-hour layover, we would connect to Nice, in the south of France, on the way to Monaco.

Amsterdam's Schiphol Airport is a big, bright delight of a major hub with plenty of shops and souvenir kiosks, spots to have a croissant plus a casino. There is even a "faux forest" on the second level with artificial trees and the piped in sounds of birds with couch-like reclining chairs for those who need a "natural" respite.

None of this was enough to satisfy my overtired female traveling companion, who became especially frustrated when we were turned away from the airline executive lounge. Her irritation turned into a spat. (I would hesitate to characterize it as a "lovers quarrel" since she would not long after gain the title of "ex-wife.")

Some space was needed, so I sleepwalked over to the Grand Café Het Paleis, which had just opened at 7 a.m., and slid, alone, onto a barstool.

The Grand Café Het Paleis was a majestic, traditional Dutch cafe with a high ceiling, gleaming glass, polished brass rails and marble features. An unexpected retreat for a bar in the middle of an airport concourse,

I was both feeling down and nerved up, so I ordered up a glass of Heineken Extra Cold from the frozen tap as a breakfast beer. It hit the spot as it hit the back of my throat.

When the amiable Egyptian bartender saw how fast I drank down the suds, the sweet man drew another one and served it up...along with some enjoyable banter.

I came to learn he lived in Los Angeles for a spell, was born on the fourth of July, and went by the name "Prince Ali."

Just like that, all became better with the world. By the time I rejoined my companion for the flight, I had a new, carefree attitude and a new friend in Prince Ali.

I always try to visit Ali for a beer when I connect through Amsterdam's airport, which is often because I am dedicated to flying Delta Airlines and its' codeshare partners. Sometimes the connection in the giant airport does not route me through the Grand Café's terminal.

If I had a Heineken at het Paleis and Ali wasn't there, I always left a note or my card for him. It was even more disappointing when the flight connection time made it impossible to stop at all.

I was a little short on time on one occasion for a connection to Paris. Hustling with my little son Harrison, we hurried to get through the airport's additional passport check, the line for which stretched past Grand Café.

Stuck in the line, I could just see through the opening to Grand Café, and spotted Ali behind the bar in the center. Somehow, he looked up, and we waved enthusiastically to each other, which my little boy noticed.

"Dad...you have airport friends?" he commented. "That's weird."

Maybe a prince in his imagination, but Ali, an ambassador for Amsterdam and Schiphol Airport, is undoubtedly a prince of a man. He is always smiling from his stage – the circular bar in the middle of Grand Café Het Paleis. The windowed watering hole is its own brand of oasis in the middle of the vast collection of corridors and boarding gates teeming with travelers from around the world gliding on moving sidewalks from flight to flight.

My most recent visit to Ali was in November of 2022.

"You call him a prince?" Julie, a young bartender at Grand Café het Paleis, asked me as she drew a draft Heineken for me. Julie was behind the bar in the Grand Café on an early afternoon when I passed through Schiphol Airport on my way from Los Angeles to Vienna. Ali was due for duty in only a few minutes.

"Isn't he an Egyptian prince?" I responded.

"If he says so. He's such a sweet man."

We laughed and Julie assured me Ali would be in shortly and in time for me to visit with him and still make my connecting flight.

"Ali mentioned to me he was expecting someone today," Julie said. "He said the person was a writer and was a nice person."

"I messaged him my flight itinerary so perhaps he meant me. But 'nice?' Maybe there is another writer coming...?"

Julie laughed and assured me it was me Ali had been speaking of me.

"Maybe he meant it as a warning to you!" I joked.

"No, no. Ali sometimes arranges his work schedule so he can come in and greet people he's come to know," she explained. "For nice people, anyway."

Then, as if on cue, we heard a voice call from the top of the café's ornate spiral staircase. Ali...had arrived.

Ali had come in half-an-hour early, before his shift, to visit with me. I was honored he would do that and delighted when he, for the first time, sat beside me at the bar instead of standing and serving on the other side. From his stool Ali drank Turkish coffee while we chatted.

I learned Ali worked at the Grand Café for more than 18 years and lives in Hillegom, about 30 minutes from the airport, between Amsterdam and The Haig. I cannot be certain of my geography in that matter because for all the times I have landed at Schiphol, I have never once left the airport. (There is a Café het Paleis canal-side in the city.)

Ali was excited to tell me his daughter is getting married, and he was nice enough to show me some smart-phone photos of his recent family trip back to Egypt. He studied sociology and, based on the many people who visit and embrace him at het Paleis, has put his sincere knowledge to good use as a cheer-spreading bartender.

When Ali saw me sneak a peek at my watch, he asked me for my flight time and gate. I was relieved to learn we had more time to talk before his shift started and my travels resumed.

"One evening we were about to close when there was a flight delay. 700 German football fans came streaming back into the bar," he recalled. "They took losing badly."

Speaking of soccer, Ali brought me a gift. He presented me with a FIFA World Cup blanket in the Holland team's colors and a pair of festive orange sunglasses.

I then learned Grand Café het Paleis, in soccer parlance, was in "extra time."

Ali told me the bars days were numbered. The airport had a new plan for the place. Something else would take the space.

With a fair amount of ceremony recognizing its loyal staff, the gorgeous palace closed in January and, by May of 2023, was gutted.

I do not know where Prince Ali reigns now, but he will always be a royal friend.

21

MEETING JENNIFER HUDSON

It may surprise people to know they can be in a cozy, small setting with superstar Jennifer Hudson...without even paying for a ticket. You can be among the audience at Warner Brothers Studios, in Burbank, for a television taping of her vibrant "Jennifer Hudson (JHud) Show" ...just by asking!

I did it – and it's a trip – if you don't mind a trip to Los Angeles.

JenniferHudsonShow.com will even allow you to request the date which works best for you. Once confirmed, you'll receive a prompt email with the date and time of the show, what time to arrive, where to go, and even where you park (which is complimentary – a rarity in the Los Angeles area!)

You can ask for several tickets and there is no fee at all to attend. I'll share more on my experience and what to expect in this article.

Hudson, a Chicagoan with a trumpet of a voice, famously sang her way onto the television talent show American Idol. In hindsight, it was a blessing Hudson didn't win because with faith in a divine plan...and her otherworldly talent...she went on to win Oscar, Emmy, Grammy, Tony and Golden Globe Awards. In its first year her television show has been nominated for a People's Choice Award.

Celebrity lives are well-documented. With faith and grace Jennifer Hudson has achieved success, endured tragedy, and encountered heartbreak, so when she sings, she sings from her soul. And when she smiles, it's a glimpse of God's glory. I've been bestowed the gift of that grin three times in brief moments with Hudson, the most recent of which was in the studio audience during the taping of her show.

Our first meeting, in January of 2011, was a happy accident at the inaugural sailing of one of the "Happiest Place on Earth's" cruise ships. Hudson, then 29, had christened the new Disney Dream as the luxury liner's "Godmother" during an elaborate presentation from a stage beside the ship in Port Canaveral, Florida with Disney CEO Bob Iger.

It's doubtful Iger even knew Hudson existed in 2003 when she began her professional career with a gig as a performer aboard the Disney Wonder, before American Idol. She recalled singing standards such as Lion King's Circle of Life in a shipboard show called Disney Dreams.

The Disney Dream grand opening and launch that day included the debut of the "AquaDuck," a 750-foot, sea-through waterslide that extended over the side of the ship 11-stories over the sea. My pre-teen son Harrison and I, as soon as the stage presentation was over, hustled onto the ship, in bathing suits we'd worn under our clothes, in anticipation of riding the slide before the rest of the onboarding passengers lined up for it.

Before even checking into our cabin, Harrison and I reached the sunny top deck before anyone even thought to go up there...except for two people we nearly stumbled across: an impeccably dressed, glamorous couple lingering in the shade of an awning against a high-top table.

It was unmistakably Jennifer Hudson and her beau.

So it was that in a blue swim shirt and sea-horse-patterned trunks I met the mighty Jennifer Hudson. We were the only four people on the entire deck, so it would have been awkward to not acknowledge and greet each other. Our meeting was natural. What was not anticipated was how friendly and gracious Hudson was, chatting warmly and standing for a photo. (Something that must be such a drag for celebs.)

"It's so wonderful when amazing things happen to very nice people," I told her, and acknowledged she was from Chicago.

Hudson seemed genuinely flattered to hear this from a fellow Midwesterner – albeit a stranger on the deck of a cruise liner.

Ships we were, then, that passed in the day.

Six years later, in 2017, I attended the grand opening of the Marriott Marquis, which, attached to the McCormick Place Convention Center, became the largest hotel in Hudson's hometown of Chicago. After interviewing Marriott CEO Arne Sorenson in a skyline lounge high atop the hotel, I was taken to a concert down in the ballroom below at which I stood in front of the stage and marveled at the energy and talent of Jennifer Hudson.

I recall the dazzling diamond tennis bracelet, black dress, and astonishing voice of the co-star of the television show "The Voice" as she opened with a song titled It's Your World. (I use that fast-moving ditty now for my daily I-phone wake up song.)

Fate found me backstage after the show for a meet-and-greet photo-opportunity with the superstar. The warmth of the woman once again inspired affection, and so, during our moment together, I asked the elegant Hudson a question.

"Is there something, for you, I can pray for tonight?"

"Oh, wow," she responded, placing her hand on her chest. "That's so kind of you. "Yes. Pray for David. Yes, David. Please pray for him. David."

I didn't ask for any details or context. I just swept away smiling and did exactly as I'd promised to do.

Both Hudson's romantic partner and their young son were named David, and subsequent news accounts would later report a domestic issue at their home the day before the concert.

I was in Michigan, October 2022, visiting my mother. I sat on her couch watching, on television, Jennifer Hudson sitting on a couch, hosting her new talk show. Knowing I'd be in Los Angeles two weeks later, I Googled the show's website and, through their handy online system, requested three tickets to experience a taping in the studio audience. Within two days I was notified, via email, the tickets were mine if I wanted them.

The process was simple, and anyone can request seats. The show's producers kept in touch via email with clear instructions and even allowed for guest name changes up to 24 hours before the show. Guests are asked to dress in colorful, "nice casual" apparel, avoiding black or white outfits. You'll want closed-toed shoes, no denim, t-shirts, or shorts (it can be chilly in the television studio, anyway.)

When you go to Warner Brothers Studio in Burbank for the taping, you'll arrive about 90-miuntes before the show starts so you can show your ID, present your Covid card showing you are fully vaccinated; and be tested for the virus. The testing tent is very convenient right next to the free parking garage in which show guests will wait, with seating and vending machines, before being walked over to the comfortable studio waiting room and eventually into the studio's theater-style seats.

Jennifer Hudson's television set is like the Oz Dorothy stepped into with Toto. It is brilliant and vibrant and as bright as the sun, with ethereal, moving images on big flat screens; plush carpet; a luxurious couch; and a grand piano under a chandelier. There are some personal photos of JHud and her family, and of course a grid of bright television lights hanging above illuminating all of it (including the audience members, who often appear on camera.)

Pop music is pumping through the house to liven up the audience. I noted Rihanna and Tupac, for instance, as the audience waited, of course, to hear Hudson's "Happy Place," the song used to open the show and bring out the star. But some audience members first get to co-star. The audience director called a few female audience members down to dance to a song on a wide aisle between the audience and the main stage.

After he sent the women back to their seats, over the dance music, I heard the audience director shout words I feared: "Okay, men, it's your turn!"

As one of only three or so men in the entire audience, I knew I was doomed to embarrassment.

"You, in the red blazer," the stage director demanded of me on his wireless mic. "C'mon down here. We need you."

Given the setting and the atmosphere of the room, I had no choice but to submit and embrace the situation. Within seconds I was "dancing," if you want to call it that, on a veritable stage in front of the eyes of 50 women. (I'm not certain if the cameras were taping for b-roll, but they were aimed in our direction.)

It didn't take long for the audience director to step in and attempt to rescue me. He ran up to the stage and shouted, "Red blazer guy...do what he does!" He pointed at the grooving gentleman next to me who had the natural rhythm, timing and technique to dance with style.

With nothing to do but to embrace my role as the dance floor jester, I shrugged my shoulders and copied his action as closely as I could. (I swear the man then ramped up the degree of difficulty!)

When the song came to a merciful end, as I went back to my seat, I apologized to the women in their seats along the way. "No, no," one of the women insisted, "it was cute."

"Oh God. That's what I was afraid of," I laughed, lowering my head.

The audience director then took center stage and continued warming up the crowd.

"Would you all like to take home some fabulous prizes today?" he yelled.

"Yeah!" the audience screamed and cheered.

"Well, we don't have any! But you will have a good time," he retorted. "And if we should have to evacuate the studio in any sort of emergency, please grab some of this furniture and take it with you! No sense leaving any of these Ikea treasures behind!"

He did, however, toss out occasional logoed t-shirts during commercial breaks.

"We care about you, unlike some of the other studio audience shows," the director insisted. "But I won't say which ones..." (then he mumbled "Dr. Phil" joking under his breath.)

The producer then thoughtfully let us know which day (November 21), the show being taped would air on television.

Jennifer Hudson hit the stage with elegant enthusiasm. Her opening monologue was a dialogue delivered from her perch on the couch about the upcoming Thanksgiving holiday and included some audience participation. She shared the results of the opinion poll questions producers sent to the audience members via email in the days leading up to the show. (One of the questions was: what's the dumbest bet you've ever made?)

Hudson was warm with the audience members and effusively attentive with her interview guests, which included free-spirited actor David Arquette. Hudson, on the talk show, uses her vocal range for more than singing. When amused, she occasionally bursts forward with a seemingly uncontrollable, punctuating chortle from the same diaphragm that gave us her award-winning performance of, And I am Telling You I'm Not Going, in the film Dreamgirls.

During the television taping she performed some physical comedy in the way of a cooking/tasting segment of strange combinations of foods. Plus, a trivia contest between two contestants who subsequently dug their hands into a big dish of mashed potatoes to search for prizes! (They both ended up winning flat-screen televisions slid out onto the floor right in front of them.)

Between segments, during the commercial breaks, music blared throughout the studio set while makeup touch-up professionals and producers with clip boards huddled with Hudson and collaborated at her couch. Cue cards were readied and, while it all happened simultaneously like a pit crew fueling the tank and changing the tires at a high-speed car race, I noticed a very focused JHud still swaying and bumping to the music.

One of the breaks in the middle of the show was different, though.

A floor director/producer helped Hudson up on her heeled boots, across the little carpet and down off the raised stage in the middle of the set. They led her carefully across the impossibly shiny floor and up the theater steps into a row of the audience seats and directly to me!

"You're Michael, right?" Hudson, or maybe it was the producer, asked.

I must confess it all happened fast and yet seemed to occur in slow motion.

But before I could process it I quickly, very quickly, leapt to my feet and, with a startled voice, confirmed it was me.

"I just wanted to thank you for coming to see the show," Jennifer Hudson told me.

Once again, the aura of her affection-inspiring goodness got me: I gave her a great, big hug. I was very careful, though, not to smudge her makeup (I'm not a total showbiz rookie!) Like noticing the diamond tennis bracelet in Chicago, this time it was Hudson's perfume that struck me. Everyone else surrounding us blurred into the distance.

When the embrace broke, I looked her in the eye, gestured to the surroundings, and said, "Is there no medium you can't conquer? Congratulations on the People's Choice Award Nomination!"

"Oh my gosh, pray for me," she responded, I sensed, for all of it – not just the potential award.

"You know," I told her, "You're the 'Queen of Peace."

I don't know why I said that, or what it necessarily means, but it came to me like an inspiration, and so, totally unfiltered, I shared it with her. It seemed true to me. Hudson, just like the last two meetings, seemed genuinely flattered.

"The last time I met you was in Chicago," I reminded Hudson, who'd mentioned pizza at Thanksgiving in one of the show's segments. "Don't you think we need a Lou Malnatti's Chicago Pizza Restaurant here in L.A.?"

I don't know how often she eats that deep dish treat – which, like Hudson herself, is a beloved Windy City experience and authentically represents Chicago.

"We do. That's a good idea. We sure do," she agreed, and then asked, "Can we get our photo together?"

She gestured toward the professional photographer who'd followed her up the aisle and, as I suddenly became aware of and sensitive to the constraints of her time, turned quickly to pose with her. I knew the very thoughtful producers who'd surprised me by facilitating the brief meeting, Maddie Kirshenblatt, Joslyn Martinez, and Emma Ostergard, none of whom I'd ever met in person, would get the photo to me.

Even though I was blessed to meet Jennifer Hudson in person, I think everyone who watches her show, and especially those who come to the studio audience to see a taping, come away feeling they've met her and been hugged by Hudson. (The producer said after some tapings she greets the entire audience in a line. "That's just how Jennifer is," he admitted.)

Try the show on television or come dance in Jennifer Hudson's Warner Brothers Studio – it's her happy place!

22

PROPOSING TO JENNIFER HUDSON ON NATIONAL TV

 Jennifer Hudson is a Chicago-born, gospel-singing church girl who finished seventh on "American Idol". But she went on to become a worldwide star, winning Emmy, Grammy, Oscar, and Tony Awards. Her first season of hosting a nationwide television chat show, she won the NAACP Image Award for Outstanding Talk Show Host.

Plus, her Hollywood-based, syndicated show was recently renewed for a second season. So, Hudson is on her way to succeeding and surpassing another TV-talking Chicagoan named...Oprah.

Hudson has talked about a dream to sing the National Anthem before. Specifically in one of the south sider's hometown Chicago White Sox baseball games – hopefully in the World Series.

And it was a Jennifer Hudson "double-header" for the studio audience members who'd secured complimentary tickets to attend her talk-show taping at Warner Brothers Studios in Burbank, California.

Simply by choosing and confirming a date on the "Jennifer Hudson Show" website, they were ushered into the lively, interactive experience of watching the award-winning singing star interview celebrities and positive people in the plush TV studio she designed and dubbed the "Happy Place."

Attendees on most days get to view and participate in two consecutive tapings. These are presented with professionalism and enthusiasm by the show's energetic, efficient director, stage managers and production team.

Gary Cannon is an affable stand-up comic. He serves as the studio emcee and warms up the audience with instructions and plenty of jokes. After the first show, he explained what was next.

"We are going to feed you lunch in between shows," Cannon explained to the audience. "Maybe you have heard of Mastro's Steakhouse in Beverly Hills...?"

The audience murmured in anticipation.

"...Well, the lunch will not be from there," he deadpanned.

"Could y'all bring a sandwich for little 'ole me?" Jennifer Hudson herself chimed in from the stage. Even when she's speaking, it sounds like sweet singing. Hers is not false humility. Hudson closes her shows by thanking the viewers for tuning in to "see about 'lil 'ole me'." It's even written that way on her teleprompter.

Off the air, she also voiced appreciation to the audience for staying for a second performance. This meant 180 people were at the studio from 1 pm until after 6 pm.

Hudson does not take the attendees for granted. Neither do the "Jennifer Hudson Show" audience staff members, who are very proficient and respectful. During the boxed-lunch break TV monitors show previous episodes. Plus, there is a small gift shop with very reasonably priced souvenirs. Although some get a t-shirt tossed to them by Cannon during the commercials. Or win, for instance, flat screen TVs in on-stage contests.

I brought "Lil' 'Ole" Jennifer Hudson more than a sandwich when I recently attended another taping of her show.

Being a native Midwesterner myself, I felt "Mama Hud" might treasure a true "Taste of Chicago" from her Windy City hometown. Lou Malnati's, Chicago's traditional-yet-innovative deep-dish-style Chicago pizza maker, shipped a few frozen pizzas in a cooler of dry ice via TasteOfChicago.com.

Also in the gift box was Garrett's Popcorn in a White Sox-logoed tin canister, with White Sox-decorated cookies. This is another Chicago tradition I thought she'd enjoy knowing she'd love to sing the anthem at a game.

The confirmation email the Jennifer Hudson Show sends when one requests tickets advises that attendees may bring gifts for Hudson. This is somewhat of a rarity for audience shows. Hudson's team members happily accept the gifts before the show. They then chronicle the names and contact information of those who present them.

The quintessential "taste of home" would prove more meaningful than I had imagined during an eventual conversation I had with Hudson after the shows.

Part of the unique fun of attending a "JHud" taping is the dance floor. This sits in-between Hudson's "Happy Place" cushy couch and grand piano on her stage.

During the pre-show warm-up, Cannon coaxes attendees down onto the dance floor to shake and groove to the music pumping through the studio. Meanwhile, the audience members clap, cheer and in my case, laugh.

Another hurried, enthusiastic producer came to my chair and beckoned me to the dance floor. She led me in front of one of the production team's cameras, which was now pointed at me. Then demanded, "Now dance!" It was not an invitation – it was a command.

I loved the producer's pointed demeanor and did exactly as I was told...with zero rhythm but lots of shameless energy. Little did I know while stepping lively I was auditioning. Jennifer Hudson herself was watching from backstage via that camera shot.

I would later learn she was selecting four audience members who'd "understood the assignment" and showed up for her television show taping blinged-out in their best fashion. One of the finalists, for instance, was a fellow from Detroit in an all-pink pants, shirt, and hat presentation. One woman rocked stop-sign red, knee-length boots, while another woman was draped in an orange business suit.

I don't know what possessed me that morning, but I had donned a white suit, over a lime green shirt and a white tie. Plus, red shoes and a red and green-striped Gucci scarf draped around my neck. I finished with transitions glasses the bright production lights of the studio caused to automatically darken. In the pre-show, Cannon joked at me for the fashion faux pas of wearing white before Memorial Day.

I was seated near the back of the studio audience theater seats as the show's "Happy Place" opening theme song started playing. The camera operators had taken their positions, but a producer snuck up the aisle and crouched next to me. She rapidly told me, "You've been chosen to be in our fashion segment."

"Wow, okay," I replied.

"Be ready to walk back and forth like the stage is a fashion show runway and pose. Lots of energy."

"Got it," I said, nodding.

"Jennifer is excited," she assured me.

As I smiled at the notion and nodded that I understood, the producer, about to leave, turned back with a deadly serious expression on her face. They looked me square in the eye and spoke declaratively:

"Don't let me down!"

Her urgency directed me and encouraged me at the same time. I thought to myself, "Damn, this woman is a superb producer!" She was like a Super Bowl coach sending me into the game.

As the theme music played and Jennifer Hudson took the stage, I had the anticipation adrenaline of the unknown. But the known began to hit me. I was one of about five men in a studio audience full of truly fashionable women.

They were cheering and singing and dancing and clapping as Gary Cannon and "JHud" delighted them along with the prospect of her TV star celebrity guests. Today the guests were "Breaking Bad's" Giancarlo Esposito and "Talking Dead's" Chris Hardwick. Ironically, Hardwick also hosted "Talking Saul," the post-show for "Better Call Saul," which Esposito also co-starred in.

In that environment, I was about to be pulled from the audience frying pan into the chandeliered fire for my little runway fashion strut.

What would I say? How would I have the nerve to strut on the stage?

In terms of technique, I once found myself standing with former President George W. Bush at a golf course. He'd delivered, in an acceptance speech, the famous line: "I've been accused of having 'swagger'... which in Texas is called: 'walking.'"

I recall daring to ask the President if he could teach me that swagger.

"No," he flatly answered.

Maybe I looked startled by his directness, so Bush continued by explaining his verdict. "First of all, you are not from Texas. Secondly, you're obviously already a grown man."

On Jennifer Hudson's runway, I'd have to go it alone and channel some type of moves. As the show opened, I conjured some moves which would be a twisted combination of a high school football grapevine agility drill and Irish dance.

It's all I had - I'd have to go with it.

I sat, literally, on the edge of my seat waiting, in nervous anticipation, for the "Understood the Assignment" fashion portion of the show. Thankfully for my nerves, it came in the show's opening segment.

One of the other selected "fashionistas," a woman, was called down first. This gave me a chance to observe how the bit rolled out.

But then there was no turning back.

Hudson, dressed in royal purple under a black leather jacket, stood in front of the audience on the dance floor stage. She said into her wireless microphone: "Let's see who else caught my eye." She then called my name out like a contestant on "The Price is Right."

Adrenaline – and the admonition of the producer – propelled me to perform over my skis. I thought back to the enthusiastic manner displayed when actor/director Roberto Benigni jubilantly leaped from his seat to walk flamboyantly atop the chairs down to the stage to accept two Academy Awards for his film "La Vita e Bella."

Since life, in Jennifer Hudson's studio, was indeed beautiful, I channel Benigni's explosion of excitement. I gave Jennifer Hudson and her producer nothing less.

With my hands in the air, I ran down the aisle shouting for joy.

"Oh, I see you, baby," Hudson called out. "Yes, I do. Yes, I see you. C'mon!"

She laughed and the audience "awwwd" when I put my arms around her in a giant hug and said, "Mama!" (In reference to Hudson calling herself "Mama Hud.")

Hudson then squealed with surprise and delight. Her knees buckled when I dropped to one knee to kiss her hand.

"I love you!" she called out as the audience cheered. "Bless your heart! You're so sweet!"

I thanked her and she continued.

"First of all, thank you for coming to see about me," Hudson said as we stood face-to-face.

"Thank you for letting me in the door in this outfit." I replied, gesturing to the white suit with my hand.

"Tell me, where are you from?"

"I'm from Michigan," I answered. "Near Chicago."

"Come on, Michael Patrick. Tell me what inspired your look?"

"You inspired me…"

"Listen to this," she played along, chirping the audience as I continued.

…"Because when one is in the company of royalty you have to jazz it up!"

The audience applauded and Hudson said, "Thank you. I done found me a man of quality!"

"That's right, I retorted. Will you marry me?"

"Where's my ring?" Hudson demanded over the now boisterous audience. To which I turned and pleaded: "Somebody lend me a ring!"

"Go make me happy now," Hudson said. "Walk the runway for me."

The thumping studio music pumped on and I enacted my preposterous runway walk with my arms sweeping as the lights flashed and Hudson encouraged me. "Yeah! You gonna give them a twirl? That's right! Now come on! Work it!"

Once again Hudson's cheerleader-style speaking sounded like singing.

Riding the tide, I made a dramatic move of ripping my glasses off and sliding my hands down my body as I passed Hudson on my way back to the other side of the stage.

"Thank you," she said between her apparently amused, high-pitched laughing. "Thank you! Give him a hand, y'all!"

That's when I took off my Gucci scarf and swung it above my head.

"Yes!" she called out. "There you go! There you go! There you go!"

As I reached my seat, Hudson, from the stage, called out to me, then looked into the camera: "You've got to give me some life, sir! He did that! See that's a man of quality right there. He knows what he's talking about. You can come to my happy place any time you are ready!"

The camera cut to me back in my seat nodding and smiling.

After the bright lights, music, mayhem, and performance art that is the Jennifer Hudson Show subsided, the producers kindly invited me to stick around for a photo with Jennifer at the now more darkened, quiet, living room-style stage.

"All this is not easy," I said, knowing that the commitment to a daily talk show, for someone like her used to picking and choosing gig-style concerts, movies, and appearances, is an adjustment. "You must be working endlessly."

"I am either here or at home," she agreed.

I knew Hudson was being modest because a multi-platform star like her, and a parent, has countless other demands, big and small, on her time, career efforts, and responsibilities.

"I've been hosting a radio talk show for 17 years. What you've done in 100 shows is remarkable," I expressed to Hudson. "What you've done here in 100 shows is remarkable."

"Am I doing alright?" Hudson asked. Were she not so genuine I would have presumed her question was polite, false modesty and rhetorical. But beyond the second-season renewal, Image Award and multiple other award nominations, I sensed that Hudson, as a performer, would want to master her new craft.

And with an army of professional producers and crew working on her show, I imagine, as a rookie host, she felt some responsibility to them. Every member of her team I met, including Gary Cannon, seemed supremely happy in their work and motivated.

"Am I doing alright?" leaned back into Hudson's "lil' ol her" image. I would never be so presumptuous as to offer advice to a wildly successful performer and businesswoman such as Hudson, but she made me feel comfortable in answering her honestly.

It was not as if I were offering dancing or singing advice, thank God. But as a talk show host, I was, in a small sense, a colleague of hers, and though I'd only met her briefly a few times, I sincerely cared about her success in this venture.

"I like how you are not afraid to ask the short question," I said.

She seemed intrigued by this level of "talk technique."

"Some interviewers ask long questions to show off what they know and how much research they did," I explained. "This leaves the guest very little to reveal in response. Larry King was very good with the short question. And I notice you are, too."

Hudson nodded.

I didn't want to take too much time, so I then congratulated her on her show being renewed for a second season and smiled saying: "Oprah who!?"

She demurred a little at that notion. But I do believe that Hudson's personal story of success, faith and endurance gives her a depth far beyond the showing of celebrity baby pictures and audience game show bits necessary on a "happy place" show like hers.

Hudson's first season began with a face-to-face reckoning for Simon Cowell, the "American Idol" judge who'd doubted her chops at the start of her career. The season concluded with an interview with U.S. Vice-President Kamala Harris. See what I mean by Hudson coming a long way in 100 shows. She opened by acknowledging her past...and then rocketed to her own new heights. I am eager to see where her arc goes next.

Hudson's is a soul that can, with a daily talk show, have a now even bigger impact on her viewers and the world. Jennifer Hudson is on her way to being the Oprah of her time...with the talent, sincerity, and genuine joy to create an even more expansive ripple.

Though tragedy and personal issues managed to find her, the Goddess of Disney Cruise Lines and woman who played The Queen of Soul remains a respected showbusiness untouchable. I hope she knows that's what I meant when, before we parted, I told her:

"The world needs more 'good guys' to finish first. You are an example of that and an inspiration to others."

As we parted I thought I'd ask "Mama Hud" for some advice in return. I told her I'd just moved from Michigan to California and was living in Beverly Hills.

"You're a Midwesterner like me," I reminded her. "Any advice on how to acclimate to life in 'La La Land?'"

That's when I experienced "Mama Hud's" mothering instinct. Hudson took my question very seriously. She looked me in the eye and told me, "I still haven't acclimated to life here!"

"It's important to remember who you are and bring elements of that with you."

In case you think Gospel-singing Jennifer Hudson has "gone Hollywood," guess again.

She's just conquered Hollywood!

23

INCIDENT AT THE HOLLYWOOD WALK OF FAME

I froze in my tracks in the golden California morning sunshine to stare at the driver behind the wheel of a big SUV. She was, admittedly, nice to look at – a glamorous blonde in bright pink – but I was more interested in whether she saw me. Not to make a good impression...but to keep from becoming an impression...on the sidewalk! I was strolling near the intersection of Hollywood and Vine – in fact, along the embedded stars of the Hollywood Walk of Fame, while the woman was attempting to pull out of a driveway.

I have always laughed about being "invisible to women," but wearing a purple blazer and waving though her windshield, I managed to catch her eye. It provoked a smile and a shrug from both of us. Then I went on my merry way, it would turn out, to the same place she was: a Hollywood Walk of Fame press conference on the rooftop of the Aster.

With the 100-year-old Hollywood sign in the background, the fourth-story Aster rooftop event space is in the shadow of another iconic Hollywood landmark: the 13-story, cylindrical Capitol Records Tower, which looks like a giant stack of albums or vinyl 45's.

It was on that rooftop deck, an event space with a bar, umbrellas, tables and couches, I was formally introduced to Ellen Kost, known by her on-air moniker "Ellen K" to legions of Los Angeles radio listeners – instead of encountering her from under her SUV.

"I did not see you. Did I look as lost as I was?" she laughed. "I was one driveway away from here and talking to the location about where to park and using my GPS. I looked up and there you were in your purple blazer. You were probably pissed off."

"One move of your stiletto and I would have looked like a giant, squashed grape!" I joked. Then I assured Ellen K I was not upset. Conversely, I was happy to meet her.

"We bonded over that borderline catastrophic event," she posed.

While I would have been flattened on the Walk of Fame, radio and voice over-talent Ellen K is enshrined, in 2012, with a star on the Hollywood Walk of Fame. I asked her how that feels?

"It feels like it is not real. My star is right across from the Pantages Theater on Hollywood Boulevard. I have a couple of friends who will mess with me. They will go by and bring Windex and clean the star. Family members will drop by it and send me photos of it. It just feels...not real," Ellen insisted.

Ellen K's very real radio career has included co-hosting national shows Rick Dees and Ryan Seacrest in addition to working with Wayne Brady. She is the Hollywood Insider; the voice of the Grammy Awards and friends with many of the stars on the Walk of Fame.

"I cannot believe how long I have been in radio. The lesson, I think, is, 'put it out in the universe and say it. Raise your hand.' So, I did,'" said Ellen, who has five siblings. "Radio has the excitement of being able to connect with people live. You can take a call from a listener who is crying about something and share the experience."

As we connected before the press conference started, I asked Ellen, who attended Purdue University in Indiana, what her first, memorable, "I've arrived in Hollywood moment" was?

"My most Hollywood moment happened at a valet stand where I was waiting to get my car," she recalled. "A car pulled up unlike any car I had ever seen. It was some kind of weird color with tinted windows, so I could not see who was in it. The gentleman got out but, gesturing to me, told the valet, 'Help her first.'"

Ellen explained it was her most "I've arrived in Hollywood moment" because she recognized the man who emerged from the custom car.

"It was Brad Pitt. Brad Pitt let me go ahead of him at the valet. He was in a hurry, but he let someone else go first before they took his car."

I could not help but connect the dots: "So your Hollywood career began with Brad Pitt yielding to you with his car...and brought you now to you yielding to Michael Patrick Shiels with your SUV!"

"You really brought that full circle," Ellen remarked while laughing.

Ellen K also serves as chair of the Hollywood Walk of Fame Selection Panel, and, in that role emceed the press conference I attended to announce the new class of star honorees. She hovered near the podium under an umbrella in front of a tent full of camera crews from media outlets such as "Access Hollywood", Los Angeles local affiliate TV stations...and me.

While we waited, I chatted up an amiable, stately man who was conservatively dressed, by comparison, in a professional suit and tie.

Meanwhile, Ellen K wore pink, I wore purple, and there was a digital reporter named Heather Wilson, wearing leopard-print body suit, who goes by the Instagram name "MyChocolateChipChick."

While the gentleman and I sought shade under the small tent, he asked me about my media outlets, and I explained that I was a travel writer and syndicated talk radio host. The gentleman seemed interested in the type of radio program I hosted, especially when I explained that my interviewees were often elected officials and business leaders. I decided to turn the conversation to local California politics.

"Do you think Governor Gavin Newsom will run for president?"

"Eventually, but not this time. I think he will run in 2028," he answered – and then told me Vice-President Kamala Harris, who most presumably to also be a contender, was a friend of his.

Then I asked the gentleman if U.S. Representative Adam Schiff would win his bid for the open California U.S. Senate seat? "Well, he's officiating my upcoming wedding before his election to the Senate," he answered with a smile.

It turned out the gentleman was Steve Nissen, former head of government relations for NBC Universal. After retiring from a job that had him bouncing between Los Angeles, New York, and Washington, he is now settled in as the president and CEO of the Hollywood Chamber of Commerce. And Nissen is also settling down with a marriage via the upcoming wedding he mentioned, which will take place at a friends' home overlooking the Pacific Ocean.

"With such a romantic setting, maybe you should stay right at their home for the honeymoon?" I posited.

"They were generous to suggest we have the wedding at their home, but I am not sure they'd go that far," he laughed.

I love engagement stories, so Nissen was generous enough to share his, and even showed me proposal photos on his phone. It was another exquisite setting for the surprise at a catered, private lunch in the vineyards of Ojai, with the entire scene scored by a strolling violinist Nissen secretly hired.

"She may have been a little suspicious because, for once, it seemed important to me that we be on time. I am typically very easy going," he admitted.

It was then time for Nissen to take to the podium and introduce Ellen K, who would read the list of the new class of Hollywood Walk of Fame Star inductees.

It was a very exciting and timely list of celebrities who would be honored with star ceremonies over the following year. Recent Oscar-winner and former 007 Bond girl Michelle Yeoh and Wonder Woman Gal Gadot were action-packed choices, while television's Eugene Levy and Kerry Washington were sure to be crowd-pleasers.

In music, Sammy Hagar and Dr. Dre were among those who made the list; in sports: tennis star Billie Jean King and Carl Weathers, who boxed as Apollo Creed in the "Rocky" movies and played a golf pro in Adam Sandler's "Happy Gilmore."

Ellen K is friends with many of the inductees – and then she announced the name of a friend of mine: Jim Nantz. Nantz is television's most significant, respected, indefatigable sports broadcaster. He has, for years, been the play-by-play voice for golf's Masters Tournament; the NFL and the Super Bowl; and the NCAA's "Final Four" basketball tournament. The versatile Nantz, with his professional demeanor and deep knowledge, has also been called on for duties as diverse as hosting the CBS Early Show and delivering the eulogy for Arnold Palmer.

I immediately texted Jim a photo of Ellen K at the Walk of Fame podium making the announcements with the words, "Congratulations, Star!"

Jim Nantz responded: "What's that?" "I am at the press conference announcing the honorees," I texted back. "You're getting a star on the Hollywood Walk of Fame."

Almost immediately my phone vibrated with an incoming call from Jim. I answered by offering my congratulations.

"Michael Patrick, is this some kind of gag? Are you joking?"

"No, Jim, I thought sure you would have already known. They just announced the names here in Hollywood. You are getting a star." (Ellen K later told me Nantz's nomination was strongly supported by the selection committee.)

Nantz wanted to know some of the other names announced. I looked down at the press release.

"Chris Pine, Gwen Stefani, Mario Lopez," I told him. "You know, the kind of names you think of when you think of 'Jim Nantz.'"

He laughed.

"I thought you'd know before the announcement," I continued. "I hope I didn't spill the beans or jump the gun on telling you?"

Jim Nantz answered generously, as is his nature.

"I am honored to receive this news from you. You have got to be at the ceremony."

The Hollywood Walk of Fame, free to all, is a legendary attraction at which stars, with celebrity names on them, are embedded in the sidewalks through the central Hollywood area, connecting landmark business such as the iconic Chinese Theater (with its hand and foot-prints in cement); Dolby Theater (Where the Oscars are handed out at the Academy Awards Ceremony); and other theaters such as the Pantages and El Capitan.

Costumed characters pose for photos for tips between the hot dog carts, souvenir shops and hotels such as Loews, which is connected to Ovation, with its tiered, outdoor shops with a view of the Hollywood sign. Jimmy Kimmel tapes his nightly, late-night ABC talk show in front of a studio audience right on Hollywood Boulevard and is known to frequent Hollywood's oldest restaurant, Musso & Frank Grill (since 1919), seen recently in the film "Once Upon a Time in Hollywood."

24

ANDREA EASTMAN AND THE GODFATHER

 I felt like I was hit by "the thunder-bolt."

You recall, in Mario Puzo's novel-turned-Oscar-winning movie "The Godfather," when Michael Corleone, strolling around Sicily with sheep farmers, was stopped in his dusty tracks by the sight of Apolonia herding schoolkids on a field trip?

"You have been hit by 'the thunderbolt,'" Fabrizzio told exiled mobster Michael, who was played by Al Pacino. Michael left behind a squeeze in the States – Kay, played by Diane Keaton.

"Mikey, why don't you tell that nice girl on the phone you love her? 'I love you with all my heart. If I don't see-a-you again ima-gonna die,'" sotto capo Peter Clemenza teased Michael when he whispered to her sotto voce in front of the boys, who'd gone to the mattresses and were bunkered in with him making pots of pasta.

If you are lost in the vernacular, you haven't watched The Godfather seven-million times as I have. I even made a pilgrimage to the locations where Michael Corleone's scenes in Sicily were filmed. IC Bellagio directed me to the actual Bar Vitelli seen in the movie, where Michael inadvertently meets Appollonia's father. It exists, just as it was in the film, in Savoca near Taormina.

Which brings me back to "the thunderbolt."

The thunderbolt hit me while cavorting in the Beverly Hills Hotel's typically star-soaked Polo Lounge. In the fray, I think it was comedic writer Billy Riback who introduced me to the very tall, silver-haired and silver-tongued public relations professional Michael Levine. Upon hearing I was a media type, he planted me in a banquette with a woman from Montana named Abby Moneyhun who, despite her name, was not in a 007 movie. She sat alongside her friend, a woman who'd traveled with her into Hollywood from Bozeman.

I was cozily couched next to the friend Levine introduced as Andrea Eastman. While I was admiring her super-stylish midnight designer blue suit and literally rose-colored glasses, Levine concluded his introduction by saying, "Andrea was the casting director for...The Godfather."

Thunderbolt!

Wait, what? Levine said: "The Godfather's casting director!"

I was already intrigued by Eastman's powerful presence and mystique, but that is the moment I was further struck by The Godfather thunderbolt. And I didn't need Clemenza to goad me into telling this nice girl I loved her. I loved the Godfather, loved her casting, and, over the next few weeks came to love Andrea.

Andrea, I learned, was living in a suite at the Beverly Hills Hotel until the Academy Awards in early March, a night upon which she planned to attend the Elton John Oscar Gala.

Andrea had recently seen her life characterized in the Paramount+ streaming series "The Offer." It was a dramatization of the making and production, including the casting, of The Godfather, which took place more than 50 years earlier, when she was a prodigy executive in her 20's.

"I remember it like it was yesterday," Andrea told me. "It was Charlie Bluhdorn, who, as the owner of the Gulf+Western conglomerate, owned Paramount Pictures; Robert Evans, the head of the studio; Paramount's COO Stanley Jaffe...and little old me. If you watch "The Offer," you will see that Charlie yelled at a lot of people. But he never yelled at me. We had an incredible relationship."

Andrea's relationship with The Godfather's producer Al Ruddy was even warmer. Surreal as it must have been to see herself played by actress Stephanie Koenig on the television series, Andrea told me she thought the series was well done.

Candidly, she took issue with only one factual element.

"Al Ruddy was a great producer. A terrific person. In "The Offer" it depicts us as having a one-night stand, but indeed it was a yearlong love affair," she revealed. "I am still incredibly close to him all these years later. I am close to his wife and his daughter. It was a love affair and an incredible endearing friendship."

As she shared all of this, I tried not to ask too many questions. Occasionally, though, the modest, soft-spoken Andrea would look up over the top of her glasses and tell me she felt like I was interviewing her.

"It was the happiest time of my life. I am most proud of being one on the team that cast The Godfather," she continued in a tone of voice one might use when recalling an old friend.

I was fortunate to feel like a new friend to Andrea Eastman, who'd befriended, and, in her post-Paramount career as an agent, represented, some of Hollywood's brightest stars. Dustin Hoffman, Billy Crystal, Katie Couric, Barbara Streisand, and Sylvester Stallone among them.

It was Andrea who discovered Jaclyn Smith.

"I was at a show and during intermission, I saw this woman and 'Bang!'"

Andrea said she asked Smith if she was an actress.

'No, but I want to be,' Smith answered.

"I gave her my card," Andrea recalled.

And just like that Jaclyn Smith had a career and went onto be one of "Charlie's Angels."

Eastman also told me a darling story about how Streisand was initially resistant to taking a role as Hoffman's spouse in the movie "Meet the Fockers."

"She didn't want to do it, so I tried to price her out of it, but no matter how high I went the producers kept saying 'yes,'" Andrea insisted. She then gave the hint of a humble smile.

That movie also starred Robert De Niro, who played young Vito Corleone in "Godfather II."

"I interviewed Robert De Niro before he was Robert De Niro," Andrea told me. "He didn't say much...but he didn't have to. He had a presence."

Andrea, due to sensitive circumstances she seemed discreet about, chose to leave Paramount Pictures just before The Godfather won the "Best Picture" Oscar. "Someone disrespected me," she allowed. "But I was ecstatic it won Best Picture. We were all a family and still are, including the author Mario Puzo," she insisted.

The Academy of Motion Picture Arts and Sciences honored Andrea at their Academy Museum of Motion Pictures in Hollywood, which celebrated the 50th anniversary of the Best Picture-winning Godfather movie with a special exhibit.

I walked through the temporary Godfather Exhibit, with the iconic Nino Rota film soundtrack score piped-in throughout, to see hand-edited pages of the original screenplay and script; costumes, such as the leisure suit worn by Michael Corleone in the "Havana" scenes and the silk and chiffon dress Mama Corleone danced in at the First Communion on Lake Tahoe.

The dental aesthetic device Marlon Brando wore to accent Vito Corleone's jaw was viewable under glass and the life-sized set of the Godfather's desk office was set up for photographs. It was more exciting than the "Oval Offices" set up at each of America's Presidential Museums.

"The ultimate lineup was iconic," read a display. Eastman's name and legacy, including casting Pacino (whom one of her studio bosses referred to as a 'little pip squeak'), was prominently displayed in the elaborate exhibit's "Casting and Performance" section of the extensive "Godfather" series of rooms. A film on the wall showed rehearsals with a closed-caption graphic across the bottom reading "Every member of the Corleone family was thoroughly researched, tested and selected."

"CASTING AND PERFORMANCE" the room's entrance plaque was headlined.

"Initiated by Andrea Eastman...casting for The Godfather entailed hundreds of auditions and screen tests and became a point of contention. But the ultimate lineup was iconic: Marlon Brando, James Caan, Richard Castellano, John Cazale, Diane Keaton, Morgana King, Al Pacino, and Talia Shire, with the sequel adding Robert De Niro, Michael V. Gazzo, Bruno Kirby, and Lee Strasberg, among others..."

I stood there for a moment and stared at the name "Andrea Eastman" to soak in the giant part "little ol' Andrea" played in staking that Academy Award-winning team. To think I'd gone to the museum exhibit hoping it would somehow acknowledge her. It properly gave Andrea Eastman a starring role – which is what she did for many others during her casting career and as an agent – including the unlikely star of three, Best Picture-nominated Godfather films:

"...Pacino, then a relative unknown, would instantly become a star for his measured and intense portrayal of Michael Corleone."

Fate would have it that days after my museum visit, during my month of memorable meetings with Andrea, I randomly encountered Al Pacino "Sunday brunching" with an apparent friend of his in the Tower Bar of the Sunset Tower Hotel. Tower Bar, a 1929, art deco bar overlooking Los Angeles had been recommended to me.

I had never been there, but for a reason unknown to me I woke up late that Sunday with the idea of going there. I selected a seat on the edge of the veranda which overlooks the Los Angeles skyline, but, weirdly, I also chose to sit on the side of the table facing the room instead of the panoramic view over the pool and skyline.

Shortly after Barb, the hostess, sat me, I began to relax almost to the point of being at ease. Leaning back in my chair, I barely noticed an older but suave man passing my table on his way to be seated. Without moving, or even changing expression, I realized that gentleman was Al Pacino.

It was like seeing a shark swim by: first I saw him; then I recognized him; then I processed it; and then I believed my eyes.

Al Pacino sat mid-room at a table with his long hair and back against the wall, hunched over and often looking at the screen of his phone. Of course, Al Pacino was all I could subtly see for the rest of the lunch. My table faced his, so I was sneaking peeks but not staring.

There were other giant, unbothered celebrities in the room – Ryan Reynolds and Christoph Waltz, to name two - but Al Pacino is an actor with his own orbit – an orbit I dared to enter by physically forcing myself to approach his table. This wasn't Any Given Sunday - one of Pacino's many film titles. This was a day on which I could meet "Michael Corleone." I simply had to invite myself to the party.

Nervous as a cat, I purposely pushed myself up from my table and propelled myself toward his, knowing that once I was physically committed to a visible path toward the stars' table, there would be no turning back.

My mind, facing a split-second, impending deadline, would have to invent something to say. While walking the 10 feet from my table to Al Pacino's, so many of his screen roles flashed through my mind: Serpico; Aldo Gucci; the Devil; Tony D'Amato the Miami Football coach in Any Given Sunday; and more. But since I was in a restaurant with Al Pacino two tables away, my mind flashed through his iconic restaurant scenes:

"Scarface," for instance, when Cuban gangster Tony Montana, is his tuxedo, lashed out at all the other patrons staring at him as he defiantly described himself as "the bad guy."

Al Pacino's character, blind veteran Frank Slade, confidently approached and invited himself to Gabrielle Anwar's table and ended up dancing with her in Scent of a Woman, at the Oak Room of New York's Plaza Hotel, a bold move that perhaps I took inspiration from as I approached his table at this moment.

But most of all, I envisioned Al Pacino as Michael Corleone, in the Godfather, when Virgil Solozzo and Captain McClusky, took Michael into Louis Italian-American Restaurant in New York. We all know the scene where Michael goes to the restroom, gets the gun from above the toilet...and with bangs, smoke, and an overturned, red-checkered tableclothed table, does them in with shots to the forehead and throat.

At his Tower Bar table on this day, though, I noticed Al Pacino kept taking his indoor sunglasses on and off. He was wearing a black wool overcoat, casual track-type pants and black sneakers. The Oscar-winner did not look up when my shadow reached his table, so I tried to break the ice by saying, "Excuse me..."

When that went nowhere, I quickly explained why I stood there.

"I dined with Andrea Eastman last night..."

That got Al Pacino's attention, and he looked up.

"...I know she'd want me to send her best," I offered.

He then smiled with his eyes and his mouth.

"Andrea and I go way back," Pacino told me. "She's in town? I should call her. How can she be reached?"

I told him how to call her. Then, since I sensed it going well, asked the screen legend who'd played Michael Corleone in three Godfather films, if he'd visited "The Godfather" exhibit at the Academy Museum?

At that point Pacino's lunch partner finally chimed in...with a joke. "If people saw Al walking around in that museum, they'd think one of the statues came to life!"

We all laughed, and, in the chuckles, I sensed it was time for me to exit, stage right.

Later Pacino and his pal happened to be leaving the restaurant at the same time, so I took the opportunity to thank him again and, with less nervousness, attempted a joke:

"I kept an eye on you during lunch," I told Pacino, the man who, as Michael Corleone, offed the Turk Virgil Sollozzo and corrupt cop Captain McCluskey at that table with a pistol placed behind the toilet tank in Louis Restaurant. "If I saw that you went to the bathroom, I planned to run for the exit."

As I said it, I pantomimed my hand reaching up behind the toilet tank, as Michael Corleone did to find the gun.

"Oh yes. That's very funny," Pacino politely patronized me, managing the kind of smile he gave Carlo Rizzi just before he met his end with a wire around his neck and his feet through a windshield.

When we parted at the valet entrance, before Pacino got into his white Range Rover and drove himself off, I reminded him Eastman was back in residence at the Beverly Hills Hotel, the classic castle where, over the years since The Godfather, she'd bumped into Pacino a decade earlier – a sweet story he confirmed. "Al Pacino happened to be in the hotel's Polo Lounge when I was there. Richard, the piano player, played the theme from The Godfather, so Al and I decided to dance together to that song," Eastman fondly recalled.

Imagine, just as Pacino's Michael Corleone danced with his wife Kay, played by Diane Keaton in the First Communion scene in Godfather II (a dance reimagined in Corleone's declining days at the end of Godfather III) Andrea Eastman dancing similarly with Al Pacino at the Polo Lounge piano.

When it came to Diane Keaton, Andrea explained to me how the romantic comedy character actress ended up with such a vital supporting role in the brooding Godfather.

"We had Diane Keaton on our list," Andrea assured me. "She had only done Woody Allen movies, so to think of her playing Michael Corleone's wife was a very unusual role for her."

Andrea said there is no secret to her success in terms of casting, but she shared some of her process with me. "You make endless lists when you are a casting director. When you do a movie, you try to think out of the box. For The Godfather, it was endless casting. We worked seven days a week. I was dreaming of Italians all night every night."

She said ultimately casting comes down to instinct.

"Some actors and actresses can go to acting school forever and the don't have 'it.' 'It' is a gift. Somebody walks in the room, and they have a presence."

Andrea, in another of her patient conversations with me, revealed that it was a close call for James Caan to get the part of hotheaded Santino Corleone.

"We all worked as a team, but I am responsible for Jimmy Caan getting the part of Sonny," she allowed.

I settled in for the story.

"Jimmy was amazing in his Godfather screen test for 'Sonny,' but he was out of the movie. Francis Ford Coppola, the director, had initially promised the part to a big guy named Carmine Creedy he'd met at a party. Coppola made him an offer in a bar, but it turned out Creedy wasn't quite right for the part. He was a big guy but not menacing. He was like a big Saint Bernard," Andrea explained. "Luckily, he'd never formally signed a deal, and Coppola trusted me. He was leaving for Sicily, so he told me, 'Just cast my f-ing movie!'"

Andrea said she ran up to her office to make Caan's deal before anyone changed their mind. "Everybody in the world wanted to be in The Godfather, and we then had our dream cast: Marlon Brando, James Caan, Robert Duvall, Diane Keaton and Al Pacino."

"Andrea, once you selected and secured the cast, did you ever get to see your actors in action before the film hit the screen?"

The gentle, sweet woman tolerated yet another of my questions. And gave me a colorful answer.

"Charlie Bluhdorn and I went to visit the compound they used as the Godfather's house. When we arrived, they were in between shoots. During that time the production team has to move the cameras and adjust the lighting and microphones and so there can be a lot of time waiting," she explained.

Imagine Andrea pulling up with Bluhdorn, the corporate owner of Paramount, seeing the cast in the compound playing frisbee?

"'What's going on here!?" Andrea said Bluhdorn yelled. "'This is Paramount's money and you're playing frisbee?'"

Andrea understood the business and so she led Bluhdorn inside the house to calm him.

"But when we looked out the window, Marlon Brando and Jimmy Caan mooned us! It was pretty funny," Andrea said. "It was the happiest time of my life."

Andrea's wide-ranging career, which began after she graduated from Ohio State, has left an impact on Hollywood.

My "Johnny-come-lately" occasions spent visiting with Andrea over the month in Beverly Hills would be the "power meetings" she was accustomed to, but to me, they were significant and enjoyable. During "Award Season" residency at the Beverly Hills Hotel, we gathered time and again at Polo Lounge; and chatted on the couch in her hotel suite with an outdoor balcony overlooking the gardens in which I also came across her walking her dog one evening.

I sat next to Andrea on the second-floor dining room at Mastro's in Beverly Hills with late-night radio star George Noory and his radio executive friend Mark Rollings, along with comedian and writer Billy Ribeck. A trio played music and it was loud in there, but the soft-spoken Andrea had us all leaning in as we feasted on her tales and charm.

To illustrate how connected Andrea still is, she had an idea for Pat Boone, the singing star now living in Beverly Hills who is a friend of Noory; Ribeck had an idea for Andrea because she is friends with acclaimed director Ron Howard.

For all her legacy and power, Andrea was unassuming. I found her, at times, opinionated and decisive. Other times she was modest and even shy.

While speaking of local restaurants, Andrea mentioned she'd be interested in going to Spago.

"I would really love to see Wolfgang Puck again, if he'd see me," Andrea mused.

Puck, the original celebrity chef, is Spago's founder and a wildly successful international entrepreneur. Spago, at its previous and current Beverly Hills location, has always been Hollywood's "it" restaurant for see and be seen cuisine. Not to mention Puck's prominence as caterer to the stars at the Academy Awards Ball.

I asked Andrea to let me arrange a Spago reservation.

The response I received from Chef Puck's assistant after emailing his office was rapid, enthusiastic, and warm:

"Chef Puck would be delighted to meet with Ms. Eastman. Would you please ask her if she can some to the restaurant on February 19?"

Andrea and I, as directed took a table that night at Spago. John Scanlon, the Irishman serving as general manager of the Beverly Hills Hotel, brought Andrea to the restaurant where my son Harrison Shiels and a pal named Tim McGuire gathered for dinner.

Our conversations fell silent when Wolfgang Puck appeared at the table. He and Andrea concluded they hadn't seen each other in a decade but hugged and instantly conversed like it had only been yesterday.

Chef Puck sat down, ordered up a table full of deserts and created a craft margarita for himself with jalapenos on the spot, which he requested the server make and bring to him. The rest of us chose to "drink like Chef Wolfgang Puck," so the server brought a full round of them. We silently savored our margaritas while Puck and Andrea savored each other, laughing, smiling, and recalling good times and old friends.

The Austrian-born Puck talked about his operation exiting Hotel Bel-Air, which owned by the same Dorchester Collection group as the Beverly Hills Hotel. This caused Scanlon, who previously worked with Puck in London, to shrug that while he was with the company, was not involved in the crosstown property.

But Puck then countered by telling us about an exciting new restaurant he was involved in at a popular beach spot in Malibu.

"Will you name the new restaurant?" I asked Puck.

"If I want to," he answered with a shrug.

I could see why he and Andrea got along so well. They were both significant, successful people...but they weren't outwardly impressed with themselves. It was a joy to see the two of them have such a fine, fun time together in that special starry space called Spago.

Andrea was equally modest when the heartthrob singing star Paul Anka swept into Polo Lounge with a small entourage late one evening after his performance at the Saban Theater over on Wilshire. While we were seated in Frank Sinatra's old booth – yes, the one with the infamous telephone – Anka and company, including O.J. attorney Robert Shapiro, took a table in the back corner of the green and white-decorated dining room. (The same booth I'd seen Bono and his mates from U2 occupy one evening that month.)

Now both in their early 80's but vibrant and stylish, Andrea expressed an affection for Paul Anka, and explained she'd known him for years. Because she is dignified and classy, she declined my suggestion that she go say hello to the man who'd written "My Way" for Frank Sinatra; and Johnny Carson's "Tonight Show" theme while collaborating on hits with Michael Jackson; Tom Jones; Michael Buble; Chicago's Peter Cetera, and more. Anka, for still sold-out crowds, still performed his countless other chart-toppers such as "Diana," "You're Having My Baby," and Kodak's "Times of Your Life."

When it came to Paul Anka, Andrea, like all of us, had a lifelong case of "Puppy Love."

Since it was the night of the Grammy Awards, and Clive Davis staged his legendary annual pre-Grammy gathering after party where we sat at Polo Lounge, I knew the room would soon be full of the famous. (Stevie Wonder was among those I'd spotted seated earlier.)

Fate found us in front of Anka's table just before he left, and the sight of Andrea set Anka's eyes alight. They recalled the details of a first-class cross-country flight they once took together with amazing accuracy – Anka even recited the seat number! As Anka and Andrea spoke warmly and caught up on things Shapiro, wearing a fedora, chimed in asking Andrea why she hadn't cast him in any Godfather movies!

Another evening I saw Andrea dining with another longtime musical friend of hers Michelle Phillips - one of the original members of the Mamas and the Papas. They sat in the same Polo Lounge booth in which only days earlier she'd strategized with star news anchor Brian Williams and his wife Jane, who were in town for a meeting with Creative Artists Agency. Also, to visit their actress daughter Allison Williams, who lives in West Hollywood.

Andrea Eastman's special memories of the iconic pink hotel include a not-so-happy one, but one that does touch her heart. She was in residence with an extended stay to recover from her open-heart surgery during the pandemic. The hotel brought pleasure to her pain, as did her devoted dog Trooper.

"Sylvester Stallone flew Trooper and I from my home in Bozeman, Montana on a private jet to come to Los Angeles for my open-heart surgery," Andrea said with a swoon of appreciation. "He's a great person. I've known him since before 'Rocky.' We go back a long way."

Eastman's experience has been chronicled in a new book for travel types, children, and animal lovers entitled: "Trooper at the Beverly Hills Hotel." The coffee table-pretty book by Susan McCauley features charming illustrations memorializing Eastman's late golden retriever and the gilded hotel by Darlee Orcullo Urbiztondo.

"Trooper would prance around the hotel and go behind the front desk each morning where the staff would greet him. Trooper loved the hotel and the affection I got from Trooper in that peaceful, elegant setting hastened my recovery. The book makes people cry because of Trooper's loyalty and unconditional love for me and everyone," Eastman revealed.

The Beverly Hills Hotel's current general manager, John Scanlon, welcomed Eastman back with her new dog, a golden/dingo mix she named "Polo" in homage to the hotel's famed Polo Lounge.

As we talked, Eastman introduced me to her new canine companion.

"I rescued her from Korea, where, I don't even want to tell you, but they cook dogs alive. She's pretty cute and sweet. I love animals. They trust you and love you," she said, petting Polo, who'd jumped up from her plush pink and green Beverly Hills Hotel dog bed in the suite's vestibule at the door.

Some of Andrea's dearest clients, friends and associates rallied around, some attending a book launch event at The Beverly Hills Hotel and some endorsing her beautiful book:

Stallone said, "This heartfelt story will move you for sure." Academy Award screenwriter Marshall Brickman compared "Trooper" with "Charlotte's Web."

"It's a delightful story for children, their parents and dog lovers," according to supermodel Cindy Crawford. And Ali McGraw, whom Andrea cast in "Love Story," says "the book will touch your heart."

Eastman is an animal lover, and though she's described making the Godfather as the best time of her life, there is one scene she lobbied against: the infamous "horses head in the Hollywood producer's bed incident" (which was filmed at a mansion behind the Beverly Hills Hotel with a genuine, previously butchered equine skull.)

Eastman has rescued horses at her home in Bozeman, Montana, near Big Sky Resort, owned by Michigan-based Boyne USA. She was also featured in the book "People We Know, Horses They Love," written by NBC "Today Show" correspondent Jill Rapaport with images by her sister Linda Solomon, a celebrity photojournalist from Michigan.

And lest you think Andrea is a one-trick pony, she cast many other movies including 1970's "Love Story" starring Ali McGraw and Ryan O'Neal – a casting and picture that also gave Tommy Lee Jones his film debut.

The lesson in all of this? Keep your friends close...and your pets closer!

On Academy Awards Sunday, I walked with the afternoon crowds around the Dolby Theater on closed Hollywood Boulevard trying to catch a glimpse of the glittering stars being delivered to the red carpet via chauffeur-driven black SUV's. Occasionally a black-tinted window would open and one of the attendees would wave to the crowd.

I did the same "through the looking glass gadfly routine" after the awards outside the Vanity Fair Party presented to the tuxedoed and gowned statue holders in an elaborate, gated -off tent venue on Santa Monica Boulevard outside the Wallis Annenberg Center for the Performing Arts in Beverly Hills.

I'd watched them building the tent city for two weeks on my walks in Beverly Hills and, after dark, saw the VF logo projected up onto the ornate Beverly Hills City Hall tower. Even the landmark, art deco-style neon 76 gas station across the street was closed that night in deference to the soiree.

Andrea Eastman, in as glamorous a gown as any partygoers wore that night, had a fine time at the Elton John After Oscar Party, escorted by Scanlon.

And with that, at sunrise on a March Monday, the curtain came down on the more-than-a-month-long award season, which began with Golden Globe Awards at the Beverly Hilton just after New Years.

By the next morning, a gray and chilly one, Andrea Eastman and her dog Polo decamped from the Beverly Hills Hotel. On her way out of Hollywood, which by all accounts was a meaningful memory lane return full of personal reconnections, she messaged me from LAX. I sensed she would miss everyone, but the Dame and her doggie were boarding the Bozeman flight back to her snowy mountain "home."

Her text read:

"Thank you xx. On the plane" (followed by a crying "sad face" emoji.)

I messaged Andrea Eastman back stating that, in addition to that days' weather, Tinseltown was already less glittery without her.

Then I sent Andrea a line Nick Carraway said to "The Great Gatsby" at the end of F. Scott Fitzgerald's book:

"They're a rotten crowd. You're worth the whole damned bunch of them put together."

25

PAUL ANKA'S FRONT ROW
PROPOSAL

 Before there are destination weddings, there are dramatic proposals. New York's Times Square at midnight on New Year's Eve, the top of the Eiffel Tower overlooking the City of Light and the beach in Cabo at sunset. Maybe a ring at the bottom of a champagne glass at Joe's Stone Crab in Miami, a "Will You Marry Me?" flying banner over Dodger Stadium, or a man on bended knee at a Las Vegas nightclub near one of those cheesy wedding chapels. These are some of the time-honored options.

I love hearing engagement stories. I had a few, myself. One proposal was in a vineyard at Frog's Leap Winery in Sonoma. Another was a twilight affair in a lakefront in a gazebo with roses, candles...and a three-piece orchestra from the Lansing Symphony Orchestra.

But my first and most significant personal engagement story involves one of the entertainment industry's most successful singer-songwriters: Paul Anka.

Anka is best known for writing the song "My Way" for Frank Sinatra. He also penned "Johnny's Theme" for Carson's legendary "Tonight Show." Tom Jones' hit "She's a Lady" was a creation of Anka. And the "King of Pop" Michael Jackson's posthumously released song "This Is It" was a collaboration with Anka. He also had a hit with the group Chicago called "Hold Me 'Till the Morning Comes."

Anka, for decades, has been an amazingly energetic and likeable singing star. He performs his own hits, including "Diana," "Put Your Head on My Shoulder," "Lonely Boy," and "Having My Baby." His sentimental song "The Times of Your Life" turned a Kodak commercial into one of the most enduring television advertisements of all time.

I first met Anka after his terrific concert at Pine Knob Music Theater, a famed outdoor venue, in Clarkston, Michigan, north of Detroit, in 1989. I was producing WJR Radio's afternoon drive show with Joel Alexander, and we held a ticket giveaway promotion with the theater.

The public relations woman, Marylin Desjardins, took my parents and I backstage for a short "meet and greet" with the famed singer after his killer performance. Anka was friendly and very lively and gracious when my father Arthur complimented him about the fact that Anka had five daughters.

A couple of years later, on a summer morning, Anka phoned into the J.P. McCarthy radio show one morning. He was promoting another appearance that upcoming Sunday night back at Pine Knob. As McCarthy's producer, I took the call and therefore briefly chatted with him again on the telephone before the interview. Anka was friendly, even though he told me he just stepped off an overnight flight from Paris. Born in Ottawa, Canada of Lebanese heritage, Anka performs worldwide and even released songs in Italian.

Desjardins kindly set me up with two front-row tickets to the concert, so I made plans to attend the Sunday show. What happened next, I did not plan.

It was warm in the twilight when I made my way into the show with my girlfriend Vera Ambrose, a vivacious celebrity chef whom I had met through the J.P. McCarthy Show. She hosted a culinary television show called "Now You're Cooking" and was very popular amongst the Bloomfield glitterati. Vera was a blonde who resembled actress Mariel Hemingway. Ironically, Vera had been college roommates with Mariel's sister Joan Hemingway. Joan, Mariel, and their sister Margaux were granddaughters of Ernest Hemingway.

When I picked up the tickets left for us at the theater "will call" window, I secretly slipped the attendant an envelope.

"I am a radio producer. Mr. Anka asked me to get this to him backstage," I fibbed. I used the "assumed close" by not asking whether he was capable of getting the envelope backstage or not.

Inside the envelope was a note with a request for Anka. The note listed our seat locations in the front row. I was completely uncertain as to whether the note would reach the star. In fact, considered it unlikely, but I was nevertheless prepared. This uncertainty heightened the drama of surprise for me, too.

Vera sat down in our seats and Anka's high energy show unfolded. Then...nature called me.

About 30-minutes into the performance, I really had to go to the bathroom. Of course, I could not dare to get up just in case Anka had received the note and deigned to honor my request. I sat tight with my feet below my seat moving faster than Anka's.

And Anka is always on the move. By now his fans know he enters any venue singing his opening number "Diana" from the back of the theater. Anka surprises the crowds, who hear him singing before they figure out where he is and see him, by walking up the aisle singing into a wireless microphone, his black suit bathed in the spotlight that follows him. And during his show Anka paces across the stage only rarely standing still.

At one point, though, just after the sun set behind the grass hill behind the seats, Anka, in the middle of a song, not only crossed the stage but came down off it. Without ceasing to sing, he glided down between the stage and the front row of seats until he reached...us.

It was surreal when, between verses, Anka asked:

"Are you Vera?"

To say Vera was surprised would be an understatement. But managed to answer "Yes?!"

"He wants to marry you," Anka quickly told her, pointing to me.

Vera turned my way to see I had pulled a ring box from my pocket and had it open to present the diamond to her.

And just like that, Anka sang and danced his way back onto the stage, while Vera and I hugged.

Occasionally, throughout the rest of his show, Anka would, during a song, come over to our way and sing words of congratulations or encouragement by incorporating them into the lyrics of the songs he was performing from the stage. "Marry him!" he shouted with a smile.

The anticipation I experienced sitting through the first half of that show, wondering whether I would leave the theater an engaged man, was intense. Once I sent that note back to Anka, the matter was out of my hands. The engagement that night, in a way, was a surprise to me, too.

Flash forward 16 years.

By 2008 I moved from being a radio producer to being a radio host. I found myself interviewing Paul Anka via telephone on my radio show to promote an appearance he was making in at Caesar's, in Windsor, Ontario. After I introduced Anka, the star said:

Anka: Hi Michael, how are you?

Shiels: Great to hear your voice again! Now, you and I have an interesting history, you know.

Anka: I remember. I think that was the first time that had ever happened to me. But you tell the listeners.

Shiels: It was 1992 at Pine Knob. I was in the front row. You came off the stage, walked through the front row, and told my girlfriend I would like to marry her. That was such a generous thing to do.

Anka: Oh, I remember the set up. Obviously, I was informed. That was the first time it had happened. I have done it about six times since then. May I ask, are you still married?

Shiels: Uh, I've been married two more times since then.

Anka: I don't mean to laugh, but I should have been there for the other two!

I told Anka he would be meeting my latest wife, a brunette dentist, that night backstage after his Caesar's show in Windsor. Anka was in a dark, post-show sweatsuit by the time he received us, and we chatted for a bit before standing for a photograph with him.

Paul Anka, as fate would have it, met yet another of my wives, a blonde therapist, a few years later, in 2015. Ironically, she bought me the concert tickets as a Christmas surprise – but mistakenly purchased very good seats for Neil Diamond. Imagine my look of bewildered surprise and feigned gratitude when I opened Neil Diamond tickets on Christmas morning? She could tell something was amiss, and I gently explained she may have mistaken Paul Anka for Neil Diamond. (I found people sometimes also confused Anka with Neil Sedaka.)

We scalped the Neil Diamond tickets and my industrious little wife, being a self-described "seat snob," replaced them with a fantastic pair of tickets in Sarasota – which meant a Valentine's Day trip to Florida.

We stayed at the waterfront Hyatt Regency hotel adjacent to Sarasota's very purple Van Wezel Performing Arts Hall, which happened to be where Anka and his band were staying. We got ourselves backstage after the show and I introduced her to Paul Anka. After chatting, once again another wife and I posed for a photo with Anka.

It may sound terrible, but once back home I just layered the latest photo on top of the other one in the same frame. Eventually that photo also came down when the curtain came down on that marriage, too.

By 2021 I had managed to stay single for more than six years. I noticed Paul Anka was coming to perform at the showroom of Andiamo, an Italian banquet venue in Warren, Michigan.

But I was finished with taking wives to see Paul...and done with wives in general.

Paul Anka, though, still meant a lot to me, and I was feeling nostalgic. When I heard his music, especially his tune, "Times of Your Life," the mental slideshow flashing through my mind was vivid.

"Reach back for the joy and the sorrow – put them away in your mind. The memories are time that you borrow to spend when you get to tomorrow...Gather moments while you may. Collect the dreams you dream today. Will you remember the times of your life?"

The "joys and sorrows" Anka sang about – the shadows of misty yesteryears – played on my mind. I bought some expensive tickets to Anka's concert and reached back to invite my parents Art and Gladys, who had accompanied me to my first Paul Anka show over 30 years previous. My father was in declining health, and it turned out to be the last concert he'd attend before passing months later.

Then, not knowing how she would react, I dared to invite Vera, my first wife, and the mother of my son Harrison. The same Vera who, decades earlier, received my front-row proposal courtesy of Paul Anka himself. I was not sure how Vera would respond to the prospect of such an invitation or whether she would be sensitive to being in Anka's audience again – especially with me. To this day I feel guilt for the end of the marriage. Anka's lyrics for Sinatra's anthem "My Way" begin with the words "Regrets, I've had a few..." I can say allowing that marriage to end is the biggest of my life's regrets.

But gracious as ever, and without hesitation, Vera was game to come along. I thought it was very, very magnanimous of her. It was a way for me to express my appreciation to Vera her for all she'd done to raise Harrison in her happy, vibrant, creative home and to impress upon her that I remember and value the meaningful moments she created in the "Times of My Life."

My father always said Vera was his favorite, so he was perhaps even more pleased than I that she would attend the show.

In the days leading up to the concert, since I am a travel writer, I had been on a tour more furious than Anka surely had. In the span of just over a month, I had been consecutively to Mackinac Island; Zion National Park near St. George, Utah; Los Angeles; San Diego; Casa de Campo Resort in the Dominican Republic; the Saxony Region of Germany; Asheville, North Carolina; and Mazatlan, Mexico before arriving in Detroit on the day of the concert and heading straight from the airport to the venue. I was road-weary but ready to see Anka, the teen idol who was now an 80-year-old dynamo, light up the stage and my heart.

The four of us, who arrived separately, hacked our way through the thick crowd to take our seats – stage left – two tables back from the stage.

When I entered the venue, as I originally had at Pine Knob a lifetime ago, I asked a staff member to take an envelope backstage to "Mr. Anka." The note inside let him know I was there if he wanted to meet backstage again and let him know where Vera and I were sitting.

Just as before, I waited...

Just before "curtain," I snuck a peek at an incoming text from a number I didn't recognize:

"Hi this is Eliza, Paul Anka's violinist...."

Anka asked Eliza James to send me a message from backstage. "From PA: 'Sorry we couldn't get together this time. Hope you enjoy the show!'"

I appreciated the gesture and chalked it up to the pandemic restrictions much of socially distanced show business operated under at that time.

As is his tradition, when the house lights dimmed and the music struck up, the most energetic octogenarian in the house turned up with a spotlight on him in the center of the room, wireless microphone in hand, singing and weaving his way between the tables. Anka was dressed in a black suit with a black tie over a white shirt and had let his hair grow a little longer in the back.

Sure enough, instead of a beeline to center stage, Anka took a real "left turn" to his right with his eyes scanning the gathered up and down. He was headed straight toward the area of our table. When Anka's one-man parade reached us, he wide-eyed, smiled broadly at Vera and I mid-song...and then sashayed to the stage. Paul Anka sprinkled his stardust upon us once again.

In February of 2023 I was having drinks at the Polo Lounge in the Beverly Hills Hotel. It is not unusual to see notable people dropping in on any given night. Paul Anka, on this evening, came through the door and sat at a corner table with a couple of guests, one of whom was the celebrity attorney Robert Shapiro, who was wearing a fedora. Shapiro became nationally famous by being a member of O.J. Simpson's "dream team" of attorneys.

Anka, who lives in the greater Los Angeles area, had just finished performing at the Saban Theater in Beverly Hills. It must have been nice to perform, for once, near his home, so he settled into the Polo Lounge after his show for a late bite and a nightcap. I knew he was on his way to Florida for the customary Sunshine State stops of his winter tour.

When I could tell dinner was winding down, I re-introduced myself to Anka, reminded him of our "history," and greeted his friends. I thanked him for the memories. "Pine Knob," he said, nodding and smiling.

As we all walked out of the Polo Lounge at the same time, I said goodbye by saying: "Break a leg back in Sarasota at the Ven Wezel."

Anka stopped and smiled. "I will."

26

A DETROIT RIVER TURNABOUT

 The "Downriver" area of suburban Detroit, Michigan, has always been known for its industrial prowess – steel mills, factories, and freighters. All in support of Motor City's auto industry. But there are pockets of peaceful nature, some preserved by industrial donations, amidst what some call the "Rust Belt."

One of those sanctuaries is Elizabeth Park, a 103-year-old riverfront respite adjacent to downtown Trenton, Michigan. It sits just across from Grosse Ile, an upscale enclave island that divides the Detroit River from Ontario, Canada before it reaches Lake Erie.

Elizabeth Park feels like a narrow island itself since it is reached, by car or on foot, over small, scenic bridges. There is no cost to drive in or park along the one-way, 1.5-mile loop road that encircles Elizabeth Parks' wooded interior. The Detroit River can be seen from the road since that portion of the park is elevated making it so even some of the parking spaces provide a panoramic view.

For those who leave their cars, there are barbeque grills, picnic tables, swing sets, slides, pony rides and baseball diamonds. There are even exercise-stretching devices dotted throughout the park. But there is no retail, other than a fanciful chateau, buttressed by flowers on the bluff above the river that serves as a wedding and event venue.

The equally fanciful footbridges that connect the island are so gorgeous they are often used as backdrops for wedding, graduation, and prom photos. You're likely to see everything from Middle Eastern people smoking shisha to catered picnics.

Downtown Trenton presents events such as the annual art fair; fireworks; Jazz on the River and power boat river races which are viewable from Elizabeth Park.

I walk the park's waterside boardwalk area frequently. Both morning and evening, I observe people casting lines over the side in the hopes of catching a fish. Some come with equipment and tackle boxes, others are more casually recreational about it.

Many of the people fishing come in factions of families: including fathers and daughters. The level of involvement in the actual angling seems to depend on the age of the child. Whether they are actively casting or not really paying attention, the kids seem happy to be there.

As golf great Jack Nicklaus once said, "You know your child is ready for serious golf when he can go more than three holes without trying to catch a frog."

If I may digress, for a moment, the Nicklaus comment reminds me of an anecdote with my son Harrison Shiels. He was probably eight years old when we were on a golf trip to Crystal Mountain Resort near Traverse City, Michigan.

We were staying in one of the resort's golf-side condos. Ours was a multi-story, four-bedroom unit built into the hill among the trees along the left side of the 18th hole.

One morning I noticed the condo door wide open. I walked through the door and looking into the main level bedroom near the door, I saw Harrison. He was in his little striped golf shirt and khaki shorts, with a Scooby Doo bucket hat on. Lying face down on the bed, with his head over the side, he appeared to be looking at a blueberry muffin on the floor. A little, brown, plastic trash bin from the bathroom was upside down next to the muffin.

I stood for a moment or two surveying the surprising scene and wondering why he was motionless while intently staring at the muffin. My curiosity then got the best of me.

"Interesting," I said so as not to startle Harrison. "What are you up to?"

"I'm trying to catch a chipmunk," he whispered.

This explained why the condo door was wide open – and the slider door leading to the deck, too, for that matter.

I am not sure what Harrison would have done if he'd covered a live chipmunk with that trash can, but I admired his willingness to bite off more than he could chew.

While I walked along Elizabeth Park's riverfront promenade, a tiny version of Havana, Cuba's oceanfront Malecon, watching the culturally diverse groups of families fishing, I remembered both Harrison and my own late father, Arthur Shiels, who loved fishing.

In their later years, after he'd spent decades fishing off his pontoon boat in Northern Michigan's Sage Lake, he and my mother Gladys lived in Trenton Towers which was along the river and adjacent to Elizabeth Park.

Before they bought the cottage in Sage Lake – which we named "Arthur's Way" – my parents would take my brother and sister and me, along with extended family, to a rented cottage. It was situated among the mom-and-pop "resorts" on Houghton Lake, Michigan's largest inland lake.

Cottage rental came with a rowboat, and my grandfather would borrow the local pastor's outboard Evinrude boat motor for some horsepower. My father would go out early fishing – and sometimes in the evening – with his father-in-law and my uncles.

I used to pester him to take me and one morning, he relented. He piled my little brother Robert, and even our baby sister Lori into the boat at dawn.

The four of us motored out under gray skies in damp, cold air. It was perfect weather for fishing, but not so great when you are a soft third grader like me. I was chilly, so I tucked my hands inside the sleeves of my windbreaker jacket and clutched the fishing rod and reel through the gathered-up ends of my jacket sleeves.

At this point, you can probably imagine what I soon saw with my own eyes. The fishing pole I'd been provided by my father (of course I didn't bait my own hook, that would have meant touching a worm) – had slipped from my vinyl grasp. It was sinking, tip down, into the green water on its way to "Davy Jones Locker" at the bottom of Houghton Lake (the sinkers on the line outweighed the bobber.)

It is at moments like this that one desperately imagines they can make themselves, or the situation, "invisible." I stayed quiet and wondered if anyone, especially my father, would ever notice? My brother and sister, in their own frigid misery, either didn't notice the mishap or chose not to rat me out.

Who knows? Maybe there was a fish on the hook at the other end of that line. This is what I tried to tell my dad when, of course, he asked where my fishing pole was.

My father and I were not fishing at Elizabeth Park four decades later. Rather, we were sitting on a blufftop bench watching others with their tackle boxes casting lines into the river.

Just about 20 yards to our left, overlooking the river, was a young man who had created a romantic scene to the delight of a woman who'd just joined him. They sat on a large blanket amidst a catered dinner surrounded by candles and flowers with gentle music playing quietly and softly.

It was a beautiful scenario in the twilight.

But the sweet scene took place in the twilight of my father's life. He'd just been diagnosed with Cancer – a Cancer he was told might spare two more years of his life.

"It is a good idea to get your affairs in order," the oncologist at the University of Michigan Hospital told him.

My father and I sat on the bench talking about this and that while he puffed a cigar – and why the hell not?

"Don't tell your mother."

"I won't."

We faced east and the sky, at the western edge of the eastern time zone, was a combination of purple, pink and orange.

"I have had a good life," he blurted out. (It always seemed somehow easier for him to be philosophical with a cigar in his hand looking at water. The only thing missing was the Jameson Irish Whiskey he often sipped with the stogie.)

I was happy to hear him say this. It was a gift. And then he continued.

"Yeah, I had three good kids and you all turned out alright. I never really had any trouble with any of you."

The statement revealed his true priority.

I knew this was a generous exaggeration, also, because most of any trouble he had with his children was with me.

My mother did get the worst of me once, at only pre-school age, and it had to do with Elizabeth Park. My pre-school, or nursery school as it was known then, scheduled a field day at the end of the school year.

The picnic day of partying, pony rides, sack races, ice cream and balloon tosses was scheduled to take place in Elizabeth Park. Whether the school heavily promoted the event or not, probably no other student anticipated the day more than me. I could barely sleep the night before.

The sandman must have sent me some winks, though, because I awakened to the sound of a spring rainstorm lashing my bedroom window. The next sound I heard was the absence of my mother's voice. Typically, at that early hour, she would have been urging me to get up, brush my teeth, wash my face and get dressed.

This time, the dawn silence was deafening.

But there would be plenty of noise – from me – when she eventually told me the rain had washed away my wishes. There would be no field day. This was a development I vociferously refused to accept for hours. It was a development I did not understand. Why not go forward with it?

It was also the morning an inconsolable little boy, who would grow up to be a writer, learned the distinction between the definitions of "postpone" and "cancel."

One morning, as a fully-grown adult, I was walking along the river from my mother's apartment in Trenton Towers to the Elizabeth Park boardwalk.

It's about one mile each way through the leafy neighborhood, over one of the park's fanciful bridges and down to the end of the boardwalk where a fence separates the park from the marina along the Grosse Ile Bridge.

The sun was out on a Sunday morning as I slipped through the sidewalks' occasional shade. I was about to pass an apartment building on my left when I would see a woman emerging from her car which she'd parked along the curb on the street.

The woman was walking from the car on an angle toward the apartment building, on a course that would intersect and pass by me as I continued along the sidewalk. There was plenty of room for both of us as at mid-morning we were the only two on the street.

Without altering my steps my navigation proved accurate. The woman passed me without a word or look. I too passed her, without a peep.

Passing so closely without even acknowledging each other was a split-second decision on both our parts.

My excuse? As a man, I felt I should defer to her and follow her lead and anticipate her body language so as not to seem intimidating to her alone on a street – even in the flash of passing. I felt immediate remorse, though. I should have at least nodded.

The fact that she chose to pass me without any acknowledgment was not terribly surprising. It stopped short of being disappointing – more like something I shrug off.

Never breaking stride, I continued south along the street.

And then...

I heard a woman's voice well behind me break the Sunday silence.

"I'm sorry," she said, in a plaintive tone.

I turned to look back without stopping my slow stroll.

"Good morning," she then offered, as she made her way toward the apartment driveway.

"Hey, thanks," I replied. "Good morning to you in this sunshine! That was sweet of you."

Just as I felt a tinge of awkward regret for ghosting past another human being, so, apparently, did the woman. She may have been very busy but had the dignity to correct her mistake of omission before I did. For this, I salute her. I imagine her inner dialogue was similar to mine:

"Oh, I should have said 'hello.' That wasn't right. I feel badly. Oh, I can still correct it. But now it's awkward. Should I do it anyway? I have to – I won't feel right unless I do. I mean, I could just go on with my day and eventually, I will forget about it. But I am not that kind of person. Oh, here goes!"

Then "I'm sorry," spilled out.

Hopefully, my body language in response sent her the message: "I know, I know. I felt the same way and I should have said 'hello,' too."

The late Catholic priest Father Jake Foglio, a New Yorker who spent much of his life at Michigan State University, preached, gently, that one should never walk past another person without offering some kind of acknowledgment. "You don't have to be animated when you say 'hi,' but you at least have to nod or give a little wave," he insisted.

He also felt a simple smile was powerful.

The woman walking near Elizabeth Park reinforced a few life lessons for me that morning:

Never pass another person without at least a nod or smile, if not a wave or the word "hello."

It is never too late to correct a mistake of manners or politeness – even if it feels awkward.

The other person might be feeling just as uncertain as you about greeting you. Go first!

27

NASHVILLE HOT LICKIN'

 On my first visit to Nashville, the 'Music City' transported me back in time and across America as the melodies and spirited live performances gave lift to the lyrics. Listening with a longneck of Bud Light as a sunny afternoon slipped away my imagination drifted to destinations mentioned.

"I saw miles and miles of Texas," sang Wendy Newcomer, decked in a skirt and satin western top on stage with the band at Robert's Western World – the classic country, historic honky-tonk. I took a sip and recalled a recent 10-hour-drive from San Antonio to El Paso across a barren moonscape of miles. My first stop in El Paso was Rosa's Cantina – memorialized in the Marty Robbins gunfighter ballad "El Paso," where of course they played the hit song often.

Getting behind the wheel the next morning I cued up Glen Campbell's "By the Time I Get to Phoenix," so I smiled when I saw the Glen Campbell Museum that day in Nashville, too.

Music can be life's soundtrack, coincidentally or not, and so sometimes the tunes can bring back, shall we say, less ebullient memories.

Lyrics like George Strait being exiled to Tennessee because "all his exes live in Texas; or, to again speak locally while in Nashville, when Waylon Jennings sang "T for Texas; T for Tennessee" about the "no-good woman who made a wreck of me" and drove him out of Atlanta.

Merle Haggard implored the listener to "tell him something bad about Tulsa" so he won't go back to face an old love.

And where was "Lucille" going when she "picked a fine time to leave" Kenny Rogers? Was she "Eastbound and Down" like Jerry Reed sang?

When it comes to melancholy melodies do the songs provoke feelings? Or...is it moods that give birth to the music?

"Both," said Jay McDowell of the Musicians Hall of Fame and Museum in Nashville. "Art allows that for us. It's personal and different for each of us going through it or listening. The singers we turn to for those feelings help us express our feelings."

Nashville-based songwriter Jenn Schott penned, for Mickey Guyton, one of Billboard Magazine's 10 Best Country Songs of 2015 which included the lyric: "You said 'goodbye' with words cold as ice I was shaking watching you go. I couldn't breathe. I just couldn't see past you leaving me here all alone..."

Schott sat, strumming her guitar, telling me about how she co-wrote "Better Than You Left Me" with another songwriter Jennifer Hanson and Guyton herself.

"The day Jennifer and I wrote that song we had never met Mickey before. Mickey came in and sat down and said, 'You're never going to believe what's going on in my life.' For the next 30 minutes she shared her heart with us," Schott revealed. "Mickey was a genuine, open-book and while she was telling us all of that we ended up writing Better Than You Left Me in about 90 minutes."

Schott described it as a "song of strength" that was cathartic for Guyton. "The hope of a songwriter is to write something that is true to the singer and resonates."

Upon hearing the story, I told Schott, "God forbid you write a song about the details of my life!"

"Truth is usually much better than fiction," Schott goaded me back.

As she strummed her guitar, I thought about what Schott had written "Feel It in the Morning" for Rascal Flatts; and "Two Lanes of Freedom," the title track on Tim McGraw's Grammy-nominated album. This was a once in a lifetime moment with songwriting royalty, so I dropped my embarrassment and decided to give it a shot.

"Let's write a song about me real fast," I suggested.

Schott, with long, very light brown hair, wearing blue jeans, a white sweater, and an olive-colored quilted coat, took a swig of her decaf coffee and played along. I, ala Mickey Guyton, then spilled a few personal points to her:

"Married four times...vagabond who lives on the road a bit...radio performer...is that enough?"

"I already know the title," she chimed.

"You do?!"

"I do: "Four Wheels Four Wives.""

It was savant-like as if she'd performed a magic trick. Then she began to play the guitar and sing the brand-new song:

"Four wheels...four wives...four dozen roses...

Good car...good life...I don't know where the road goes..."

I asked Schott how she did that?

"Being here in Nashville you get schooled in the craft. I learn every single day – even after 22 years," explained Schott who also performs at The Listening Room and Bluebird Café.

I don't know if she will move forward with "Four Wheels Four Wives" but maybe there will be a Grammy Award in Schott's future with it – courtesy of my country song-style life.

During my day wandering Nashville her melody and lyrics for Four Wheels Four Wives played over and over in my head as did some of the destinations I visited with those four former spouses (two blondes and two brunettes). Honeymoons, vacations and getaways played like retrospective music videos: Nassau and New York City; Ireland; Bermuda and the Big Island; Kauai and London for instance. Each of those places has music which conjures up memories of them – as do the brides I'd traveled with.

But on this day, I kicked up my heels and then put my heels up at Nashville's new Hyatt Centric Downtown, a flashy, fun, high-rise hotel which, as the name describes, is in the center of the action - as is Nashville itself.

"'Music City' is within 500 miles of 50-percent of the U.S. population," said Hyatt Centric sales director Bret Hoffman, who pointed out that the hotel's welcoming lobby mimics a living room in the South. A close look reveals the wallpaper is subtly pattered with Tennessee State bird – a fact you can confirm at the nearby Tennessee State Museum. "Our staff will point you to Nashville's hot spots."

The vision and drive of developer Michael Hayes put the music and art-filled Hyatt Centric within walking distance to the Country Music Hall of Fame; revered Ryman Auditorium; concerts and hockey games at Bridgestone Arena; Titans football games; Hattie B's Hot Chicken, and Broadway – Nashville's neon answer to the Las Vegas's glowing "Glitter Gulch."

But music, not gambling, is the name of the game here where Broadway's bustling buffet of all-day live entertainment is served up family-style.

My standout scene was a father and daughter dancing the afternoon away in front of the rooftop band at a big bar called Lucky Bastard. I am sure he felt like one...and I'm certain his little girl will never forget the fun.

Another vivid visual is seeing sidewalks full of performers pulling musical instruments all over town like cowboys slinging six-shooters.

"My guitar centers me...and this is my good luck guitar - it's one that got some of my music recorded," Schott had told me while strumming the strings of that beauty that also created hits for music stars Billy Ray Cyrus, Pam Tillis, and more.

Tap your toe to classic country music in Robert's Western World or step into sprawling show bar restaurants with open-air and rooftop patios founded by Kid Rock, Jason Aldean, Blake Shelton, Miranda Lambert, Luke Bryan, and Dierks Bentley. Also, don't forget the no-frills "honky-tonks" like time-honored Bluebird Café; Redneck Riviera; and Winners and Losers (the bar Toby Keith sang about loving in the lyric of his hit song.)

The depth and quality of musicians playing all day long with no cover charge is astonishing – but bring a pocket full of cash because you will be inspired (and encouraged) to tip these top-class performers. And God bless the beauties sporting spirited Southern and Western wear. Nashvillians, though, without dampening your ardor, would have visitors know locals don't wear cowboy boots...even though you can buy three-for-one (that's pairs, not boots) at shoe shops on Broadway.

"There is a perception that Nashville is all 'boots and leather,'" Hoffman admitted, "but it's called 'Music City,' not 'Country Music City.'" It's now a clean, youthful, fresh, stylish and slick city.

You can get your weathered, downhome fix at the Johnny Cash; Patsy Cline; and Glen Campbell Museums. Plus, of course, the Grand

Ole Opry House (20 minutes from downtown) for a great backstage tour or another historic (since 1925) performance.

"It's overwhelming. When you walk down Broadway you hear all different types of live music surrounding you and coming from every direction," said McDowell. "It is exciting to see music stars come into the Musicians Hall of Fame and Museum and be fans. I do get starstruck. Aritmus Pyle, who survived the Lynyrd Skynyrd plane crash, came in yesterday. Graham Nash has been by. I gave Don Everly a tour once. In Nashville you might see Taylor Swift dining across the room."

First timers – start with "medium" spiciness anywhere you try Nashville Hot Chicken (for decades the city's official food) and then work your way up according to Jim Myers, who serves a version of the authentic Prince's Hot Chicken Shack original recipe at his charming Elliston Place Soda Shop. "The hot sauce and cayenne will burn you from here to tarnation."

Did you just hear ..." hunka hunka burnin' love..." or "...ring of fire..." in your head?

28

NINE BRIDGES TO KOREAN CULTURE

Jeju Island is a resort destination below the Korean Peninsula. There I was on the veranda of Nine Bridges Golf Club, following a round at what then was a new course on the island. The club was ultra-exclusive, with a $500,000 membership fee.

So fancy were the various buildings and adjacent villas that the service elements were below ground and connected by tunnels. None of the members or guests ever saw a kitchen, or an office, or any rubbish whatsoever. Instead of a halfway house, the golf course had two elaborate stone buildings after each six holes so golfers could sit and enjoy invigorating fruit drinks, Soju whiskey, sushi or even shark fin soup.

Fellow golf writer Evan Rothman and I had just had the honor of playing golf with the club president – a Korean man they affectionately called "Georgie." At the seventh hole, we noticed a large, tarantula-like spider walking across the green. Georgie, nonplussed but with little hesitation, walked over to the spider and stood over it. Then he pulled his pointed divot-repair tool from his pocket, and, like a Ninja Warrior throwing a Chinese star, whipped the divot tool down with a quick flick of his wrist. The pointy tines of the tool went right through the center of the spider!

Evan and I, standing next to each other, went slack jawed at the impressive, deadly accurate feat. We watched as Georgie then picked up the tool and turned it upside down at eye level to examine the spider. It's eight little legs were wiggling like crazy.

I grabbed Evan by the arm in horror: "He's not going to eat it, is he!?"

Georgie flung the wounded spider into the nearby jungle of trees, and we played on.

Evan left Georgie and me with the American public relations woman, Ann Victor, on the veranda following the round. Georgie's English was very broken, but we managed to communicate. We were having drinks, and I was feeling very internationally cosmopolitan learning about Korean culture and geopolitical policy issues concerning the "Hermit Kingdom" of North Korea. Once again, in the exotic setting, I felt like "Bond, James Bond."

Georgie changed the topic from politics and, sitting up straight, asked me in a growling voice: "You...shower?"

"What's that?" I asked in return.

"You shower?"

"Uh. Yes, sir. I do. I do shower."

"Then you....shower with me!" he exclaimed.

I froze. And I looked at Ann Victor, who'd taken me there as a journalist.

"Ann," I said, giving her intense eyes, "there must be something lost in translation?"

She just shrugged.

"We go," Georgie said, pointing at the clubhouse "Shower!"

"Ann?" I said, as he led me away from the table. I was trying to play it cool, and be a polite guest, but walked up the stone steps with trepidation through the garden.

"I think you should be honored," I heard Ann offer from back at the table, her voice trailing away from behind. "He wants to show you the club."

The main clubhouse at the top of the hill was the size of a stately, small hotel and had a Zen-like, Far East quality to it. I tried to relax.

Once in the door, instead of turning toward the locker rooms, Georgie turned left, leading us through a special door. Based on what I began to observe, Nine Bridges Golf Club had two locker room areas: a smaller one for guests; and an elaborate, expansive private one for its executive members.

Still feigning sophistication, I kept my eyes closely on Georgie because no one else was around that afternoon at the exclusive enclave. Inside the locker room's spa facilities, Georgie gestured for me to undress.

"Shower now," he said, handing me a tiny Korean bath towel, which was about the size of a face cloth!

I tried to cover up with my fig leaf of a towel. I am sure it looked silly when we moved, without clothing, to a large, peaceful atrium with three, large square Jacuzzi tubs cut into the slate floor. The room had floor-to-ceiling windows which let in natural light from the verdant forest surrounding this wing of the clubhouse.

Surely there was some Asian ritual to be followed, but I hopped in the closest reflecting pool to me and got below the water level as fast as I could. Then George took his time climbing in. From the far side of the Jacuzzi, I tried not to look.

"George," I said, trying to send a signal, "I notice you have an all-female caddie corps here. They are all sweet and gorgeous. And cute, too, carrying their 'Hello Kitty' handbags."

I was completely uncertain as to whether Georgie understood my signal, or anything I said in English, since he merely threw his head back and laughed and smiled.

"Do you know 'man's gold?" he asked.

"Man's gold?"

"Yes, man's gold what is? You know?"

I slowly shook my head "no."

Georgie then tried to explain to me, in his broken English. I was able to glean, from his tale, that Korean men stand naked in cold streams first thing in the morning to enhance virility.

"Man's gold," he said again, standing and displaying how the men dip their testicles up and down below the surface of the water.

I wish I could have seen the expression on my own face. As for Georgie, he once again threw his head back and laughed!

29

MILAN'S DUOMO DREW ME IN

 Hotfooting it under a time constraint, I could not wait in a long line of tourists queuing to enter the dramatic Duomo di Milano, so I decided I would enter by attending Mass the next morning – when there is no line or entrance fee to enter the world's fourth-largest cathedral. With much more patience than I had, the soaring Duomo was built over six centuries beginning in 1386.

Thanks to the trusted advice of IC Bellagio.com, Italy's top custom, personal tour designer, I was staying right around the corner in the city center off the piazza in a former palazzo now known as the Park Hyatt Milan.

I checked the posted Mass schedule outside the Duomo and planned to return for 7:15 Mass the next morning. I then spent the remainder of the evening checking out Milan's fashion scene, eating arancini and drinking Peroni Nastro Azzurro at street side cafes. My day culminated by luxuriating in the steam room and heavenly, candle-lit soak tub of the Park Hyatt's soulful spa. (The Hyatt's concierge also managed to procure for me the most elusive ticket in town: a viewing of Leonardo da Vinci's 15th century mural "The Last Supper.")

The 7:15 am Mass came early. I had to delay enjoying the Park Hyatt's elaborate breakfast buffet (included with the room) in La Cupola under a 30-foot glass dome in order to get around the corner to Mass. I discovered all the main front doors of the cathedral were sealed, though.

The historic Duomo's massive footprint covers more than a city block, so by the time I found the small, open door around the building's backside and made my way through the vastness to creep up to the elevated back altar – I was very late for Mass. And my rubber shoe sole squeaked with every step on the marble floor which disrupted the small group of worshippers gathered. (I know because they all turned their heads to look.)

When I finally found a pew I heard the Lord's Prayer, which comes late in the Mass, was already being recited. That's when I realized my mistake – the Mass, for which I was already late, had started at 7 a.m. not 7:15. (Arriving when I did was like turning on Star Wars after the light saber fight.)

Mass, which was spoken in Italian, ended quickly, so I decided to stay and wander the now empty Duomo. The Mass-goers were gone and the tourists had not yet been allowed in. I gazed at the 40 gothic columns supporting the ceiling 148 feet above which covered the sculpted statues, compelling works of art, and relics – including a nail from the crucifixion – below it.

The Duomo's design has been controversial: Mark Twain liked it, but Oscar Wilde didn't. I, full of solemn wonder, had the place to myself and was snapping photos until an attendant seemed to come from nowhere and took his turn snapping...at me: "No photo, per favore. No!"

Embarrassed yet again I began to sulk toward the exit. The sunrise light was streaming through the 68-foot, colored stained-glass windows. But it was a tiny green light way back in one of the empty side altars which caught my eye. When I got close to investigate, I realized it was one of the old-fashioned signal lights over an ornate, wooden, phone booth-sized confessional box. I admired the craftsmanship by peeking into the darkness behind the curtain...but was then startled by a sound coming from inside.

"Pronto," a little voice called out. "Pronto."

My Duolingo app study of remedial Italian had taught me "pronto" means "ready." Someone sensed I was there, so I felt compelled to respond and enter the box. Once inside I found myself kneeling in front of a window face to face with an old, Italian priest. It'd been two years since I'd done this, so I began wobbly reciting the customary formulaic recitation of, "Forgive me, Father, for I have sinned...."

The white-haired priest stopped me, gently, and asked me, with a shrug and a heavy accent, "Please-a...speak slowly. My English is, eh...."

In the subsequent confession of my sins, I spoke as much Italian as I could manage – and the priest conveyed his inspirational message of reconciliation effectively in his broken English.

"I have been missing Sunday Mass," I confessed.

"Why?"

"Dormie," I offered, hoping that he'd get my meaning that it was merely out of laziness.

"Why are you here now then?"

"Well...I would like to, eh, 'reconnect.'"

The priest nodded. Then he spoke, again in deliberate, broken English – each word slowly and carefully chosen individually with no cadence. He looked in my eyes with each word as if to check if I understood his meaning. "God is very patient. He is waiting for you. He will not go anywhere without you. You see?"

"Si, padre. Grazie."

"Eh, you must think of Mass as if you are making an appointment with a lover. Meeting with a lover would be very important to you, so you would make an appointment, yes?"

"Si," I nodded, though I suspected I was turning red.

"On Wednesday maybe plan ahead as to when you will attend Mass on Sunday. Make it an appointment."

It seemed simple enough and heartfelt.

At the end he gave me a card and instructed me to read the "Act of Contrition" aloud in Italian, which we did, with him guiding me, together.

"L'atto di contrizione... Oh mio Dio, mi dispiace davvero..."

It was a divine duet.

And with that, my sins, even being late for Mass in squeaky shoes and snapping forbidden photos (among others) were forgiven.

I emerged from the confessional box touched and surprised. Upon reflection, which the Duomo easily inspires, I became amazed at the chain of events which steered me to that solitary moment.

I misunderstood the Mass time and, because I was extra late after initially being unable to find an open door, I lingered longer in other areas of the huge but empty cathedral (instead of hustling back to the Park Hyatt's breakfast.) It was then and there I "saw the light" (the green one) and "heard the calling" ("pronto.") Coincidence? You decide.

30

BOND VILLAIN AND LIFEGAURD PRINCESS

Actors who actually live in and around Hollywood, California are accustomed to seeing tour vehicles driving people past the "stars' homes". These are tours that originate from the Walk of Fame area near Hollywood's iconic Chinese Theater. Those vacationers have chosen to visit Tinseltown and see the big screen scene, where they might also be part of a studio audience for the taping of a game show or sitcom.

Sometimes performers are sent to shoot films on location. Sir Michael Caine, for instance, reportedly agreed to appear in the low-brow "Jaws 4" in part because it was filming in the Bahamas. Though he earned good money for the role, sadly, Caine paid the price of being presented with an Academy Award in absentia for an earlier film back in Hollywood while he was stuck on set.

Caine was in the process of moving from Los Angeles to London.

London is a favorite location for Famke Jansen, who appeared in a 007 movie and the "Taken" and "X-Men" films.

"I love London. I'd like to make that my second home," Jansen told me, via phone, from her home in New York City. "I love traveling. I am a nomad and have been wandering my whole life. It would be hard to tie me down and keep me in one place."

Visitors to London can jump into 007's world privately or in a group through various walking and bus tours. The Langham Hotel's front entrance stood in as the Casino de Monte Carlo in "Goldeneye," for instance. Jansen's menacing character played the card game chemin de fer against Pierce Brosnan's James Bond in the scene.

The film "Goldeneye" used London's Somerset House, on the Strand, to represent St. Petersburg, Russia.

Bond's creator Ian Fleming lived in Mayfair, and while some make a pilgrimage to his home there, it is more fun to visit the Dukes London Hotel and have a vodka martini – shaken, not stirred. This is where Fleming drank and crafted Bond's preferred tipple (which was actually "stirred, not shaken," in his books.) The Vesper is also on the cocktail menu at Duke's.

007's distinctive MI6 British Secret Service headquarters is plainly visible, and reasonably approachable, along the River Thames.

Jansen's roles have found her filming on-location in Cape Town, Istanbul, Malibu, Monaco and more. Some of her other "Bond villain" scenes in "Goldeneye" were set in Cuba but filmed in Puerto Rico.

"I did a DNA test and I have a little bit of Irish in me. I love the Irish," said Jansen, who starred with Irishmen Pierce Brosnan as 007 and Liam Neeson in "Taken." Brosnan and Neeson played action heroes in those films and their sequels. Jansen played Zenia Onatop with Brosnan's James Bond and Lennie, the wife of security specialist Neeson's Bryan Mills.

"Taken" fans can easily visit the Malibu Pier, the Pacific Ocean setting near Los Angeles for Jansen and Neeson in the "Taken 2" and "Taken 3" films. The white dual-towers of the 780-foot pier, along the Pacific Coast Highway, have been recognizable since they were built in 1905.

Jansen's family, at the end of the film, had milkshakes on the end of the pier at Ruby's Shake Shack, which is now called Malibu Farm Pier Café.

I asked Jansen which of her two Irish action co-star heroes – 007 or Mills, was more formidable?

"I'm not sure either of them could handle Xenia or Lennie...or Famke, for that matter," was her plucky, confident answer. "I like Pierce and Liam both personally, so I don't want anyone to be mad that I picked the other. Liam is taller, so we'll give him that."

Jansen's, striking, fearsome character, Xenia Onatop, was a Russian spy who raced 007 in dueling sportscars on the winding roads above Monaco by day and attempted to outplay the tuxedoed British agent in the Casino de Monte-Carlo by evening. By night, she tried to strangle the by-then-naked 007 in the steam room by crunching his midsection with her thighs.

"Reading that script, knowing that is what I was going to have to do, was interesting," Jansen recalled. "I wondered...how do I train? How strong do my thighs have to be? It was a fun journey."

Onatop didn't kill 007, but there were, in the film, other victims of her, shall we say, Venus Fly Trap. Did those memorable, lethal, erotic scenes affect her dating life?

"I am sure some people have strange ideas about me personally as a result of it. I have been spared that expectation...or at least people haven't been honest about it. It was a fun character, and I am grateful for it and what it did for me, said Jansen.

"I was a Bond girl and know there is a lot of stigma that comes with being one. I turned it around for myself in my own journey. You take in life whatever opportunities you can get and try to make the best out of that."

What does an empowered woman like Jansen think of 007 under the modern, "me too" misogynist microscope?

"The 'Bond' genre has been out of date for a long time but they've been so clever in constantly reinventing themselves. At some point we'll probably see a female Bond...so we'll have 'Bond boys.'"

I spoke to globe-trotter Jansen cross-country via telephone. Emmy-nominated TV star Brooke Burns took my call from across town in the Los Angeles area.

"I stay within my five-mile radius of picking my kids from school," laughed Emmy-nominated TV star Brooke Burns, who appeared on "Baywatch" and "Melrose Place," two hit shows set near her home in the Los Angeles area. She said she likes to hike the area's scenic canyons and trails. "The weather here in Los Angeles is often beautiful so I like to be outside in God's nature."

Despite her hometown girl-next-door image, the actress had her "Grace Kelly moment" when she married the son of the Australian Prime Minister.

Burns also remembers traveling to Detroit to tape the finale of the series "Motor City Masters," a show about car designers. "I remember the local food. We ate very well. It was my first time visiting there and I did a little tour on the sky train for the birds-eye-view," said Burns, referring to a ride on the People Mover. "There were sections of the city where you could see there had been struggles, but it was great to see the city coming back to life."

Since Burns' Detroit visit, the city has become a very popular tourist destination. In a previous era, the Motor City was known as the "Paris of the Midwest." In recent years, a number of its architecturally significant buildings, which have gone into disrepair or even abandoned, have been restored and repurposed, which has brought revitalization the Detroit.

Shinola Hotel, named for the popular Detroit-based watch company of the same name that has become a badge of honor for those supporting the city, is a stylish, Mad Men-era, beauty with, of course, a watch shop in it.

The Foundation Hotel was created inside a former fire station, and the architects were careful to keep the big fire doors which now open to the street in the summer for gourmet alfresco dining in what used to be the firetruck garage.

With its gilded grandeur, Book Tower is like stepping back in time...until you check into one of its extended-stay apartments at "The Roost". They are bright, with blonde-wood floors, contemporary furniture, and straight-edged, modern luxury.

The former WWJ AM radio station has become a Cambria Hotel, which left touches and memorabilia of the golden age broadcasting studios intact.

It's as if Detroit has emerged from a decades-long coma.

Burns, herself, had to perform a Lazarus act and resurrect herself more than once. She survived a car crash, a swimming-diving accident and a snow skiing wipeout.

"I live life enthusiastically. It is true. I have had some accidents in my life, including a near-death experience when I broke my neck in my swimming pool. That was pretty extreme. I had a friend with me who was a paramedic, so he saved my life and mobility," Burns explained.

"I am one of those people that when I wake up and can put two feet on the ground, I am a grateful person. Grateful to be alive."

The lucky Burns has hosted TV game shows "Dog Eat Dog;" and "Master Minds.

31

BEVERLY HILLS BLONDE

 Thursday nights, June through August, the city of Beverly Hills, California presents "Concerts on Canon," from 6-8 pm. The free shows take place on a stage under the sky in Beverly Canon Gardens. It's a manicured, fanciful, 33,000-square-foot public courtyard beside the understated, luxurious Maybourne Hotel.

The gardens connect Canon and Beverly Drives. The water features, fountains, flowers, trees, and sculptures make the space a lovely place to "hang." Plus, there is a public parking underground garage (first two hours free), restrooms and both high-end and affordable food options.

Almost daily I will see people playing chess, groups of older men playing a dice game, or people reading in the gardens. I sometimes bring my laptop computer and write amidst the plants and people.

The architecture and lighting surrounding the gardens are both fanciful and stately. The pink, script eight-foot tall, three-dimensional

"Beverly Hills Beautiful" sign at the Beverly Drive entrance, as a photo spot, is a must for anyone who comes to town.

I walked through the "Golden Triangle" of Beverly Hills. This includes Rodeo Drive, to the Beverly Canon Gardens on a partly sunny Thursday evening in early June. My aim was to enjoy whatever type of music would be performed that evening. It didn't really matter to me who the performers were - I was there for the tunes and the fresh air. Plus, exquisite, eclectic people watching.

The window shopping along my walk – which, when I looked through the big glass windows of the Four Seasons Beverly Wilshire's THE BLVD meant "people watching" - added to the entertainment. Blocks and blocks of street-front restaurants such as Wolfgang Puck's Spago; Avra; Il Pastaio; Nate 'n Al; Wally's; and many more lively spots are sprinkled in the see-and-be-seen scene.

As for shopping, Gucci; Tom Ford; Prada; Hermes; House of Bijan – with its yellow Rolls Royce parked out front; and 100 designer line the blocks. Don't confuse Jimmy Choo with Mr. Chow or the Mr. C Hotel!

The Beverly Hills Courier, published weekly in print and online, is an excellent local information source, as the Beverly Hills Experience free mobile app presented by the Beverly Hills Historical Society.

Beverly Hills, Los Angeles, and all of coastal Southern California experience an annual weather condition described as "May Gray" and "June Gloom:" two months of almost never seeing the sky or sun.

I am certain I was suffering from a So Cal seasonal affective disorder on the evening in early June when I wandered over to the "Concert on Canon."

The sunken garden sprawled out before me as I decided where to sit. Some sit along the colonnade under the balconies at tables with food and drink service. These seats are like the "luxury suites" for the concerts. Others sit on folded chairs placed on the grass in front of the stage. Some, like the woman in the red hat who chased her three small children around, unfold blankets on the grass picnic-style. Some just stand and stroll.

I chose to stretch out near the stage on the concrete steps and used the top step as a back support. It was only minutes before the concert, which turned out to be "Linda and Friends – a Ronstadt and Laurel Canyon 1970's Rock Review," was to begin.

I sat in solitude and let my eyes stroll the scene – people watching the elegant and eclectic people who turned up or passed through. One of the most intriguing was striking: a smiling man in a buttoned-up trench coat and fedora hidden behind dark sunglasses. He looked like Dick Tracy and seemed harmlessly cartoonish. Nevertheless, I kept an eye on him.

Lounging among the lavish I had my own little space on the steps surrounded by the beautiful people.

The musicians were in position. The lead singer stood on the side of the stage about to be introduced by someone I presumed to be a city official who was approaching the microphone.

But it was not the official's voice I heard next.

"Do you mind if we sit here, too?"

I swiveled my head and looked up to see it was a seriously beautiful blonde who had asked me the question. She had long hair, perfect makeup and was dressed nicely but appropriately in summer white. And was accompanied by what appeared to be her mother, who was also fashionable. They were the type of women seas part for.

I was taken aback because there was plenty of space along the step both beside and below me. The blonde woman did not need to ask me if she and her mother could sit there, but she did, anyway.

The gesture struck me as exceedingly polite. And maybe her way of saying hello was to ask, "Do you mind if we also sit here?"

"I would be lucky if you did." I responded with a smile.

She smiled back, and they both sat down.

There was not much else to say, especially since the pleasantries between us and on stage gave way to the music. I think it was a song by the Eagles, maybe?

The blonde was to my left, meaning that when we all looked at the stage, she and her mother were looking on an angle away from me.

But she surprised me again at the conclusion of the first song when she turned back to me.

"It's nice music, right?"

"It's nice music and a very nice setting," I answered.

Our random proximity became a bit of a communal affair – we just happened to be sitting next to each other.

After the next song finished, I felt like it was my turn to say something to her.

"...Of course, I'm too young to remember any of these songs from the 1970s."

She laughed and shrugged. I resisted any temptation to make any reference to her age – or her mother's.

I stayed for another half an hour listening to the tunes and the set-ups by the lead singer. When she began to introduce the band members individually between two of the songs, I applauded and then decided it was time to move on.

To be courteous, I tapped the blonde lightly on the shoulder as I stood so she could see I was leaving.

"Thank you for being friendly," I told her.

Like everyone I say that to she seemed surprised. But the truth is I never take friendliness for granted.

"Safe home," I said, stepping away.

Her stare then caused me to pause for a beat. She gave me a very long look directly into my eyes – her expression seemed as if she were touched by my sentiment.

"You too," she said, very warmly, but purposefully and intently.

I walked off into the twilight having enjoyed the music, the setting, the fresh air and the human connection with a woman who no doubt gets her share of head-turned attention in any room she graces.

I found her to be an angelic woman and daughter.

She was part of my "Midsummer Nights"

32

MISSING VUE ORLEANS

 I looked up during the entire short walk across the street from my luxury lodging at Loews New Orleans Hotel over to Vue Orleans. A 34-story view of the Loews Hotel, Mississippi River, French Quarter, Superdome, Canal Street, Garden District and other New Orleans landmarks awaited from a new, 34-story, indoor/outdoor deck.

"I am afraid of heights," I joked to the Vue Orleans docents after I toured my way through the colorful, musical ground-floor exhibits of the interactive attraction and eventually reached the elevator doors. You can safely describe Vue Orleans as "immersive." A major reason for that is the warm welcome and helpful presentations given by each of the staff docents I encountered along the way, such as the two I joked with at the elevator: Alexis and Crystal.

"Once you set foot in New Orleans you fall in love and you don't want to go back," said Alexis at the elevator reception stand outside the theater. "It was just one look into my eyes, and you got stuck. You fell in love with us."

"Is it that obvious?"

"You haven't stopped smiling since you started talking to us...and you're blushing."

"Guilty as charged. Should we get hitched?" I joked.

Crystal chimed, "I can be the witness!"

I confessed to the ladies I'd already been married four times.

"That's okay. Fifth time is the charm," Alexis laughed. "We can go to the chapel right now. Since you like New Orleans so much, we can have our honeymoon right here."

My fun and playful elevator entrance conversation with Alexis and Crystal, who are lifetime New Orleanians and were dressed in their uniform collared shirts and vests, continued.

"You know you've missed three elevators now," Crystal pointed out.

"I'm afraid of heights," I deadpanned.

Meanwhile Alexis was making "wedding night plans."

"We can go get a daquiri and crawfish to start the evening. After that we have to go get a drink somewhere."

"A drink after a drink?"

"Yep. There's no stopping alcohol here. It's five o'clock everywhere," she said with a wink and a smile before Crystal chimed in.

"Bourbon Street gets sticky. It gets stuck to your shoe and stuck to your heart. I have met a lot of people who came to visit and got stuck here. You can get immersed and stuck here in a good way," she warned. "Alexis and I are never leaving."

Alexis nodded and added, "The culture itself here is way different than anything you'll find anywhere. Different from Texas, Florida, Atlanta...you name it. We have our own culture."

Part of the culture is the aforementioned drinking and partying – and everything that comes with it. Street performers with snakes and costumed people and strings-of-bead-covered brides and drummers banging on buckets, to offer a few striking snapshots.

"I am not shocked by anything. It's New Orleans," Alexis stated. "Everywhere you go expect something crazy to come out."

Crystal countered, "Some things are amusing...and some are disturbing. Take Alexis, for instance. She practices voodoo."

"Don't say that! I do not!" Alexis protested. "People take voodoo bad but it's not. Some people can do good and some do bad with voodoo. I don't do either. I have a pure heart."

I asked Alexis and Crystal, who seemed to be authentic fonts of information, if it's hard to handle hurricanes that pass though the Big Easy?

"You have to get Hurricane snacks. Some popcorn and chips. Maybe make it classy with some wine," Alexis advised.

Crystal countered, "Before the storm charge up your devices. Download movies. And fill your bathtub up with water. You never know how long the power is going to be out. I overprepare by making sandwiches and such."

I eventually bid Alexis and Crystal adieu and went into the elevator which, in itself, is a show. The glass panels covering the walls, on the way up, provide a video presentation showing scenes of historical, vintage New Orleans. Thirty-four stories zoom by and the doors open to reveal two more stories. The first, an enclosed, 360-degree, windowed viewing floor with occasional video screens to caption what landmarks below you may be looking down over and out to the horizon.

A fun virtual game puts you in the pilot house and at the helm of a container ship. It tests your ability to steer the freighter through the tightest bend of the entire Mississippi River, the actual banks of which are visible below right out the nearby window.

There is also a banked video screen and seating area showing a brief film called "Rising Up: Black New Orleanians Leading the Nation in the Pursuit of Equal Rights."

One story up is the top floor: an open-air, glass-walled balcony – again 360-degrees – with a small café.

Unless you run into Alexa and Crystal like I did, you'll naturally be inclined to hurry to get through the main-level exhibits and onto the elevator to see the scenic panoramic payoff at the top at "Vue Orleans" from its' 34-story summit.

But New Orleans is a sensual town, so, resist temptation to finish too quickly and let Vue Orleans take you on a timed-entry, tantric, touchless trip through its colorful exhibits before you reach its climax.

The New Orleans food scene can also be described as decadent. While the main level exhibits serve as a starter to whet your appetite, and the observation tower is the main course, New Orleans itself is a dessert to dive into after you've learned about it and surveyed it from the sky.

"In New Orleans when you're eating breakfast you are wondering what you're going to have for lunch. At lunch you're thinking about dinner. During dinner you're discussing where to go for drinks," said Drew Mills, Food and Beverage Director for Loews Hotel, which can be prominently seen from above atop Vue Orleans.

But you wouldn't skip the turtle soup to get to the catfish at Commander's Palace Restaurant in the Garden District, so let's have a look at the Vue Orleans ground level exhibits – my favorite of which revolved around food.

"Story Café" is made to look like a diner counter where you can sit at the stools and view entertaining videos on the menu board by PBS Chef Kevin Belton and "Louisiana Eats" host Poppy Tooker. The exhibit plaque reads, "Find out why we eat red beans and rice on Mondays, king cake on Fat Tuesday, bananas Foster at Sunday brunch, and discover the story behind the dishes."

You can walk through and linger at similar interactive audio and visual participatory displays featuring local artwork presenting music, history and culture. You also have a chance to virtually "meet" legendary New Orleans figures such as Irma Thomas, the Preservation Hall Jazz Band, Henriette De Lisle, Giacomo Cusimano and Tillie Karnofsky.

If Vue Orleans ended there (and you exited through its' gift shop) the exhibit would be worthwhile and memorable. In truth, every docent staffer I met was very proud to present the exhibits and excited to engage me. I learned later they'd been hired based on their enthusiastic, special personalities. This friendly, welcoming, helpful element breathed true life and spirit into Vue Orleans.

Timed-entry tickets are $30.

Loews Hotel New Orleans is in the arts district just across Poydras Street from Vue Orleans which is at the foot of Canal Street, the wide thoroughfare which divides the city. I love Loews because its decor incorporates New Orleans architecture and history in music in tasteful, subtle ways. Its corner location, with large, ceiling to floor windows surrounding a lobby and restaurants keep guests connected to the city, its weather and its people.

As big as Loews is, it feels like a neighborhood hotel and is very close to everywhere you might wish to walk to – day or night. This includes the French Quarter, Natchez River Boat; Café du Monde; Saint Louis Cathedral; The National World War II Museum and Jefferson Square; Preservation Hall; Sazerac House; the Treme neighborhood and even the Superdome.

A long walk back from Lafayette Cemetery #1 in the Garden District deserves a liquid reward. Handcrafted cocktails can be found at

Loews' Bar Peters at the corner of Poydras and Peters. This is also the name of the hotel's American brasserie – where the Poydras Market stood for a decade beginning in 1838.

Vue Orleans, in one of New Orleans' most recognizable (if dated) high-rise buildings, is in plain sight from the upper-story guestrooms of Loews – making it a mutual admiration society.

I looked out an 11th story window in the Loews Hotel at part of the New Orleans skyline. To my left I could see the imposing, soaring shelter-like structure of the National World War II Museum. Down at street level I saw unsheltered people lined up in the light rain to get into Mother's – a no-frills, decades-old po' boy-jambalaya-red beans-and-rice restaurant on the corner across the street.

"I think they pay people to stand in line there," deadpanned Drew Mills when he saw me notice people waiting. Mills is the food and beverage director for Loews New Orleans Hotel.

"I ate there twice yesterday," I then confessed to him. And sensing a bit of competitiveness from Mills I asked him if it was difficult to be the chef at Loews – or any hotel – and its Peters at Poydras brasserie in a city with such compelling cuisine?

"No one comes to New Orleans to just stay in the hotel, so we get our guests started and end the night with them. And if it rains or something they're good," he admitted.

A week before my visit I'd heard television food critic Andrew Zimmern say New Orleans is the only city that, at the mere mention of its name, you can taste.

Even though he is in management, Mills loves pouring handcrafted cocktails in the hotel's comfortable, elegant bar on the spot where the Poydras Market stood.

"The bar is where I get to meet guests and find out what they're here for and where they want to go. When I can give people hints on where to go it's fun. New Orleans has its own personality," explained Mills. A number of classic cocktails were invented in New Orleans, but Mills insists, despite the uber-traditional simple dishes slung at Mother's Restaurant, the New Orleans food scene has evolved.

"The whole culinary background for New Orleans is a giant slow-moving cycle. It got very popular as a melting pot city. You had all kinds of demographics and cultures coming together and it became a food scene. But New Orleans cuisine has been recreated. The door is open now. There are no rules. Chefs are being as creative as they can."

I told Mills that, in addition to Mother's, I'd made pilgrimages to some of New Orleans oldest and most time-honored restaurants. These included Arnaud's; Napoleon House; Galatoire's (where I had to endure dining room-wide waitstaff singings of "Happy Birthday" to three different tables during the span of one meal); Commander's Palace and Antione's (1840).

"You can still hit the old spots but the new restaurants opening are refreshing. If you came here expecting everything covered in crawfish cream sauce you will be surprised to find even Asian influenced dishes and restaurants," he countered. "Creole food is being refined and the flavors cleaned up, but it scratches the itch for the dishes you remember."

In terms of culture Mills described New Orleans as the "Northern-most Caribbean City."

Due to its storm-ravaged, sometimes weathered, authentic condition, Mills calls New Orleans the "City that Care Forgot." But he never forgot The Big Easy.

"I know what it means to miss New Orleans," he said, invoking the lyrics of the famed droopy jazz ballad by the same title. "I lived in New York, and I moved to the Philippines and while I was there the only thing I could think about was coming home."

As difficult as it was to tear myself from the luxurious Loews, I left Mills and set out on foot for the day hoping to, James Joyce-style, come back later with a stream of consciousness head full of stories. New Orleans, of course, in all its historic, eccentric, musical glory, turned out to be a page-turner.

I started the day in the best possible way with a café au lait at Café Du Monde. With the coffee and a bag of three hot, crunchy beignets I found myself completely at ease in the covered, open-air patio under the green and white-striped awning between Jackson Square and the Mississippi River.

There was a sidewalk casual quintet pumping out jazz-versions of tunes such as "You Are My Sunshine." The music made my morning but annoyed some a type-A stress-ball with a red Ohio State shirt on who, right in front of his kids, barked at the attendant at the coffee stand. "This music is driving me crazy!"

He'd truly come to the wrong place, because "music" and "crazy" are two of the main reasons to come to New Orleans!

Everyone else was applauding the band...or were they trying to dust the white powdered sugar from the beignets off their hands. (There was a pile of powdered sugar left in the bottom of my beignet bag, which I poured into my coffee.)

When the clapping stopped one of the band members, holding a plastic bucket, shouted a rhyme:

"Applause is nice...but it doesn't get us beans and rice."

He was, in his funny way, reminding the crowd to tip the musicians.

"Don't forget Phillip...fill-up the bucket!"

The ragtag band struck up an instrumental while he went around the railing allowing people to toss pennies or pence into the pail.

They passed the basket, too, at my next stop: 9 a.m. Mass just across Jackson Square at the Cathedral-Basilica Saint Louis – the white, triple-steepled, iconic landmark. Masses were first celebrated on the site in 1718 and the current structure is America's oldest cathedral in continuous use.

After Mass in the gloriously decorated cathedral under its soaring ceiling and chandeliers, I chatted briefly with New Orleans Archbishop Emeritus Alfred Hughes.

"Your Excellency you know you are now sending the faithful out onto Bourbon Street and into one of the most tempting cities in America," I posited.

"It's always a challenge to speak the Gospel here in the French Quarter but it is what I am called to do. Even here inside the cathedral Satan can be at work in subtle ways trying to get ahold of us and feed our ego by tempting us to misuse the gifts of God," he warned.

How did he know my plans for the day?

"Well, it's all in the pursuit of experiential journalism," I justified to myself.

I then, myself, processed down Bourbon Street looking for just the perfect place to have my pre-noon first drink of the day. I passed the gate of civilized, gentrified Musical Legends Park, which I recommend as a very easygoing, open-air, family-friendly jazz listening experience among life-sized statues of legendary musicians.

Just a block from there a guy sat on the curb banging noisily on upside down plastic buckets as if they were a drum set. Of course, he had one bucket right-side up to collect tips from passersby. Who's to say what is "music," I suppose.

In order to evade the noise, and because it appeared to be a unique experience, I ducked into Jean Lafitte's Old Absinthe House. It was dark and quiet, the walls covered with thousands of business cards. I ordered a traditional Absinthe Frappe to find out if the worm-wooded, hallucinogenic "green fairy" might enhance my James Joyce "Dubliners" day in the French Quarter.

As the absinthe in my glass was just turning milky after soaking through the sugar cube spoon, I thought I was already hallucinating when a gentleman seated down the bar with his wife and another couple offered to pay for my $18 drink.

The resulting conversation revealed – again, maybe a hallucination – that the man was a Canadian from Houston who once drove Route 66 from Chicago to St. Louis in a 1950's-era car while wearing a zoot suit. (He showed me pictures on his phone to prove it unless they were also part of a hallucination?)

I began to feel as if I were in a movie. A sensation encouraged by the fact countless movies and television shows are filmed around New Orleans at any given time, according to Marybeth Romig, an assistant vice-president with New Orleans & Company, the city's tourism organization.

I had coffee with her in the Loews Hotel lobby as she was on her way to meet with the producers of the NBC Today Show to plan a live broadcast from Jackson Square featuring Jenna Bush and Hoda. It was a busy month for Romig. Mardi Gras had just finished and the NCAA Basketball's Final Four was on the way.

TV, movies, or not, I found constant amateur entertainment just walking the streets. Little pop-up bands played for tips on curbs and in doorways, and even individual soloists sang for their suppers. Each afternoon there was a rousing band in front of the cathedral that played until dark and wrapped up with an extended version of the requisite hit "When the Saints Go Marching In."

Just as they concluded, a "second line" wedding procession paraded around the corner and down the street dancing and cheering and whooping it up with a marching jazz band. I've never attended any wedding reception anywhere in which the guests had more fun than this moving wedding party.

Here's the kick – it was exactly like the jazz funeral procession I'd seen on the streets earlier in the day! The "mourners" held photo placards of the deceased and some had bouncing parasols over their heads as they danced and paraded down the streets between people with python snakes around their necks and iguanas on their shoulders offering selfies for money.

If you take your jazz seriously, take in a 45-minute, pure, profes-sional performance at tiny, hidden, historic Preservation Hall – the beating heart of New Orleans music. The intimate sessions run all day long with timed-entry tickets. Preservation Hall is like French Laundry in Napa where there is no artwork, flowers, or ambient music to distract from the food.

Preservation Hall is a no-frills, music appreciation listening expe-rience. It's like you've been allowed into a dilapidated laboratory to sneak a peek at master craftsmen preserving their art by sharing it.

Maison Bourbon bar is my favorite live jazz venue because it's on the corner which allows for people watching while listening to the Lee Floyd Band's banjos, drums, trumpets and Satchmo impressions. I ordered a Hurricane and settled on a stool.

In between songs, during a quick conversation with some people next to me, I mentioned the phrase "south of the border." Someone on the stage heard me, thought it was a request, and the quartet spontaneously struck up a bluesy version of the song South of the Border!

"I'd better be careful what I say," I joked.

When the band took a break, I asked Lee Floyd if that song was part of their repertoire?

"We've never played it before," he said.

I was astonished that with no advance warning and no conversation between them, they were able to perform that song, each playing their own instrument, from scratch.

After starting with absinthe, I decided I'd "drink for the cycle" that day and consume the cocktails New Orleans was famous for (not counting the giant daquiris sold at the countless chicken shacks throughout the French Quarter.)

At Dickie Brennan's Bourbon House – maybe the most beautiful bar and restaurant in New Orleans on the corner of Bourbon Street and Iberville – I tried a milk punch.

"What's a milk punch?" I asked the bartender.

"It's like a milkshake with bourbon," the bartender barked as if he wanted to milk punch me!

My own "research" revealed a milk punch has spicy brandy, bourbon, sugar, vanilla extract and creamy, cold milk.

I walked to Antoine's, the oldest restaurant in New Orleans, for a gin fizz – complete with an egg white mixed in - something I would likely not have occasion to drink anywhere outside New Orleans.

I sat for soup in the darker, big, back room (very different from the smaller, gentle, bright street-front entry room) with its walls full of generations of photos of celebrities who'd dined there. My server, a gentleman named Murphy Ruiz, had encountered some of them during the decades he worked at Antione's while his wife ran the wine cellar.

Murphy was training a new, also tuxedoed server named Megan who was nevertheless plucky and attentive. She already seemed to know her way around, and it turns out she should. She, as his daughter, was literally raised in the restaurant. Megan encouraged me to explore the wine cave and the rabbit warren of various private rooms

– one was once a jail. While I did so I met her "Uncle Skeeter," who has been working at Antione's for 40 years.

Having walked through the antique Court of Two Sisters very old, open-air dining space – known for its jazz brunch and turtle soup - I was looking for Fritzel's European Jazz Club on Bourbon Street. When almost in front of Sinners and Saints Restaurant, I met a young woman who, lord have mercy, smiled, handed me a card and asked me to come see her perform.

15 minutes later I found myself stage-side in Rick's Cabaret – one of, it seemed, Bourbon Streets more respectable, so-called "gentlemen's clubs." (I hardly think one can describe a strip bar named "Barely Legal" as a "gentleman's club.") But I digress. And I guess I confess, that at Rick's Cabaret I sipped a Bud Light and watched a woman named Billie (maybe) who danced around a pole.

Standard stuff for that type of entertainment until she managed, using the pole, to get herself about six feet up off the stage and, like a David Blaine levitation trick, seemed to be hovering in the air!

I finished that one, a quick beer and, on my way out, over by the bar, told Billie how amazing her dance was. Then I asked Billie how she did it?

She wouldn't reveal her secret, but Billie did tell me, "The trick is practice and confidence. I've only fallen twice."

She seemed proud of her talent and pleased that I'd noticed.

"New Orleans is different," she said. "We are all performers."

Back on Bourbon Street I met another performer of sorts – a trickster. He was amiable enough when he approached me and asked me, "Will you give me $20 if you tell me only your first name and I can then spell you last name? Only tell me your first name....and I will be able to spell your last name."

I don't know if I was tired or just enjoying the spirit of his enthusiasm, but I agreed.

"My first name is Michael. Now you're telling me from that you will be able to spell my last name?"

"Yes, Michael, I can," he nodded, and then continued: "y-o-u-r l-a-s-t n-a-m-e."

He was as proud of himself as Billie was, so I happily handed him the $20.

I succumbed to one more guilty pleasure that evening. I had been out all day and into the night exploring and, in doing so, strolled about 10 miles according to my pedometer. On my way back to Loews Hotel I passed, not far from Café Du Monde where the day started, a storefront massage service offering foot-rubs and massages.

I'm not sure, for $12, whether it technically qualified as reflexology, but the man out front woke up a woman who was sleeping in the back of the room to give my feet a 10-minute recharge. But I gave her $20, too.

33

WHY I FELL FOR THE BEVERLY HILTON

I fall in love, at least a little, even after just a short stay, with almost every place to which I travel. This is the story of how two bellmen touched my heart and put a tear in my eye upon my recent departure from a historic hotel that feels like home. Stick with me here until the last reel.

My infatuation with the Beverly Hilton Hotel began as a child – long before I'd ever been to California, much less Beverly Hills. For some reason I recall a voice over and graphic among the closing credits of television shows stating, for instance: "Guests of the Merv Griffin Show stay at the Beverly Hilton Hotel."

That example makes sense to me now since as an adult I learned that talk show host Merv Griffin, who also produced "Wheel of Fortune" and "Jeopardy," bought Barron Hilton's Beverly Hilton flagship hotel (est. 1955) for a spell beginning in 1987.

"Mr. Griffin wasn't really a hotelier," whispered one of the Beverly Hilton staffers who worked under both owners. (One of many I've met, by the way, who've toiled loyally at the property for decades.)

It is just this kind of accidental intrigue that makes the Beverly Hilton, a functional, practical luxury hotel so deliciously dated. It is my home away from home. It's become a very significant, sentimental place in my life. I met the "hotel" for the first time during its quiet, seemingly empty pandemic days, when its restaurants and services were closed but its heart still beat.

I vividly recall, on the Thanksgiving Day in 2020 when Covid caused California restaurants to close indoor dining, being in the fresh air on my fifth-floor balcony with a bag of Mexican take-away and a split of champagne. (The Beverly Hilton has great, big balconies with lounge furniture and a table.) Though I was alone that afternoon, I was soaking in the sun - warm and happy.

I've since hosted my syndicated morning radio talk show a number of times from that room. On the air I have channeled and extrapolated that showbiz magic I'd heard so long ago, ala announcer Johnny Olson, to say: "When in Beverly Hills, 'Michigan's Big Show starring Michael Patrick Shiels' Broadcasts from the Beverly Hilton Hotel."

My syndicated radio broadcast is performed happily in the shadow of the superstar events the Beverly Hilton serves as home to including the Hollywood Foreign Press's annual Golden Globe Awards and corporate CEO confabs such as the 2022 Milken Institute Global Conference.

The speaker list included New York City Mayor Eric Adams; Steve Ballmer; GM CEO Mary Barra; Maria Bartiromo from Fox Business; Deepak Chopra; Jamie Lee Curtis; U.S. Treasury Secretary Steve Mnuchin and Meet the Press's Chuck Todd. This is just a fraction of the huge number of business, media and political heavyweight speakers.

During the pandemic, pop star Justin Bieber performed a New Year's concert not on the International Ballroom Stage, but instead on the ballroom's roof playing to socially distanced hotel guests watching from the hotel's 566 rooms and balconies plus a worldwide live-stream audience.

President John F. Kennedy made the Beverly Hilton his "Western White House," footsteps President Barack Obama followed in when he took the top two floors in 2009 and 2010.

I could go on, but you get the picture. And when you stay at the Beverly Hilton, you feel like you're "in the pictures," especially when a photographic mural of camera-flashing paparazzi greets you at the parking deck.

Every hotel of distinction with any longevity has had its share of celebrity guests (and ghosts), but the Beverly Hilton, at Wilshire and Santa Monica Boulevard at the crossroads of Beverly Hills, adds to its legacy every day.

"On the evening of the Golden Globes, for instance, or a really high-end event, you're going to have the who's who of Hollywood and the world walking through our doors," said Ryan Paterson, Beverly Hilton's director of sales and marketing.

"For the guests it can feel spectacularly abnormal to see some of the faces who pass through here. For the staff it has come to feel quite normal. We're all just people. So, there are interesting experiences where people you know out in the world are suddenly standing in the same room with you. But you can come and have a comfortable, approachable stay."

The Hilton's Aqua Star pool, opened by Esther Williams, is an enclosed enclave for fresh air lunch meetings protected from the paparazzi. On my most recent visit, while swimming, I may have seen Kristen Schaal, from "30 Rock," "Flight of the Conchords" and "Bob's Burgers," being photographed poolside. Later that same day, in the Lobby Lounge, I had a brief chat and photo with Fox News anchor Brian Kilmeade. I know I saw basketball and TV star Shaquille O'Neal, because, at 7'1, one doesn't miss "Shaq."

"We try to be discreet but, in some cases, you see the 'who's who' of the world. We host major conferences, heads of state, CEO's, actors, celebrities and musicians. Culture, television, fashion...you feel the history when you walk through the doors," said Paterson, a Golden State native who recently returned to Southern California for the position during his 18th year with Hilton.

During his time away taking assignments across America Paterson said he was always aware of Beverly Hilton's historical significance within the company and its culture. He admitted he now occasionally takes a moment to listen for the history and appreciate the scene.

"Sometimes I walk out to the Aqua Star pool in the morning and get a coffee and just look over the space before my day starts. It's an iconic California experience at 7-in-the-morning when the weather is already comfortable. I look out over that pool where I know so many moments have happened. And depending on what hour you go, instead of coffee there might be people having a cocktail. Or in the middle of the day there might be families out there. It's the biggest swimming pool in Beverly Hills and a big part of our experience...while being a small part of our overall experience."

A canyon of guestrooms, lounge chairs, cabanas and lemon trees set the scene. Ambiance is created by classic standard tunes, surf scenes projected onto the big white wall beside and over the pool and , colored lights at night. And the Circa 55 indoor and al fresco dining (Frank

Sinatra liked the corner table) make the bright Aqua Star Pool setting an old Hollywood glam experience.

At the pool's edge Mercato makes casual confabs and conversations in sunglasses seem so intriguing. (Michigan's Governor Gretchen Whitmer, touted to have presidential potential, lunched there last winter before an attending an event in the one of the hotel's conference spaces.)

While its newer, adjacent, sister hotel the Waldorf Astoria and some of the neighborhood's competing, brand name properties are plusher and posher (sometimes I find 'uber-luxe' to be suffocating), they are a different style of hotel product.

The Beverly Hilton, if a bit streamlined, simple, and institutionally corporate, is not dated per-se, because it's a historic timepiece: user-friendly, modern, functionable, and approachable. The Beverly Hilton's role and its' familiar place, playful place in Hollywood is undeniable.

"Our hotel is part of the community. Beverly Hills is very luxurious – very classy – but it can be many different things to different people. It's a place for everyone. A family can vacation here in the summer but a musician or actor that's very recognizable to the whole world will feel comfortable here as well. It's just that kind of special place," said Paterson.

"There is a historic element from the timeless architecture and the type of success the residents must have had to land them in Beverly Hills. But I've also been pleased at the 'down-to-earthiness.' I know that sounds counterintuitive. But I go on walks in the neighborhood. I encounter friendly faces and local business owners. There is a homey feel."

Like Paterson, who described the hotel as "right at the gateway of Beverly Hills," I've walked out the door and every direction from the Beverly Hilton day and night.

The shopping, dining and drinking, people-watching and neighborhood strolls are entertaining. The Beverly Hills sign in Beverly Gardens Park may be the second-most photographed to the Hollywood sign, and a further stretch of the legs through the neighborhood will get you to the placid fountains of Will Rogers Park.

In the fashion of the Hollywood Walk of Fame, Beverly Hills offers Rodeo Drive's Walk of Style. A series of bronze plaques honors the likes of Tom Ford, Giorgio Armani, Salvatore Ferragamo, and Gianni and Donatella Versace, all styles you can take home with you at the boutiques throughout downtown and in the Golden Triangle of stores across from green-fronted, gilded Gucci.

"We're right at the gateway of Beverly Hills. If you're going shopping, I suggest you walk to Rodeo Drive and Uber back with all your purchases," Paterson laughed.

The window shopping is museum-quality and there are "Instagrammable" pieces of public art. Plus, Beverly Canon Gardens is, day or night, a scenic spot to chill – especially when its decorative lights are ablaze. Speaking of ablaze, while walking on Crescent Drive you're likely to encounter the most dazzling 76 service station you've ever seen with its old-school deco design and neon lighting.

You'll deserve a bite or a drink along the way. Mornings I may stop at Nate-N-Al's Delicatessen to have breakfast where the late radio and television talk star Larry King also dined. Celebrity Chef Wolfgang Puck's Spago is world famous. The Polo Lounge in the Beverly Hills Hotel (across from Will Rogers Park) is undeniably old-school-cool. And the chicken parmesan at Dan Tana's has been enjoyed by every actor from George Clooney to Jack Nicholson. (You'll need the walk back to burn any percentage of it off!)

Maybe you'll save your calories until the end of your walk to enjoy the Beverly Hilton's rooftop Sant'olina Israeli/Mediterranean cuisine with a view. Stroll through the bar with the iconic circular windows you've seen from the street and slip out onto an open-air roof full of twinkle lights and charm. You can survey all of Beverly Hills and the mountain scenery and toast yourself with cocktails named for Merv Griffin and one dubbed the "Peter Lawford Suite."

The Beverly Hilton has a small 24-hour fitness center if you prefer to exercise on property, too. The lower-floor gym and pool are accessible by elevator so you can sneak back and forth. Guestrooms are stocked with white robes or there is a changing room at the back of the pool if you don't ever want to be caught even the slightest bit disheveled. (Especially when you see the glamorous, black and white, golden age movie star photos lining the hallway.) The Bellezza Salon and an Upgrade Lab for holistic spa treatments are down there, too, for further, "backstage primping."

"You can have a staycation here at this urban resort destination or explore Southern California," Paterson said, mentioning specifically the beaches and Getty Center. He's right – if you're driving, sightseeing or going to business appointments, the Beverly Hilton's physical location is quite convenient to anywhere from Pasadena to Downtown L.A. It's easy an easy spot to get in and out of traffic wise, unlike, say Hollywood or Santa Monica.

Parting, for me, especially after my most recent broadcast visit, was sweet sorrow.

I thought about what Paterson had told me:

"Our general manager Sandy Murphy has created a place where we lead with hospitality. We treat people as if they are in their home away from home."

He was right. When it was time to check out, I felt as if I was locking up my home for a trip while knowing I'd be back.

So, from my modern, bright, clean, white room I took one last long look off my balcony over the Aqua Star Pool and across Beverly Hills - all the way to the Los Angeles skyline - and then headed for the lobby.

Paterson had also told me that it's the loyal, vibrant hotel staff that sets the Beverly Hilton apart. "We have classic photos on the walls, but the staff members here have actually seen so much happen," he said. "Renee, for instance, one of our bellmen has been here 40 years. He is a mainstay of the Beverly Hilton and is even featured in Hilton television commercial."

The amiable Renee was near the front desk when I checked out along with his friendly colleague Frank. Chatting with them they, in their Hilton uniforms, chirped back and forth like Abbot and Costello about which of them has worked the Beverly Hilton longest.

"I have been here 44 years," said Frank, in his accent.

Renee smiled when I told Frank his 44 years may edge out Renee by four, but it was Renee who was seen in the television commercial.

"There is no business, like show business," the modest Renee teased.

Luckily it was a quiet morning so they had time to tell me tales of how they would facilitate letting Sean Connery in through the back door. "Like a sneaky 007 secret agent?" I joked.

Conversely, they spoke about the elegant Fred Astaire waltzing right through the main lobby.

And unless I misheard his accent, Frank told me a story about a now very well-known movie star, a single, struggling actor decades ago, at the time showed unsuccessful interest in Frank's then girlfriend. Frank chased the actor off and the woman eventually became Frank's wife. The actor became a megastar with a very successful high-profile, long-running marriage of his own (who shall remain nameless.)

"What happens when he comes into the hotel here all these years later and sees you?" I asked Frank.

Frank pantomimed a threatening, menacing face. Then he grinned. "No, no just kidding. When I see him, he remembers, and he asks about my wife. We both have a laugh big about it," he revealed with a smile and a twinkle.

"Now who is the one in show business?" I joked to Renee, who nodded and was always smiling.

Since I couldn't get enough of their tales, and there were no other customers waiting, Frank gave me an encore story. The fake angry face Frank teased the actor with, in his youth, must have been a real one. (After all, it scared the actor away from his girlfriend the first time.) But Frank was frank when he told me in his early days working at the hotel he would walk the aging, legendary actor Jimmy Stewart's dogs for him.

"And sometimes, when Mr. Stewart visited the hotel, I would walk him home to make sure he got there safely. He lived right over here," Frank explained. Frank figured he was 18 or 20-years old when on one occasion, while they were walking and talking, the white-haired Jimmy Stewart, who'd inspired millions by playing George Bailey in "It's a Wonderful Life," stopped walking. The man who played George Bailey in the film that inspired millions, "It's a Wonderful Life," turned to look Frank in the eye and ask him a question.

"Why are you such an angry young man?"

The halting question from such a gentle man embarrassed Frank and caused him to reconsider his attitude. Stewart then counseled him with one piece of advice.

"Be patient. Just be patient," Stewart told him.

"To this day I remember that advice because it changed my life...right on the spot," Frank told me.

At the beginning of this column, I referred to first hearing the name of the Beverly Hilton in the closing credits of television shows. One of the other common catch phrases in the credits of those TV shows mentioned that guests or losing contestants had received "parting gifts."

When we'd finished chatting, before Renee and Frank let me depart the lobby, Renee stopped me to give me a "parting gift."

"Mr. Shiels, I can tell how much you love this hotel. You care about it. So, I think you should have this," he said, handing me a small item. "I only have a few left and I think you are someone who would value it."

I looked into my hand to find a small, delicate keychain with a dangling charm shaped and painted in the image of iconic white hotel with the red words "the Beverly Hilton Hotel" across the top, just as they emblazon the top of the building.

I don't know if they noticed the tear in my eye. Choked up, I was speechless. But Renee wasn't.

"You are like family," he insisted.

Then Frank handed me some "take-away." It was, by coincidence, a split of champagne. Which I took with me out into the sun, holding the bottle proudly and treasuring it as if it were an Academy Award.

34

——·——

BATMAN AT BRONSON CANYON

It was Batman that brought me to Bronson Caves. Well, the Bat Cave, actually. I'd read it was an easy hike to the "Bat Cave" location seen in the 1968 Batman television series starring Adam West. This proved to be true. It's less than a mile round trip with only a slight, gently inclining, well-marked path to see the "cave," which is actually a tunnel in the rock wall of an old quarry. The opening to the watery tunnel was fenced off on both sides the day I was there, but it was a gas to recall and imagine the show's rocket powered, black Batmobile bounding in and out of the tunnel.

The other benefit of the stroll was a stunning view of the bright, white individual letters of Hollywood Sign high atop Mount Lee looming over the canyon. Batman and Robin didn't have the place to themselves – episodes of television's Mission Impossible; Gunsmoke; Little House on the Prairie; and A-Team were set in the foothills. There were plenty of movies filmed at Bronson Canyon, too, including various Lone Ranger movies; The Invasion of the Body Snatchers; Friday the 13th; and Hail Caesar (in 2016); to name a few.

In terms of celebrity actors, Wikipedia suggests that "Charles Buchinsky" maybe have taken the name of the street and canyon to become "Charles Bronson.")

I pulled my black hood over my head with my dark glasses on and took some Dark Knight-style selfies in front of the Bat Cave.

Call me practical, but one of the best things about Bronson is parking and a port-a-potty – the two things most elusive in Los Angeles, believe it or not. Public restrooms, even at gas stations, are spotty. And if you happen to find a parking spot, deciphering the complicated, conflicting parking signs requires a law degree.

Runyon Canyon, one of the fashionable celebrity hike spots, which stretches from Fuller Avenue up to Mulholland Drive, offers only very limited street parking, from which I have seen people's cars both ticketed and towed. In fact, I actually gave a lift to a woman who turned out to be the talent director for Soul Cycle when her car was towed from outside the Runyon Canyon North Gate after she took a short stroll.

But Bronson has two parking lots and amazingly they are both free. The parking lot has two port-a johns which I recommend using before you hike (and it's a relief, pardon the pun, to find them after.)

Bronson Canyon and the caves are in the southwest section of Griffith Park at the north end of Canyon Drive.

Walking back down the little hill I noticed another welcoming path. The gate was closed for vehicles, but pedestrians were welcome to traverse the Brush Canyon Trail. The signage indicated it led to the Mount Hollywood Trail and the Hollywood Sign summit and it listed the distances. Don't quote me on the numbers, apparently that means climbing 492-feet of elevation, very gradually, up a windy and scenic, simple dirt and stone trail.

I knew I had more steps in me and was curious to see more scenery, so I took to the trail which went along a babbling stream and through some shady oak and sycamore trees. The road climbed consistently, with only brief respites of relative flatness, but I kept walking up the incline because I was curious to see what was beyond each bend. When I started to perspire in the sunshine, I flipped my light sweatshirt up and over my shoulders.

As it rose, the trail became scenic (when I reminded myself to look up – usually when I stopped to catch my breath or greet passersby). Eventually the scrubby canyon valley began to reveal itself as the trail banked to the left in a sweeping, almost horseshoe-shaped turn. I spotted an overlook spot up on a plateau at what seemed like two-thirds of the way up the mountainside and decided it would be my goal to reach it.

The last turn and stretch of road up to the plateau was the steepest, so when I got near the top the sight of a bench on the edge of the overlook revealed itself. Ah! A payoff for my puffing, huffing hike up. I could pause and ponder and peruse the miles of beauty below – over the rough, rolling canyon, past the bulky Beverly Center, and onto the beach.

Alas, however, I saw a person perched on the plateau: someone seated squarely on the seat. I saw the silhouette of a slender woman in a safari-style hat squatting on the very center of the bench. There was probably enough room to sit in the space on either side of her and her hat, but it seemed like an awkward move, even if it weren't the age of social distancing. Therefore, I resigned myself to standing still and surveying the scenery - and at least not climbing anymore – which I did so while catching my breath) – silently, and subtly to the side and behind the bench.

Without even turning her head or shoulders, she spoke:

"Would you like to sit down?" the hat-wearing woman asked.

"Oh, it's okay, I don't want to intrude. Please...relax," I answered.

"Please...sit down," she insisted in return, while turning, standing and shifting to the side of the bench.

Realizing it would be rude to do otherwise, I sat down on the left side of the bench, leaving the middle open. It was in that space she extended a sandwich bag full of fruit toward me.

"Would you like an apple slice?"

The apple slice I did decline, but in turn gave her a promise. "Don't worry, I said. I won't disturb your peace here by talking."

She shrugged...and an hour's long conversation commenced.

I think the conversation was half an hour old before we even said our names. Her name was Theresa. Mine is Michael Patrick.

"I watched you way down there walking up the trail. It was looking like a hard walk for you. I wondered if you'd make it, but then 'poof!' Here you are!" Theresa, wearing brand name designer outdoor wear on her then, fit frame, exclaimed.

"I may keep going," I insisted, sucking in my stomach. "Does that trail go up above the Hollywood Sign?"

She told me she didn't know. "I don't need to go up behind the Hollywood Sign," she said. "I live in a neighborhood down there, so I see the sign all the time."

Theresa then made a groan directed at the very word and concept of "Hollywood." But she noticed I was looking up in the direction where the sign might reveal itself if I walked further.

"Watch your step if you keep going on that trail, though. I call it 'Poop Road.'"

I lifted an eyebrow.

"People take guided horse rides from Sunset Ranch along that trail, so...you know. The horses naturally drop 'presents.' And, if you're downwind on a hot day, well..."

"Aromatic, eh?"

"I would not use that word, but you get the idea."

We watched what seemed to be a large bird glide over the chasm below.

"That's a red tail hawk," Theresa pointed out. "There is plenty of wildlife up here. Maybe you saw some on your walk up?"

I asked Theresa what I should have been looking for.

"Oh, rabbit, rattlesnakes, deer..."

"Ever seen a mountain lion here?"

"Yes," she answered, which prompted me to wonder why she hadn't initially included the lion on her list. "I once saved a deer from a mountain lion. The lion was about to run it down and eat the deer."

"Jesus, how did you do that?"

It seemed like nothing to Theresa when explained she threw a rock at the mountain lion while making noises to startle the deer and make it run.

"That was brave of you," I stated.

"I had to save the deer. The lion was stalking it and going to pounce."

" In the 'Superman' movie he was warned not to interfere in the course of human events. Theresa, you upset the food chain!"

She smiled...a little.

"And besides, you may have replaced that deer on the food chain if that mountain lion had then set its sights on you. Weren't you scared?"

"No, I wasn't scared."

"Why not?"

"I had more rocks to throw."

As I laughed in admiration, Theresa made a comment with her voice trailing off. "Besides, I know what it's like to be chased..."

I later learned what she meant.

I shifted around a little to shield the sun in order to look into Theresa's eyes as we spoke, but we mainly talked while gazing down over the gaping canyon.

"It's so green at this time," she said. "It's usually not this green. Typically, it's brown and dry. But it's very green right now."

I didn't think too much about it but I guessed Theresa's age as 50ish. About the same as mine. She was calm and the conversation quite casual. Even though we conversed, a certain percentage of our consciousness remained focused on the nature we'd come to observe and be in communion with.

"Did you see the 'Giving Tree' on your way up?" she asked.

I said that I hadn't.

"Well, they call it the 'Giving Tree' because people stick little notes in it with their wishes. It's kind of just off the path a little bit to the side and up a bit."

"I'll look for it on the way down."

"Sometimes they clean it out and take away all the notes," Theresa said.

People walked on the trail behind us from time to time that late afternoon, sometimes stopping to snap panoramic photos of the canyon in the increasingly golden late light. While they passed, and we talked, I learned that Theresa was an actress.

"I worked as a model in Miami for a while, too," she admitted. "My father, he's 94. He lives in Florida."

"In Miami?"

"Pensacola."

"That's as far as you can get from Miami and still be in Florida."

"He ran a military base there."

I had become accustomed to, in Los Angeles, meeting interesting people with compelling stories. But I had to admit that was impressive.

"He was a pilot. Landed planes onto aircraft carriers."

"Can you imagine the courage," I said. "When I hear of people who do things like that I often tell myself 'I aint never been nowhere and never done nothing.'"

Theresa nodded and agreed.

"Does he ever talk about his service?"

"I make him. I sit with him and ask him to tell me his stories. I think his life would make a good movie," said the actress.

In Hollywood, and in fact everywhere, I have had many people tell me their story would make a good book or movie. Just a few days earlier, a Persian man at Polo Lounge at the Beverly Hills Hotel wanted me to sell his story about escaping from Iran to HBO.

But Theresa was a step further. She told me she'd actually taken all those hours of stories and turned them into a book.

"Can I read it somewhere? Is it published?"

"No. It's just for us – my family - for now," she answered. "I can't let too many people see it. Once it gets out too many people might steal the story. This is Hollywood. People do that all the time. They steal stories."

Since Theresa mentioned her family, I asked her if she had any brothers or sisters.

"I am one of 15."

"15!"

"Yes, I am in the middle."

For being guarded about the details of her book Theresa told me the romantic tale of her parents – the kind of "Greatest Generation" couple that would marry young enough and stay married long enough to have 15 children.

"My father, when he was a young man, dated 'Ms. Georgia.' But then he met my mother," she explained.

"Since your mother supplanted a beauty queen like 'Ms. Georgia,' she must have been very special," I suggested.

"She was a nurse, but her real plan was to become a flight attendant. Back then in order to be a flight attendant you had to be a trained nurse," Theresa explained. "Once she married my father and they started a family she sacrificed that dream."

"Instead of being a stewardess...she married a pilot," I posed. "Don't all flight attendants want to do that?"

Theresa laughed...a little.

I noticed the sun sinking some and thought about whether I would have time to summit or not. I was worried my car would end up locked in the parking lot if I got back down too late. I recalled a sign saying the park gates would be closed at sunset. Nevertheless, I continued the conversation.

"Do you think you are like your father?" I asked, in a question that was really more of an observation and a presumption.

"Well during the Screen Actor's Guild strike I picked up and went to live in Florence. In Italy," Theresa said while shrugging.

"Are you still in showbiz?" I asked, again in the form of a question that really was more of a conclusion.

"I am an actress," she answered.

The cliched follow-up question begging to be asked, typically, is, "What have you been in?" It's a question I have learned to resist acting. Theresa, though, with her plain-spoken sharpness, headed off the potential question.

"You've seen me in some things," she offered, from behind her sunglasses and under her hat.

"Did you like Florence?"

"My friends thought I was crazy, but I saw the strike as an opportunity. There was no reason to be here – no work – so I got on a plane and went. I didn't even know where I was going to stay."

"It worked out?"

"I was there six months. Six marvelous months. I'd like to go back."

I told Theresa I had recently been in Florence and toured the Tuscan countryside's wineries. She spoke of Siena, the medieval town outside Florence.

"I've been to the Palio."

"It looks wild," I said, speaking of the ancient but annual, circular, bareback horse race in the city center – the Piazza del Campo – twice each summer.

"The riders don't even matter. The horses run whether the rider is on or not. They fall off!"

"It looks very crowded and colorful in that square. A manic swarm of people similar to the Fiesta San Fermin in Pamplona for the 'Running of the Bulls,'" I suggested.

"I was able to watch the racing from above. From the window of the Mayor of Siena," Theresa told me.

"Wow, that must be quite a vantagepoint. Like a luxury suite. What an opportunity," I remarked.

"Well, it started out that way. But I was at a horserace, and I was the one who ended up doing the running!"

I kept quiet and didn't have to ask what she meant, as she continued.

"As soon as my friends left me alone in his office to go to the bathroom the mayor chased me all around that room!"

"Around and around the room like the Palio race below," I remarked. I was hoping, as I said it, that it wasn't unsympathetic or disrespectful.

"Right," Theresa said, probably missing the irreverence.

"Italian men," I said.

She nodded. "He was all over me. When my friends got back, I told them not to leave me alone with him again."

"Good thing your father wasn't there," I deadpanned, pardon the pun. "He would have flattened the mayor."

"Yeah," she said with her voice trailing off. I suppose the thought had never occurred to her. "Anyway, my Florence fantasy life came to an end and I left Florence when I got called for an acting job in India."

"So, I went from Florence to Mumbai. Talk about culture shock. India had so much poverty. I'd never seen anything like it. And it was contrasted against such wealth."

This topic – wealth inequity – turned an inspiring conversation toward politics, a place from which it never quite recovered. Our chat, which began in such a natural, earthy way, spiraled into Covid conspiracies; vaccine and mask-wearing mandates; and even how the contrails left behind the commercial airplanes streaking above us across the early evening sky were bad for your health.

There was a flavor of suspicion and pessimism to it all. I didn't judge Theresa, and in many ways, I agreed with her despair about the division that's been created in humanity. If only everyone could sit where we sat and see what we were seeing – nature at its most majestic – all the way down to the Pacific.

While Theresa decided to walk back down the mountain, I decided to hike up a little higher...on my way to the Hollywood sign. (The trail allows hikers to view the sign from both below it and above. It's about a seven-mile, partly paved round trip from the parking lot to the sign for selfies – longer if you decide to view the sign from both below and above, which I highly recommend.)

I was one or two bends from reaching a direct, panoramic view of the Hollywood Sign, but I had to turn back because I recalled seeing a sign stating that the parking lot would close at sunset. I didn't want to end up with my car locked in the parking lot...nor did I want to be alone on the mountain in the dark with its escarpments, cliffs and...wildlife.

In the middle of the trail on the way down, though, in the softening, golden twilight, a woman performed yoga poses in front of the scenic panorama while a cameraman filmed her.

I thought to myself: "There is no business like show business."

35

COAST TO COAST WITH GEORGE NOORY

"From the City of Angels near the Pacific Ocean" is the way radio star George Noory opens his late-night broadcasts. When his spooky overnight radio show is not on the air, he might very well be found holding court in Hollywood.

The Polo Lounge at the Beverly Hills Hotel has always been one of the most aspirational, exciting places on "planet Hollywood." Golden age, modern age, you name it - it is the posh place to see and be seen. While the Bolognese, McCarthy Salad and souffles may be the time-honored stars of the menu, the room, managed by Pepe de Anda, oozes generations of glamour.

When I started frequenting the Polo Lounge, Jimmy, in his white tuxedo jacket behind the bar, heard what I did for a living. "I have another radio host who is a regular," he told me. "His name is George Noory. Have you ever heard of him?"

Heard of him? Noory has spent the last 21 years hosting the "Coast to Coast" overnight, supernatural talk show on more than 650 radio stations across America and Canada!

Noory originally worked in radio and television in Detroit, my hometown, at WCAR and WJBK TV... but a decade before I jumped into the industry at WJR, WCSX and WCZY. By then Noory had already moved to St. Louis where he adopted the on-air persona as "The Nighthawk" on the radio waves of KTRS in the "Gateway to the West."

Jimmy, a bartender but always a diplomat, kindly promised to introduce me if my Polo Lounge path should cross with Noory's. I had, for 17 years, been hosting a morning talk show syndicated on 13 radio stations throughout Michigan. On many of those affiliate stations, Noory's "Coast to Coast" AM show precedes me and leads into my morning show. So, in a sense, at those radio stations, we are on-air "stablemates." Nevertheless, to be mentioned as a radio host in the same class as Noory was flattering.

A few weeks later, scrolling through social media, I spotted a post by Gail Gabriel. I hadn't seen her for 30 years, but I remember working with her a bit on the producer's staff at WJR in the Golden Tower of the Fisher Building in mid-town Detroit. She produced the overnight show for longtime luminary Bob Hynes.

Gabriel, on her Facebook page, posted "happy birthday" wishes to Noory. This coincidence intrigued me, so I sent Gail a private, direct message with the customary pleasantries. Then I asked her"

"I notice you posted a greeting to George Noory. Do you happen to know how to reach him?"

She responded by answering: "Of course I do. He is my brother."

Small world, indeed.

Gail gave me her brother George Noory's email address to reach out to him.

"I am nervous," I confessed to her.

"He is a great guy and so are you," she graciously insisted. It was sweet of Gail to write this, but still I was respectful, deferential and polite when I sent an email to Noory. I later learned that Gail thoughtfully also wrote to her brother advising him that I would be in touch and asking him to meet me.

I introduced myself in my email message to George Noory. I, concisely mentioned that Gail gave me his address because I, too, was in radio and from Detroit. I detailed the story about Jimmy the bartender at the Polo Lounge and that I hoped to run into him there someday just to say "hello" if it would not be an inconvenience.

The mysterious Noory responded to my introductory email.

He sent a five-word response:

"I will be there Saturday."

I sensed I would be bothering him, or pushy, if I wrote back to ask, "what time?". So, I planned, alternatively, to hang at Polo Lounge Saturday evening, which is never a bad idea, anyway.

This gave me a few days to also study-up on Noory to show respectful interest and help with small talk, should he decide to engage me beyond a handshake.

I already knew, as successor to the late Art Bell, Noory's overnight radio show explores current events, conspiracy theories, UFO's, life after death, shapeshifters, remote viewing, demonic possession and angels, Bigfoot and other mysterious subjects.

I didn't know he'd served nine years in the Naval Reserves and that the young Noory, in Minneapolis and St. Louis, was a prodigious news director and Emmy Award-winner. Noory authored a number of enlightening books such as Worker in the Light; Journey to the Light;

Talking to the Dead; Mad As Hell. Also, an examination of what really happened to the missing Malaysia Airlines Flight 370 entitled Someone is Hiding Something. He even penned a novel called Night Talk, the protagonist in which is, you guessed it, a late-night talk-show host.

The father of three appears on television's Beyond Belief with George Noory and is frequently seen on Ancient Aliens.

Arriving and walking up the Beverly Hills Hotel's permanent red carpet always feels glamorous, but I then slipped softly into Polo Lounge, intending to not crowd Noory's apparent routine.

As Noory advised, he was there, seated at the most prominent, green banquette table covered with white linen-covered next to the piano. The table faces the maître d' stand at the door past which Hollywood dealmakers, recording stars, and golden or modern age actors pass.

As recognizable as Noory is, he managed to spot me first.

"C'mon over, Mikey," Noory said, gesturing with his hand. I found it to be a very warm welcome.

Noory possesses a dark-haired aura at 72 – just like the classically-decorated, yet ageless, Polo Lounge itself, which is 82 years old. Its' outdoor courtyard is filled with colorful fauna and bejeweled in twinkling lights. Noory's intense eyes contrast with his friendly nature and the warm voice millions of listeners have depended on during dark nights.

"Mike, you just missed Paul Anka," Noory told me, pointing to the corner. "He was at that table."

When it comes to show biz, Polo Lounge's big legacy makes for a small world. Anka, a singing superstar, wrote the hit ballad "My Way," for Frank Sinatra.

"This was Sinatra's table," Noory told me sliding his hands across the linen between us. He also pointed out a sealed mount near the lamp atop the banquette upon which a telephone used to sit.

It is alleged that Sinatra, on a June night in 1966, used the phone mounted there as a weapon, hurling it at the head of a patron at the next table who asked Old Blue Eyes and his entourage to quiet down. It took two days in the hospital for the man to come to; and (maybe) lots of dollars to settle the dispute.

Noory adores Sinatra now but told me he had never been a fan of the "Chairman of the Board," even after seeing Sinatra perform a concert in St. Louis.

"It wasn't until I started sitting here at his table," Noory insisted.

"Well, your radio program each night is all about auras and ghosts," I offered. "Maybe when you sit here Sinatra is channeling you?"

Noory, who drinks Jack Daniels whiskey because that what Sinatra sipped, did not refute my theory. "Sitting here in his booth...singing his songs...amazing."

Noory does, on occasion, literally channel the crooner. He sings standards when performing stage shows across the country. Some Sinatra, some Elvis, and some storytelling between the songs. Noory produced and emceed a lunch presentation in at a Burbank ballroom with his singing star friend Pat Boone, the Elvis of his time, who lives in the Beverly Hills neighborhood.

On another night back at the Beverly Hills Hotel with Noory seated at Sinatra's table, a quiet Sunday evening, the radio star turned toward the piano player next to the table and softly sang along with Tony Cobb, that night's Polo Lounge performer. Tony's father was the Oscar-nominated actor Lee J. Cobb.

"....promise you'll never leave me alone...love me. Love me completely now and forever, as I love you..." he warbled with an impressive ability to hit the wide range of notes needed for that ballad. "It's the song I close all of my stage shows with," Noory told me. He said, when he sings the closer, he wanders through the audience hugging and dancing with fans.

The piano playing Cobb enjoyed every minute of their impromptu performance playing off each other.

"Kid, I love the Polo Lounge. I just love this place." Noory turned back to me and stated with sweet sentimentality.

At my age of 55, I like it when Noory refers to me as "kid." In that respect, of age and careers, if he is channeling Frank Sinatra, I am happy to channel Paul Anka.

The Polo Lounge piano, on Saturday nights, is manned by Jon Alexi, who brought his musical talents north from an upbringing in Mexico City. He is one of the intriguing people Noory, in what is now many meetings at Polo Lounge, has generously introduced me to.

"When you noticed Mr. Anka was in here," I asked Alexi in front of Noory, "did you play his songs on your piano?"

Alexi answered that over the years of playing at Polo Lounge or private parties with guests the likes of Lionel Richie and David Foster, he learned artists prefer not to hear their own tunes.

"George," I then asked, "if you walked into a shop and your radio talk show was playing, would you mind?"

"I certainly would not mind," he chirped back.

It may seem surprising that Noory, a radio host devoted to discussion of shadow people and the world of the dark magic and mystery, is a very visible regular at Hollywood's most high-profile "Pink Palace." He recognizes each of the white-jacketed servers who greet him by name.

And whether it is Pat Boone or any generation or genre of luminaries, Noory is interested. The former "Nighthawk" keeps a quiet eye on the Polo Lounge door. I have seen Kelsey Grammer, the star of "Cheers" and "Fraser," approach Noory to chat; as did hockey's "Great One" Wayne Gretzky.

When Noory tried to send Al Pacino a cocktail, the Academy Award-winning Godfather actor thanked Noory for the gesture but explained he does not drink.

"Pacino asked me if he could have the cash equivalent," Noory joked.

Former NBC News anchor Brian Williams sat down at Noory's table for a spell, as did singer and actress Linda Hart, from television's Dukes of Hazzard and Desperate Housewives, and film features Get Shorty, and Tin Cup.

We sat one night with our radio friend-in-common Kerri Kasem, the activist, model and daughter of the late "American Top 40" and "Scooby Doo" voice performer Casey Kasem, who, like Noory and I, began his storied radio career in Detroit. Another Michigan native, comedian Tim Allen, starred in the show Home Improvement. Noory's friend Billy Ribeck, who occasionally drops by and tells showbiz tales, was the warm-up comedian for Allen's show.

Noory's Michigan connection, appropriately, also goes into the afterlife. "I was the last person to interview Jimmy Hoffa before he disappeared," he revealed.

If Noory, like Sinatra, has his own "Rat Pack," Mark Rollings, who got his radio deejay start in Michigan but met Noory in St. Louis and went on to own radio stations before moving to L.A., is his closest confidant. Rollings has had a rollicking Hollywood experience and lived "the life" as they say in showbiz.

"George," Rollings asked him one night at the table, "have you ever seen Elton John?"

"Sure...I saw him at the bar over at Craig's," answered Noory non-chalantly, referring to a West Hollywood restaurant originally funded by George Clooney. We laughed because Rollings question was had Noory seen Elton John perform, like most mere mortals. Then Noory continued, "Russell Crowe once stopped me in the Polo Lounge and said, 'You are the guy I see on the "Ancient Aliens" TV show!' I answered him, "...And you are the 'Gladiator!'"

I have been at Noory's Polo Lounge table to witness U2's Bono stepping in. The Irish rocker headed to the corner table in the dining room. I wanted to wish him a St. Patrick's Day but resisted interrupting him. Bono had been in Polo Lounge often in 2023 as U2 rehearsed in nearby Burbank for their 20 concerts to open the amazing new "Sphere" concert venue in Las Vegas that autumn. Bono was famously kind to the Polo Lounge service staff, even penning a personal, touching letter to a waiter who'd lost his father.

Norman Lear, at age 100, rolled by one night in his trademark hat, after a career of creating more than 100 of the most formative and memorable shows in television history, including All in the Family and Sanford and Son. Two talk radio hosts, Noory and I, were speechless at the sight of Lear as he passed the table wearing his trademark hat.

Talk host met another talk host when Noory appeared on Larry King's CNN television show. King started out, like Noory, hosting a syndicated overnight radio show. Later in his life, King, doing television, lived in Beverly Hills and bumped into Noory socially from time to time.

Noory, who likes lavender dress shirts under his blazer, is a creature of habit. Noory and Rollings dine frequently, at least weekly, at Carmines, a tiny Italian bistro on Santa Monica Boulevard near Beverly Hills in West L.A. Why Carmines?

"Sinatra and Dean Martin frequented the place," Noory answered. Then he showed me the bullet holes near the ceiling when Sammy Davis Jr.'s gun was used to shoot at an exit sign during an all-night, rat pack poker game.

Speaking of card playing, Noory and Rollings follow the Rat Pack footsteps to Las Vegas, too, at Noory's beloved Palazzo Casino Hotel. Palazzo is part of The Venetian complex where a memorial plaque out front pays homage to the Rat Pack's presence on that property when it was The Sands.

I watched, in the Palazzo high-stakes gaming salon, the poised Noory calmly dismiss losing a hand of blackjack by saying, "It is what it is."

Noory and Rollings are fast friends and business partners, too. In addition to commercial messaging on "Coast to Coast AM," together they founded ParanormalDate.com and ConspiracyDate.com.

Whether or not Noory's listeners find love on the web, they know he will spend every night with them.

"There are some people listening to my show who are alone. They need someone there for them," Noory explained.

For a man who broadcasts in what Sinatra called the "wee, small hours of the morning," Noory insisted he gets virtually no sleep – three-hours-a-day – and in terms of time-off takes only occasional long weekends. He even works holidays.

"I love every minute of it. I have not taken a vacation in 20 years. My vacation is my radio show. That's my 'relaxing.' I enjoy it," Noory insisted.

Noory enjoys talking, and listening, on the air during his show, but he does not spend much time talking about his show. Believe me, as a radio host myself, I have asked Noory lots of questions, some of which he answers.

"Am I being interviewed here?" he joked. Then he looked at his longtime pal Rollings and, in a dramatic voice, said, "We tell him too much."

I am flattered that, after our initial meeting, Noory invited me to join him at Polo Lounge on a regular basis. I am a fair foil for his jokes.

"Don't you own any black jackets?" he asked, wincing at the sight of me showing up in yet another of my candy-colored blazers.

Noory offered his coat to a woman who was about to be refused entry to Polo Lounge because her stylish, designer top left her midriff bare.

Noory even once stuck up for me when my big mouth and a poor joke riled up a menacing movie producer who took a verbal shot at me from the next table.

He is very much a gentleman, which is the same style in which he hosts his radio program.

While his predecessor Art Bell was acerbic and had the tempestuous spark of a bare wire, Noory's Midwest mode is more genteel. The show's phone lines are jammed nightly with callers ringing in from east and west of the Rockies on the "First Time Caller" and "Wild Card" lines. Noory encourages his often off-beat guests and wacky callers as a therapist might. "Go on," he says, without a hint of mockery or irony.

Does Noory believe them all? He answered my question with a story.

"I had a police officer call my show one night and tell me about a time he responded to a call that a man was having a heart attack. He said got to the house before the EMT's and when he knocked, a little old man opened the door allowing him to rush into the house. Once inside he found an old man face down on the floor. When he rolled him over, it was the man who opened the door. When he turned around, the other guy was gone. And the man on the floor was dead."

These kinds of tales go on through four hours of airtime each night on "Coast to Coast AM."

Noory told me he splits time between St. Louis and Los Angeles. He flies occasionally to Denver to tape his television show and, like Sinatra, "jets himself to 'Crapsville" on Vegas weekends. But, outside of performances in places ranging from the high desert of Palm Springs to Columbus, Ohio, Noory is not keen on travel.

"I can barely stand two hours in an airplane," he insisted.

When I once asked him where he lived in L.A., Noory was cannily less candid, answering only: "west of the Rockies." This is the traditional, intriguing way - "east or west of the Rockies" - he and his predecessor Bell identify welcome listeners who call in to the radio show.

"What do you say if someone calls from in the Rockies?" Rollings once teased.

Noory's voice is all over the United States and Canada and worldwide through streaming. And, I suppose, in the resulting dreams and nightmares which come from listening.

—— • ——

EPILOGUE

Call me an amorous travel writer, because I fall in love, at least a little, with almost every place I visit.

The thrill of arriving at a new destination feels, to me, as if I have been introduced to a glamorous and mysterious stranger.

In a metaphoric manner, I "shake hands" with every new thrilling city I visit.

We make eye contact.

For those first moments in a new locale, my senses are heightened, just as they are when having a glass of wine with a potential new friend. I tread lightly through the streets as I would a conversation, excited, yet polite.

I catch a whiff of a town's perfume at the same time I notice its jewelry.

My head is turned – and turns – and all the while I know that there is so much more beneath the surface – so much I will never fully know.

It is as if the entire town is a special event to which I have been invited. Or a party I have crashed.

I put on a jacket and tie on my first evening in Paris before gliding out of le Warwick Hotel on Rue d'Berri. I felt the historic "City of Light" deserved my respect through proper attire on this, my opening night.

Indeed, I felt as if I were in a Broadway show when, moments later, I stood in the middle of the Champs-Elysees, gazing up the avenue up and down at the Arc de Triumph through the clipped chestnut trees, glittering shops, and street-side brasseries toward the obelisk in front of the Place de la Concorde. The Eiffel Tower, appearing delicate and bejeweled in lights, was also visible. One would wish to be dressed for such an occasion!

Thus began my tradition of dressing up on the first night in a new world city: Istanbul, London, Rome, New York, Lisbon, Bangkok, Monte Carlo, Jerusalem, Tokyo, Beverly Hills, San Remo, Dubai, Auckland, Hamilton, Bermuda, Sydney, Ibiza, Milan, Toronto, Durban, Miami, Havana, Glasgow, New Orleans, Honolulu, Bangkok, Las Vegas, Washington D.C., and Seoul...it was splendid to meet each of you! And to snorkel amongst the blue-footed boobys of the Galapagos Islands.

My love affairs with lavish locations have resulted in a mental scrapbook or powerpoint of priceless places.

I discovered "white port" in the town center of tiny Sintra, Portugal: an insanely romantic, storybook setting in the hills below a gleaming, ornate palace tucked amid the pink rooftops. Lord Byron, in 1809, described Sintra, the summer home to the Kings of Portugal, as the world's most beautiful city.

A representative of the Societe des Bains de Mer - essentially the Monaco tourism authority – once took me inside the stately Monte

Carlo Casino a few hours before its late afternoon, daily opening for a tour. A casino official brought out a rack of gaming chips so we could stage an authentic photo shoot for the magazine story I was writing. I was dressed like 007/James Bond wearing a white dinner jacket at the Baccarat table.

It was more casual, but similarly iconic, to sit outside Mabel's Lobster Claw, a seafood restaurant frequented by former President George H.W. Bush, after a satiating lunch of a lobster roll and blueberry pie, in the northeastern seaboard village of Kennebunkport, Maine.

My room at the nearby Cape Arundel Inn provided a picturesque view of Walker's Point, where two First Families have frolicked on Bush's famed speedboat, "Fidelity IV." I met both former Presidents a number of times when writing the book "I Call Him Mr. President, Stories of Golf, Fishing and Life with my Friend George HW Bush" with their friend, fishing buddy, and golf professional Ken Raynor.

It seemed that all of Glasgow had boarded trains and buses to come to the soccer stadium at Parkland Ground in order to see the Scottish National team take on Lithuania. Thousands of fans welled up with emotion while singing their anthem, "The Flower of Scotland," and then, at half-time, they crooned along with the Scottish pop band "The Proclaimers" when they performed their hit "I'm Gonna Be (500 Miles)" on the field below.

I have a "when in Rome" policy when eating on the road, so I had a local meat pie - and placed a bet on the game - both from the same window at the concession booth under the grandstand!

Was I really standing atop the landmark Sydney Harbor Bridge looking down at the white, billowing roof of the world-famous Opera House only hours after taking a two-day, sleeper car train trip across the Australian Outback? The rumble of the bridge below my feet and the safety harness reminded me I was.

It was hard to believe I was, in my sandals, walking in the footsteps of Jesus Christ through the Old City of Jerusalem, in Israel, where the most important locations of the world's three major religious are virtually adjacent to each other inside the walls.

Did I really attend six Space Shuttle launches at Kennedy Space Center in Cape Canaveral, Florida, watching the action from next to the big clock you see on television – the closest spot from which a credentials civilian can view the launch pad?

Higher in the sky I stood at the top of the iconic seven-star Burj Al Arab Hotel, which is shaped like a massive sailboat, on the Dubai beaches of the Arabian Sea in the Persian Gulf.

Later that day, after being driven over the desert dunes to lunch in Oman, I met an Italian couple on holiday. He was a police detective in Rome, and she was a movie star in Italy, and had been in some films with her friend Claudia Gerini, essentially the Pamela Anderson of Italy, who played, among other things, Pontius Pilate's wife in Mel Gibson's movie "The Passion of the Christ."

"Claudia Gerini," I exclaimed, even though the actress spoke no English. Then I pointed to my heart and hit my chest with my open hand. "Claudia Gerini makes my heart go 'boom, boom, boom!'"

"No, no, no," she said shaking her head and wagging her finger. "Claudia Gerini il diavolo di amore!"

I looked at her blankly, but I could see in her expressive eyes and the grasping motion of her hands she wanted me to understand her.

"Claudia Gerini...sex devil!" she blurted out.

"Ah," I said nodding emphatically and thumping my chest with my hand again, "Claudia Gerini diavolo di amore! BOOM, BOOM, BOOM!"

I bought the badge off an olive-drab-uniformed, suddenly smiling security guard at Ankor Wat near Siam Reap, Cambodia. He was initially intimidating but eventually endearing.

I never expected to be in these places, or in these situations. But when it came time to leave, I did so with a bittersweet sense of melancholy. I would love to do it all over again. Of course, as in any romantic relationship, I can only remanufacture the golden, spontaneous moments in my mind, but returning to places I have visited feels like going back in time.

I find when you are nostalgic for something, you are actually nostalgic for the person you were at the time you are reminded of. Who were you then? How did you feel? Who were you with? What was important then?

If I stand in a certain, memorable, unchanged spot, it is as if I can almost have a nostalgic visit with the "self" I was long ago. This is a sensation which was explored by Alec Baldwin's character in Woody Allen's film "To Rome with Love."

It is a lingering spirit which will always call me back, even if only for a moment. Sometimes I am reticent to return to a place at which a perfect, magical visit occurred.

And, after all, there are other places in this big world with which to fall in love.